Mastering DC: A Newcomer's Guide to Living in Washington

BY SHERYL NOWITZ

© Adventures Publishing 1994

For information regarding sales of this book, please contact:
Adventures Publishing
1-800-594-1371

© 1994 by Sheryl Nowitz. All rights reserved.
© Adventures Publishing. All rights reserved.
Published 1994. Second edition.

Printed in the United States of America.
Design and Layout: Gregor Nelson Design
Printing: Automated Graphics Systems

Library of Congress Number: 93-070397
ISBN: 0-9631935-1-1

All rights reserved. No part of this book may be reproduced or transmitted in any form or by any means, electronic or mechanical, including photocopying, recording or by any information and retrieval system without written permission from the publisher, except for the inclusion of brief quotations in a review.

Although the publisher has made every effort to ensure that the information included in this book was correct and verified at the time of going to press, the publisher does not assume and hereby disclaims any liability to any party for any loss or damage caused by any errors or omissions, whether such errors or omissions result from negligence, accident, or any other cause.

Acknowledgments

When I first began writing *Mastering D.C.* in the summer of 1991, I would not have believed that I would be working hard at a second edition over two years later. The research, writing and marketing of this book has been a wonderful adventure. Best of all, the adventure keeps going.

As always, I could not have done this without the significant contributions of a number of friends. All the phone calls, strategy sessions, fact checking forays and editing marathons would have been too much for one person to handle. I cannot thank them enough, I can only acknowledge their contributions here.

Bill Henry has been involved with the book for almost two years now, writing a brief guide to local movie theaters in the first edition and doing substantial research and writing in this edition. Listen for him occasionally on the Derek McGinty show and if you ever need a movie critic, Bill is your man.

Tom Gearty joined up six months ago. His wit, tenacity, insight, cheerful disposition and great ability to manage lots of things at once have made him a pleasure to work with. His cartoons are just the thing to give you a lift when you are wondering if it will ever get done.

Bobbi Rosen, Barbara Klein, Bonn Macy and Jeff Itell did a terrific job proofreading the final galleys. Terry Fisher, Don Graff, Esra Acikalin and Matt Firor helped out pounding the pavement researching the neighborhoods. Carol Lindeman's maps and illustrations are still charming and helpful. Christina and Gregor of Gregor Nelson Design did a great job with the new layout and the updated cover. Adele Robey of Phoenix Graphics created the original cover design.

And last, but certainly not least, Tony Klein spent countless hours editing this edition, offering suggestions, love and support. Rarely a day would go by over the last two years when I didn't bounce at least an idea or two off him about the book.

For my husband, Tony and my parents, Reeva and Bernie Nowitz.

Contents

■ Chapter 1 | *Neighborhoods* — 1

Housing Resources — 1
Rules of Thumb — 3

Washington Neighborhoods
  Capitol Hill — 8
  Southwest/Waterfront — 11
  Adams Morgan — 13
  Dupont Circle — 15
  Woodley Park — 17
  Cleveland Park — 19
  Van Ness — 20
  Foggy Bottom — 21
  Georgetown — 23
  Glover Park — 25
  Cathedral and McLean Gardens — 26
  American University Park and Spring Valley — 27
  Friendship Heights — 29

Virginia Neighborhoods
  Arlington — 30
  Rosslyn — 31
  Court House — 33
  Clarendon — 33
  Ballston — 34
  Pentagon City — 35
  Crystal City — 36
  Alexandria — 37
  Fairfax County — 39
  Falls Church — 40
  Fairfax City — 41
  Reston — 43
  Herndon — 44

Maryland Neighborhoods
  Montgomery County — 46
  Bethesda — 47
  Silver Spring — 49
  Prince George's County — 51
  Takoma Park — 52
  Mount Rainier — 54
  Greenbelt — 55

Contents

■ Chapter 2 | *Getting Around* — 59

Maps	59
Driving	59
D.C. Taxicabs	61
Traffic Circles	62
Parking	62
Surviving Rush Hour	63
Highways	63
Virginia: Streets and Roads	64
Maryland: Streets and Roads	66
Metrorail	66
Metrobus	71
Other Commuter Lines	72
Airports	73
Walking	74
Bicycling	75

■ Chapter 3 | *Settling In* — 77

Furniture	77
Antique Stores	79
Thrift Shops	80
Clearance Centers	81
Renting Furniture	82
Beds and Futons	82
Discount Department Stores	83
Pots, Pans & Dishes	84
Appliances	84
Hardware Stores	85
Wiring In (Phone Service and Cable TV)	85
Natural Gas	86
Electricity	86
Newspapers	86
Specialty Newspapers	87
Local Magazines	88
Newsstands	88
Bookstores	88
Food Markets and Gourmet Stores	91
Ethnic Markets	93
Membership Clubs	94
Bakeries	94
Food Co-ops	95
Shopping Malls	96

Filling the Closets ... 97
Business Clothes ... 98

■ Chapter 4 | *Dealing with the Bureaucracy* ... 101
Drivers' Licenses ... 101
Registering Your Car ... 102
Obtaining Insurance ... 110
Dealing with Your Income Taxes ... 111
Registering to Vote ... 112

■ Chapter 5 | *Food and Fun* ... 115
Restaurants
American ... 115
American Pub Food ... 117
Barbecue ... 118
Burgers ... 119
Chinese ... 119
Ethiopian ... 121
French ... 121
Indian ... 123
Italian ... 123
Jamaican & Caribbean ... 124
Japanese ... 125
Kosher ... 125
Mediterranean ... 126
Mexican and Tex-Mex ... 127
Pizza ... 128
Seafood ... 130
Thai ... 132
Vegetarian ... 132
Vietnamese ... 134
Lunch Spots ... 136
Power Meals ... 136
Romantic Restaurants ... 137
All-Night Diners ... 138
Bars ... **139**
Irish Pubs ... 142
Gay Bars & Restaurants ... 142
Coffee Bars ... 143
Clubs ... **145**

Chapter 6 | *Beyond the Job* — 149

Organizations to Join	149
Volunteer Activities	153
Non-Degree Classes	155
International Washington	157
Sports & Recreation:	158
Bicycling	158
Running	159
Tennis	159
Golf and Miniature Golf	160
Horseback Riding	161
Hiking	161
Swimming	161
Boating and Sailing	162
Ice Skating	163
Skiing	163
Health Clubs	164
Professional Sports and College Sports	165
Theater	169
Concerts	171
Jazz	172
Comedy	174
Movies	174
Special Events and Festivals	176

Chapter 7 | *Washington Weekends* — 179

Entertaining Visitors	179
The Weekend Tourist	179
The Beach: Ocean City, Dewey Beach and Rehoboth	182
Annapolis	186
Baltimore	187
Charlottesville	190
The Shenandoahs	191
Williamsburg	191
Civil War History	192
Amusement Parks	193

Chapter 8 | *Resources* — 195

Index — 209

THE DISTRICT OF COLUMBIA
WASHINGTON, D.C. 20004

SHARON PRATT DIXON
MAYOR

Welcome to Washington!

On behalf of the more than 600,000 residents of the District of Columbia, it is a pleasure to welcome you to the nation's capital.

We're proud to be the national--indeed, the international--capital of the world, and we want you to feel at home. You will find that there is so much more than just monuments and museums.

We invite you to explore the grand buildings on Capitol Hill and Constitution Avenue that house the inner workings of our democracy. View the majestic symbols of international diplomacy along Embassy Row. Enjoy the rich tradition and diversity of our many neighborhoods. Washington is a city full of hidden treasures.

We are proud to be citizens of this great city and know that you will soon be just as proud.

We're waiting to welcome you!

Sharon Pratt Kelly

A Note to the Reader

Thousands of people move to Washington each year, as I did several years ago. The first edition of *Mastering D.C.* was written with them in mind. The idea was to provide practical advice and a quick introduction to the neighborhoods, restaurants and amenities of Washington. Right from the start, I made the decision not to accept advertising (which could have earned substantially more money) so that I would not be influenced by any sponsor.

As you will note, this second edition continues that tradition so I can provide you the best advice and recommendations I can. The second edition expands the scope of the book to include even more neighborhoods.

Also, even if you think you are now a seasoned veteran here, virtually a native, think again as you look through these pages. You may be surprised at what you do not know.

Most of all, I hope you enjoy reading *Mastering D.C.*, that it is fun and helpful.

Editor's Note: As the book was going to press, the chain of People's Drug announced that it would be using the name of its parent company, CVS.

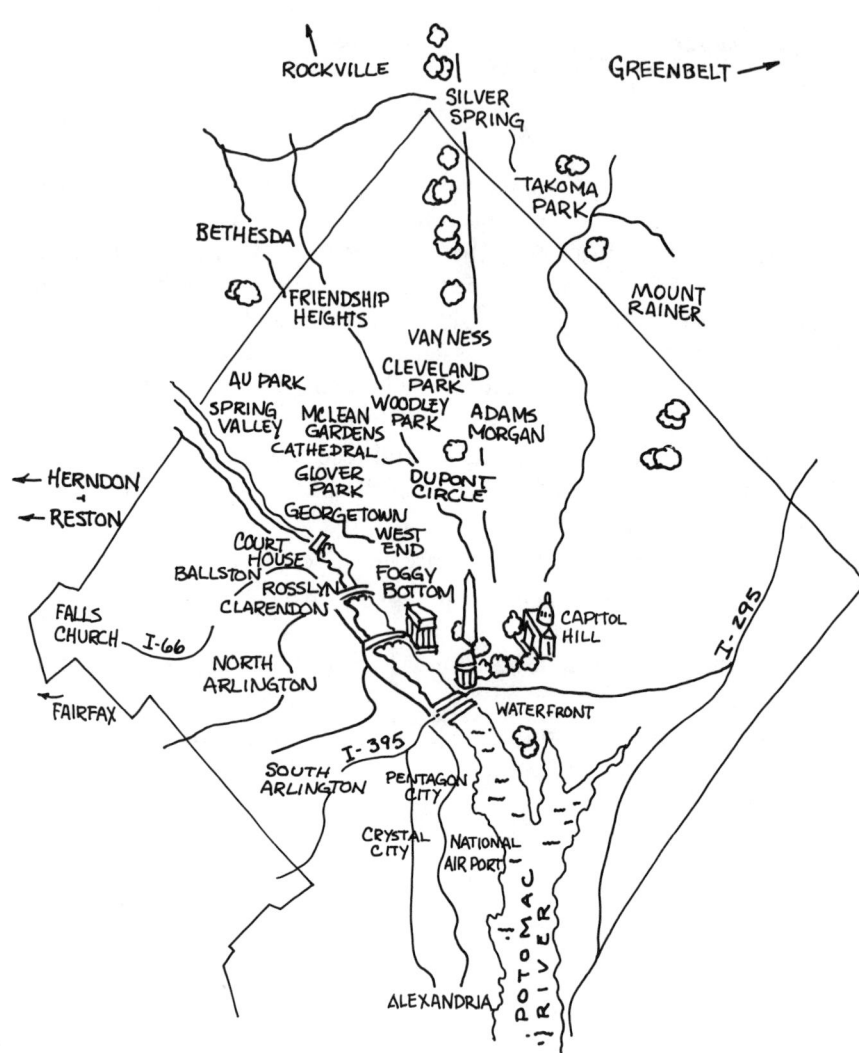

Washington Area Neighborhoods at a Glance

Chapter 1

Neighborhoods

Like any big city, Washington has many different neighborhoods, each with its own distinctive personality. If you love politics and want to live in the same neighborhood as thousands of congressional staffers, you can move to the Hill. If you prefer a diverse, multi-ethnic world, you will find Adams Morgan a perfect fit. If you want to be within minutes of Downtown, but live in a quiet, seemingly suburban area, you can look into Woodley Park, Cleveland Park or McLean Gardens. Further out, the Virginia and Maryland suburbs offer easier parking, mall shopping, lower taxes and a longer commute.

The Language of Washington Real Estate

Each city has its own terminology to describe apartments and other living arrangements. Washington and its environs have the typical options, but the great number of younger and/or not-so-well-paid people living in the city create additional alternatives.

Efficiencies One-room apartments, usually 400 to 600 square feet, generally including a small alcove and a large closet. Efficiencies are normally found in high-rise buildings. You may know them as "studios" elsewhere or as "bedsits" in London. Prices range from $500 to $700 a month.

Junior one-bedroom apartments Basically, efficiencies with an extra room—usually the size of a large closet—for a bed and bureau. Rents start at about $600 a month.

One-bedroom apartments Pretty self-explanatory: apartments with a bedroom, living room and kitchen. Monthly rent usually falls in the $700 to $900 range.

English basements Basements in rowhouses that have been converted into apartments. Usually these one- or two-bedroom apartments have separate entrances. In the District, the windows often have bars for safety. Rents tend to range between $850 and $1100, depending on size and location.

Two-bedroom apartments Surprisingly enough, these apartments can be hard to find. Rental prices can reach anywhere from $900 to $1500 a month.

Group houses If you already have a large group together or you want to live with several people or more, you can move into one of the many "group" houses available for rent. Usually each person has an individual room and everyone shares the kitchen, bathroom and common rooms. Houses in the suburbs also generally have a small lawn and accompanying backyard. Rent is most often under $500 a person. Group houses can be the best option for newcomers. Living with several people puts you immediately into a social circle and helps ease the anxiety of making the transition to a new city. If you are looking to live in a group house, you should expect to undergo an interview.

Commonly Used Abbreviations in Classified Ads

a/c or ac	air conditioned	apt	apartment
avail	available	bkyd	backyard
bldg	building	b/k	block
br or bdrm	bedroom	bsmt	basement
CAC	central air conditioning	CATV	cable TV
conv	convenient	cpt	carpeted
dr	dining room	d/w	dishwasher
effic	efficiency	F	female
flr	floor	fr	from
frpl or fpl	fireplace	h/w	hardwood floors
hse	house	gar or grg	garage
inc/inclg	include/including	kit	kitchen
lg or lge	large	loc	location
lr	living room	lux	luxury
lvls	levels	M	male
mo	month	mod	modern
newly ren	newly renovated	nghbrs	neighbors
nr	near	pvt	private
pkg	parking	prof	professional
rec ctr	recreation center	refs	references
shr	share	TH	townhouse
+ util	plus utilities (water, gas and electric)	w/	with
w/d	washer and dryer		

Rules of Thumb

Rents and housing prices vary according to the type of neighborhood, proximity to Downtown and accessibility to the Metro system. Some rules of thumb are:

1. Generally, the further away from the city you look, the less expensive you will find the housing and the more space you will get for your money. Housing in Maryland and Northern Virginia is generally cheaper than the equivalent in the District. To get the best bargains, you have to locate close to or just outside the Beltway (Wheaton, Silver Spring, Glenmont, College Park, Laurel, Greenbelt, Capitol Heights, Alexandria south of Old Town, Springfield or Falls Church).

2. The suburbs offer more public services than the District and a wider variety of convenient shopping. Taxes are also lower.

3. If you choose to live in the District, having a car can be unnecessary and even a nuisance. Having a car in the suburbs, on the other hand, can be a necessity, particularly as you move further out. The public transit options in and near the District are terrific while parking is scarce and often expensive.

Safety

Safety is an important consideration for many newcomers when choosing a place to live. If you are interested in finding out the nitty-gritty about a particular area, you can call the local police (phone numbers provided below) to find the latest crime statistics.

District	202/727-4383
Montgomery County	301/279-8000
Prince George's County	301/499-8086
Arlington	703/358-4252
Alexandria	703/838-4636
Fairfax County	703/246-7800
Falls Church	703/241-5054

Where to Look for Available Housing:

■ Newspapers

Many Washingtonians find their apartments through *The Washington Post*. Fridays, Saturdays and Sundays are the best days to check its classified section for the real estate ads. *The Washington Times, The City Paper, The Northwest Current, The Washington Citizen, The*

InTowner, Hill Rag, Roll Call, The Washington Blade and *The Journal Newspapers* also contain classified sections.

Several free guides published by area realtors list available apartments. One of the most extensive listings is the 600-page, *Metropolitan Washington Apartment Shoppers Guide*. Free copies can be picked up at People's Drugs, Giant Food Stores and Safeways. A biweekly newspaper, *Apartments for Rent*, is available at most Metro stations, Giants and Safeways.

If you are looking to buy, the two Washington dailies each have special real estate sections (*The Washington Times* on Fridays and *The Washington Post* on Saturdays). *The Journal Newspapers* are worth a special mention since this chain of daily suburban papers prints a special Friday "Home Report" section, each geared toward the suburban city or county it represents.

■ Community Bulletin Boards

Hill staffers post advertisements in the **Rayburn, Cannon, Longworth, Dirksen, Hart** and **Russell** office buildings on the bulletin boards outside the cafeterias. People also post notices for available apartments on community bulletin boards at **Chesapeake Bagel Bakery** and **Bob's Ice Cream.** Chesapeake Bagels has locations in Alexandria at 601 King St.; on the Hill, at 215 Pennsylvania Ave., S.E.; in Dupont Circle at 1636 Connecticut Ave., N.W.; in Foggy Bottom at 818 18th St., N.W.; and at 4000 Wisconsin Ave., N.W. Bob's dishes up ice cream at 2416 Wisconsin Ave., N.W.; 236 Massachusetts Ave., N.E.; 3510 Connecticut Ave., N.W. in Cleveland Park; and 4706 Bethesda Ave., Bethesda. You can also check the bulletin boards at **Food for Thought** and **The Yogurt Patch** (both are on Connecticut Ave. near Dupont Circle), a block above Chesapeake Bagels. The extensive bulletin board at Food for Thought makes entertaining reading even if you are not looking for a place to live.

The National Institutes of Health's bulletin board (9000 Rockville Pike, Bethesda) hangs outside the hospital's cafeteria (Building 10). At the **Brookings Institution** (1775 Massachusetts Ave., N.W.; 202/797-6000), you will find housing listings outside the cafeteria. **The World Bank** (1818 H St., N.W.) keeps a housing bulletin board so extensive that it even has its own staffer and telephone exchange. You may want to call ahead (202/473-1186) to smooth the way. The bulletin board at the **International Monetary Fund** (700 19th St., N.W.; 202/623-7000) is limited to staffers, but accepts submissions from anyone.

■ Real Estate Companies

If you are pressed for time during your apartment search, you may want to consider using a real estate company; their fees are frequently paid by the landlords. And if you are looking to buy, you will need to tap into the expertise of local real estate agents. On the Hill, you can stop by **John Formant Company** (202/544-3900) at 225 Pennsylvania Ave., S.E., where John and Kelly have listings of a variety of houses and apartments all over the Hill.

If you are interested in finding a place in Dupont Circle, Adams Morgan or Georgetown, try calling **Tutt Real Estate** (1755 S St., N.W.; 202/234-3344). Tutt manages apartments in these neighborhoods. Tutt can also help you find condominiums or houses in the area, if you are ready to buy.

Others

McEnearney Associates	800/548-9080
Potomac Properties	800/992-5950
Long & Foster	703/359-1500
Century 21	703/821-3121
Pardoe & Graham	703/734-7020
Shannon & Luchs	202/326-1000

Other Housing Resources

Quixsearch Apartment Finders at Tysons Corner (8383 Leesburg Pike; 800/486-3279) is a free apartment finding service for the entire Washington/Baltimore area. You give them your preferences and their computer database will offer a selection of apartments. While the process can sometimes be done over the phone, Quixsearch suggests that you visit in person. The office is open Monday through Thursday from 9:00 a.m. to 7:00 p.m., Friday and Saturday until 5:00 p.m. and Sundays from noon to 4:00 p.m. There are five other Quixsearch offices in the metropolitan area. You can call the number above for the location and hours of the nearest office.

Apartment Search (800/260-3733) will also help you find an apartment free of charge. Apartment Search has offices all over the area: Dupont Circle, Bethesda, Rockville, Greenbelt, Silver Spring, Alexandria and Baileys Crossroads. Each office has access to listings for the whole metropolitan area.

Universities also provide off-campus housing resources which are open to the public. **American University's** (202/885-3270) housing resource center is on the first floor of the Mary Graydon Center

(4400 Massachusetts Ave., N.W.). Apartment listings and information about the area are posted on the walls. Free telephones allow you to begin your search right there. In addition, AU has a computerized listing program that matches apartment hunters' wants and needs with available apartments.

George Washington University has a community resource center (202/994-7221) on the fourth floor of the Marvin Center. The center is open weekdays from 9:00 a.m. to 6:00 p.m. and on Saturdays from 10:00 a.m. to 2:00 p.m. For a dollar, **Georgetown University's** housing office (202/687-4560) will provide you with an up-to-date listing of apartments and group houses. The housing office is located on the first floor of Harbin Hall on the main campus and is open weekdays from 9:00 a.m. to 5:00 p.m.

Relocation Companies

If you are planning on buying a house, you may want to consider using a relocation service to help you find a home. Most major real estate agencies have a relocation services division or a relationship with an independent relocation company.

If you want an extra measure of attention and do not mind paying for it, you should consider contacting an independent relocation service. **The Relocation Company** (6820 Elm St., McLean; 800/336-0910) charges a flat fee of $200, whether it takes a few weeks or a few months to get settled.

Places to Stay Before You Have One of Your Own:
■ University Dorms

During the summer, many local universities rent dorm rooms by the week. American University comes highly recommended. You should opt for a room with air conditioning—Washington's hot, sticky summers are not at all fun without it. Below is a list of housing offices you may want to contact. Many of these rooms are booked by April, so sign up early.

American University Summer Housing   202/885-2669
Butler Pavilion, Room 407
4400 Massachusetts Ave., N.W.
Washington, D.C. 20016-8039

Catholic University Housing 202/319-5277
Office of Resident Life/St. Bonaventure Hall
620 Michigan Ave., N.E.
Washington, D.C. 20064

George Washington University Housing 202/994-6688
Rice Hall, Number 402
2121 I St., N.W.
Washington, D.C. 20052

Georgetown University Summer Housing 202/687-3999
100 Harbin Hall, N.W.
Washington, D.C. 20057

Howard University Office of Residence Life 202/806-6131
2401 4th St., N.W.
Washington, D.C. 20005

Women can stay at the **Thompson-Markward Hall** (202/546-3255) just across from the Hart Building at 235 2nd St., N.E. Rooms rent for approximately $130 a week, which includes breakfast and dinner. Every woman has her own room (with phone); bathrooms and showers are communal. There is a two-week minimum stay.

Roommates

Word of mouth is the best way to find a roommate if you already know people here. If you do not, you can put an ad in *The Washington Post* or *City Paper*. *The Washington Blade*, a weekly newspaper serving the gay community, also has "housing to share" ads in its classified pages.

If you are having trouble finding a roommate, you can contact matchmaker Betsy Neal of **Roommates Preferred** (202/547-4666). Betsy will quiz you about your living preferences and habits and then suggest some possibilities. If you decide to pursue them, she will charge you $50. She is easy to work with and has an excellent track record. If you are not happy with your new roommate, Betsy will find you another at no charge.

The Roommate Network (1431 21st St., N.W.; 202/296-5340) provides a similar service for professionals. Its computerized database matches potential roommates based on criteria such as age, sex, pets, level of neatness and smoking habits. The cost is $50 and they guarantee to work with you until you find a roommate. After you find a roommate, there is a two-month trial period to make sure everything is okay. For more information, you can call their 24-hour information hotline at 202/296-5326.

Moving Companies

The national chains all have local agents here. They will take care of everything from packing to storage to final placement. The local big boy is **Beltway Movers** (301/420-2200) which provides all the amenities and services of the national companies.

Because of all of the highway restrictions, movers might not be able to take the main route to your new home. Therefore, before moving day you may want to help the mover map out a route to take into the area.

■ National Moving Companies

Allied Van Lines	800/422-7356
Atlas Van Lines	800/245-5898
Bekins Van Lines	800/868-0273
Mayflower Transit	800/368-3320
Starving Students	800/537-7983
United Van Lines	800/325-3870

Unpacking

If you would like some help unpacking and organizing your belongings, you can call **Welcome Home Unpacking Services** (800/366-3878). Welcome Home will help you unpack and settle into your new living space. Prices generally average $50 an hour.

☐ WASHINGTON NEIGHBORHOODS

Capitol Hill

Capitol Hill, simply known as "the Hill," is home to thousands of bureaucrats and staffers. This charming neighborhood on the eastern side of the Capitol has seemingly endless blocks of rowhouses and many small parks. The Hill underwent a period of gentrification in the Sixties and is now considered one of the city's prime neighborhoods. Many staffers are lured into living here because of its proximity to "the action" (not to mention their offices). As a result, since staffers are notoriously underpaid, you can easily find very affordable housing— for as little as $400 a month in a group house. One of the best aspects of living on the Hill is that some of D.C.'s best landmarks are within easy walking distance. The Capitol, the Supreme Court,

*Chapter One | **Neighborhoods***

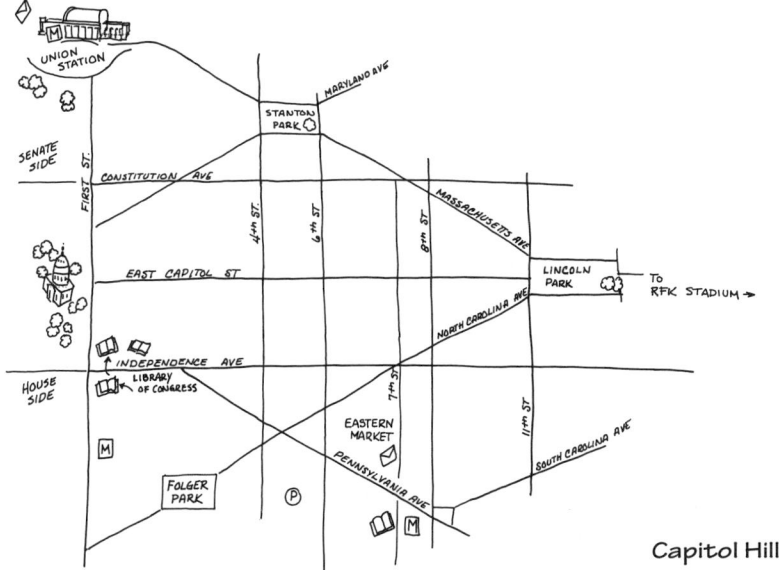

Capitol Hill

The Folger Shakespeare Library and the Library of Congress are all right there. The Smithsonian, the National Art Gallery, the Botanic Gardens, the Mall and Union Station are only a short distance further.

If you do decide to find a place on the Hill, you must keep safety in mind as you scout out potential places to live. A staffer living in Northeast just above Union Station summed up living on the Hill by saying, "It is great just for convenience's sake—I can just walk to work. But you also have to put up with cars being broken into, stolen car stereos and some shady characters."

During the past few years, several shootings and attacks on residents have made newspaper headlines around the nation. When it comes to safety, remember that the closer you live to the Capitol, the safer you are. The area surrounding the Capitol is protected by both D.C. and Capitol police. Rents vary accordingly—you can expect to pay the most for locations within a few blocks of the Capitol. The further out you go, the lower the rent.

Since Capitol Hill has few large apartment buildings, most of the available housing can be found in rowhouses. These rowhouses can make great group houses. Since renting an entire house, suitable generally for four people, costs around $1,500 a month, group houses are extremely popular, especially among Hill staffers. If you are looking for an apartment, you will discover an abundance of English basements on the Hill.

This expansive neighborhood is filled with expensive mom-and-pop grocery stores where residents can do their shopping. Many residents prefer to shop at **Eastern Market,** Washington's oldest farmers' market, where you are guaranteed to get fresh produce, meat, poultry, cheeses, fish and baked goods. Expect to pay dearly for the freshness and novelty of these shopping experiences. The blocks surrounding Eastern Market are also full of gourmet shops. Directly across from the market, **Prego** (210 7th St., S.E.; 202/547-8686) sells Italian delicacies, **Misha's Place** (210 7th St., S.E.; 202/547-5858) specializes in Russian food and **Provisions** (218 7th St., S.E.; 202/543-0694) offers deli food and gourmet coffee together with an array of kitchen gadgets. Down 7th St., the aromatic **Roasters On the Hill** (666 Pennsylvania Ave., S.E.; 202/543-8355) roasts and sells fresh coffee. A rival farmers' market turns the Redskins' home turf (RFK Stadium parking lot 6) into a fruit and vegetable-lovers' paradise on Thursdays and Saturdays between 7:00 a.m. and 5:00 p.m., year-round, and from July through September on Tuesdays, too. Prices here tend to be lower than those at Eastern Market. If you do have a car, you can go either to the **Safeway** (202/636-8640) at Fourth and Rhode Island Ave., N.E., or the one at Kentucky and 14th St., S.E. (202/547-4333).

If you live on the House side, you are in Southeast. Just above the Library of Congress and the House office buildings, Pennsylvania Ave. has several blocks of commercial activity. Local shopping favorites include **Roland's** (202/546-9592), a small neighborhood grocery store and **Chesapeake Bagel Bakery** (202/546-0994). **Le Bon Café** (210 2nd St., S.E.; 202/547-7200), right around the corner from the Madison Building, serves cappuccino and sandwiches. If you have a big appetite, you may prefer **Burrito Brothers** (202/543-6835), at 205 Pennsylvania Ave., S.E. **Taverna the Greek Islands** (202/547-8360), **La Lomita Dos** (202/544-0616) and **The Tune Inn** (202/543-2725) crowd this strip and are local favorites among Hill staffers. Further up Pennsylvania Ave., towards the Eastern Market Metro station, you will find another cluster of restaurants and a **People's Drug** (202/543-3305).

Massachusetts Ave., the main thoroughfare on the Senate side (Northeast), contains an array of restaurants including **Tortilla Coast** (202/546-6768), **American Cafe** (202/547-8500) and **Armands** (202/547-6600). **Capitol Hill Supermarket** (3rd St. and Massachusetts Ave., N.E.; 202/543-7428) provides the most convenient grocery shopping. Nearby Union Station has a nine-screen movie theater, a huge food court and several restaurants and bars.

Commute to Downtown Fifteen minutes by Metro

Post Office National Capitol, 2 Massachusetts Ave., N.E. (202/523-2628); Southeast Station, 327 7th St., S.E. (202/547-6191)

Libraries Library of Congress, 1st St. and Independence Ave., S.E. (202/707-5000); Southeast, 7th and D Sts., S.E. (202/727-1377); Northeast, 7th St. and Maryland Ave., N.E. (202/727-1365)

Police Station First District, 415 4th St., S.W. (202/727-4655) Substation, 500 E St., S.E. (202/727-4660)

Recreational Activities The neighborhood's parks turn into playing fields on warm weekends. The Mall has an exercise circuit at the corner of Independence Ave. and 4th St., S.W., as well as huge lawns great for running, walking or biking. There is an indoor public swimming pool at 7th St. and North Carolina Ave., S.E.

Southwest/Waterfront

While Capitol Hill residents tend to reside in rowhouses, those living in the Southwest/Waterfront area are more likely be found in a high-rise apartment or on a boat. With the opening of more Green line stations and the new federal office building near the intersection of M and South Capitol Sts., the Southwest neighborhood may be the next hot growth area in the District.

Aside from such notables as Supreme Court Justice David Souter and Senator Paul Simon, your neighbors in Southwest include **Fort McNair** and the progressive **Arena Stage** (202/488-3300). Located at the corner of 6th and Maine, the Arena Stage has three theaters and hosts a variety of performances ranging from the classics to cutting edge drama. In this area you will also find some of the city's best opportunities for seafood—a row of restaurants lines the waterfront, capped by the **Maine Avenue Wharf** (1100 Maine Ave.), where you can choose from an unlimited selection of fresh seafood right from the boats. In addition to walking along the river, residents can stroll the short distance to the Waterfront, L'Enfant Plaza and the Smithsonian museums along Independence Ave. Southwest is home to many government offices, including the Food and Drug Administration, the Department of Health and Human Services, NASA headquarters, the Energy Department, the Department of Transportation and lots more. Convenience alone makes this an attractive neighborhood for federal workers.

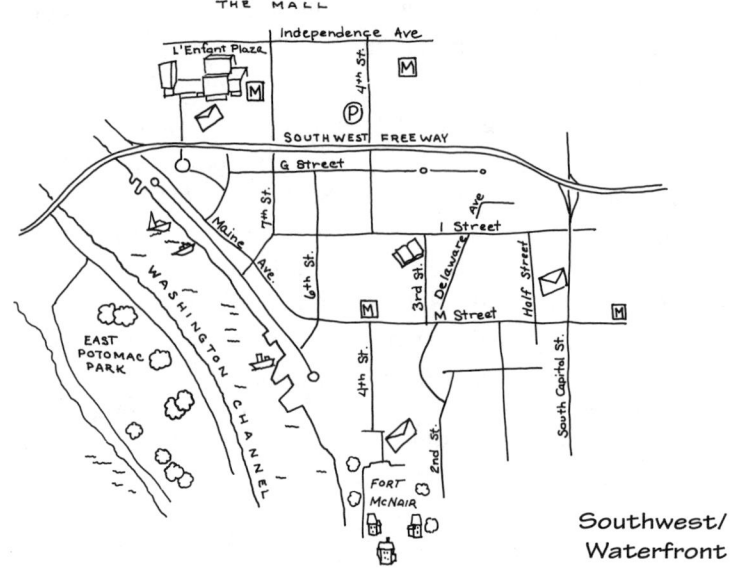

Southwest/ Waterfront

Rents for one bedroom apartments start at $650 a month. Since most of the apartment complexes have garages and lots, parking is not a problem. However, you should be prepared to pay an extra $30 to $50 more per month. **The Southwest Mall**, at 4th and M Sts., S.W., provides residents with the usual shopping options. There is a **Safeway** at 401 M St., S.W. (202/554-9155) and **People's Drug** nearby (202/863-9227).

Unlike the tonier areas of the District, the high-rises occupy blocks adjacent to public housing areas and the property crime that occurs throughout the city can be found here. Most residents I spoke with raved about living in the area, but the common perception for a lot of people living outside of Southwest is that it is unsafe. As one resident put it, Southwest shuts down in the evening, unlike Georgetown, Adams Morgan and Dupont Circle. The area's night life is mostly restricted to the waterfront restaurants and the area near the Arena Stage.

Commute to Downtown Ten minutes by Metro

Post Office Fort McNair, 4th and P Sts., S.W. (202/484-0969); L'Enfant Plaza, 458 L'Enfant Plaza, S.W. (202/523-2013); Southwest Station, 45 L St., S.W. (202/523-2408)

Library Southwest Branch, Wesley Place and K St., S.W. (202/727-1381)

Police Station First District, 415 4th St., S.W. (202/727-4655)

Recreational Activities There are several small parks in this neighborhood and the Mall is just a brief walk away. In addition, there is a major D.C.-run recreation field and facility at the corner of South Capitol and Eye Sts., S.W.

Adams Morgan

African-Americans, Hispanics and others live side by side in this ethnically-diverse Northwest neighborhood. Quiet by day, but crowded at night, 18th St. and Columbia Rd. criss-cross through the heart of Adams Morgan. Specialty shops, bars and some of Washington's best ethnic restaurants crowd a several block stretch along 18th St. and Columbia Rd.

Adams Morgan is an area in perpetual transition. Over the past decade or so, real estate investors have begun a campaign to renovate

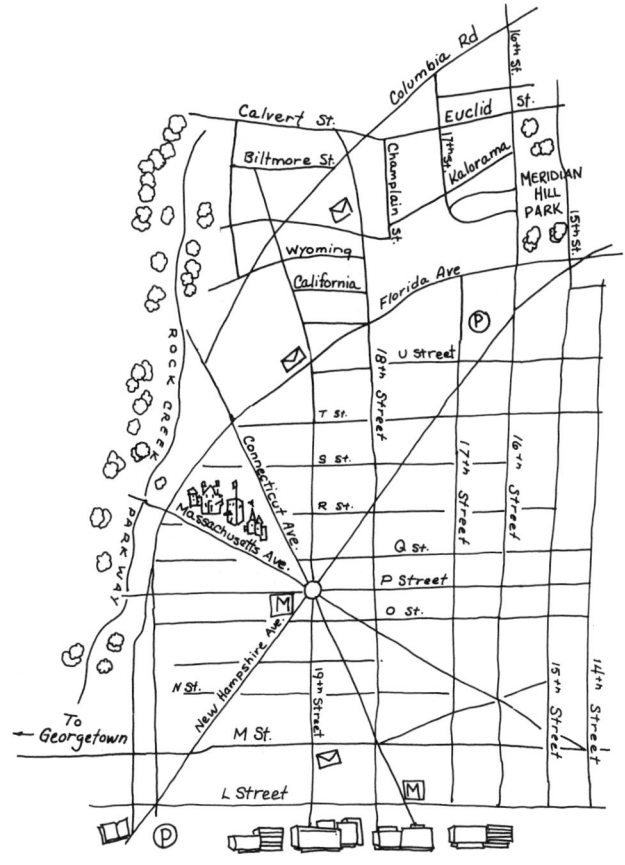

Adams Morgan and Dupont Circle

and modernize the neighborhood. You will find many townhouses that have either been made into group houses or subdivided into apartments. As in any transitional area, safety conditions can change very quickly from one block to the next. Adams Morgan's safest areas are between 18th St. and Connecticut Ave. Keep your eyes open and be sure to visit your prospective neighborhood at night to gauge for yourself.

In May 1991, Adams Morgan and Mount Pleasant made national news because of "civil disturbances." After an Hispanic man was shot by police, tension between the Hispanic community and the police mounted, resulting in two nights of looting and burning that spread beyond the Hispanic community when others took advantage of the unrest. Mayor Kelly ordered a series of curfews and a heavy police presence. While the situation has since calmed down, much of the tension remains. The District is now in the process of trying to strengthen relations with the Hispanic community.

Unfortunately, no Metro station serves Adams Morgan directly. The Dupont Circle and Woodley Park Metro stations are both a 15-minute walk from the heart of Adams Morgan. Metrobuses, however, do run up and down 16th and 18th Sts., providing access to all parts of the city.

As in many of Washington's popular neighborhoods, parking is a constant challenge here. Finding a parking spot can be especially tough on weekends, when thousands of Washingtonians invade Adams Morgan to visit restaurants and bars. Never leave anything in your car anywhere, but be especially careful here; several Washingtonians warned of having non-valuable but visible items stolen out of their cars.

The largest supermarket in the neighborhood is **Safeway** (202/667-0774) on Columbia Rd. just east of 18th St. Many residents complain about its unkempt appearance and woeful produce. The neon sign, which rarely can manage to light up all seven letters at one time, serves as evidence. A better selection of fruits and vegetables can be found at the neighborhood farmers' market on Saturdays. You cannot miss this open-air market at the intersection of Columbia Rd. and 18th St., right in front of the Crestar Bank.

Corner grocery stores and small ethnic markets fill in the gaps. **So's Your Mom** (1831 Columbia Rd., N.W.; 202/462-3666), with its trademark big kissing lips, sells deli goods from New York. Salvadoran and Mexican cheeses can be purchased at **La Queseria** (2412 18th St., N.W.; 202/232-1100). Latin American groceries are sold at **El

Gavilan (1646 Columbia Rd. N,W,; 202/234-9260) and **Americana Grocery** (1813 Columbia Rd., N.W.; 202/265-7455). **Merkato Market** (2116 18th St., N.W.; 202/483-9499), probably the most exotic market in the neighborhood, sells Ethiopian spices and other specialty foods.

A variety of ethnic restaurants crowd 18th St. and Columbia Rd. A meal at many of these places can easily cost less than $15 a person. (For a more complete discussion of these restaurants, you should turn to Chapter 5). For dessert, Adams Morgan has its own **Ben & Jerry's** (202/667-6677) at the corner of Euclid and Champlain St., N.W.

Adams Morgan Day is one of the city's best annual events. Usually held the second Sunday in September, this huge street fair celebrates the cultural diversity of the neighborhood with an abundance of food and music.

Just off the southeastern corner of Adams Morgan, the area along U St. from 16th St. out to the U St./Cardozo Metro is widely considered an up-and-coming part of town. This section, sometimes called the U St. corridor, has become home to a young, artistic crowd, with businesses to match. Many of these establishments draw on the resident artists to design and decorate their interiors, with varying degrees of success (and strangeness). While this part of town is not as safe as neighborhoods due west, it is becoming a more safe, desirable place to live and visit.

Commute to Downtown Ten minutes by Metro (Woodley Park)

Post Office Kalorama Station, 2300 18th St., N.W. (202/483-5042); Temple Heights Station, 1921 Florida Ave., N.W. (202/232-7613)

Library Mount Pleasant, 16th and Lamont Sts., N.W. (202/727-1361)

Police Station 1624 V St., N.W. (202/673-6930)

Recreational Facilities Public tennis courts are on 18th St., between California and Kalorama Sts. The Marie Reed Center (202/673-7771) has an indoor swimming pool at 2200 Champlain Ave., N.W.

Dupont Circle

Dupont Circle epitomizes the best of city living—busy sidewalks, a rare open parking space on the street, an abundance of high-rise buildings, art house movie theaters, small idiosyncratic stores, art galleries and a multitude of bars and restaurants. Its diversity and culture cater to the artsy, international and gay communities. "Dupont Circle is one part of town where you can walk anywhere you want to get to. The neighborhood has lots of movie theaters, bars, restaurants and bookstores and is not more expensive than more residential areas," boasts one resident. A mix of students (mostly grads) and young professionals are also drawn here.

Dupont Circle sits just above Downtown and below Adams Morgan. Technically, this neighborhood spans the area between 16th, 24th and N Sts. and Florida Ave., but its high real estate values have led realtors to extend its boundaries and list many other nearby areas as Dupont Circle as well (including Logan Circle and Shaw). Many of these peripheral areas offer slightly lower rents, but are not as safe or as distinctive as Dupont Circle.

The neighborhood on the western side of Connecticut Ave. houses several hotels and many embassies and art galleries. The embassies lining Massachusetts Ave. between Dupont Circle and Observatory Circle have helped this street earn the name Embassy Row. It can be an excellent route for jogging or taking a romantic walk.

Most of the more affordable rental housing appears on the east side of Connecticut Ave. The variety of Victorian townhouses and apartment buildings offers a virtually complete selection of housing solutions. Rents are among the highest in the city, although not quite as pricy as Georgetown. As a result of the high real estate values, you will not find many group houses in Dupont Circle. You should look for them instead on the fringes of the Dupont Circle area to the east of 16th St.

If you plan on living here, you really do not need a car. In fact, you are better off without one. Most addresses are a few blocks from either one of the two entrances to the Dupont Circle Metro station. Garage parking can be outrageously expensive: between $150 and $200 a month at many buildings—that is, if you get off the waiting list and qualify for a spot.

Grocery shopping can be done at either of the two **Safeways** in the area: one at the corner of 17th and Corcoran Sts., N.W. (202/667-6825); the other, a **Townhouse Safeway** discreetly tucked away at the corner of 20th and S Sts., N.W. (202/483-3908). Several corner markets and gourmet stores cater to busy city dwellers. Close to the circle, you will find the **Metro Market** (2130 P St., N.W.; 202/833-3720) and **Lawson's** (1350 Connecticut Ave., N.W.; 202/775-0400). Both **Chesapeake Bagel Bakery** (1636 Connecticut Ave., N.W.; 202/483-5600) and **Bagels Etc.** (2122 P St., N.W.; 202/466-7171) draw in bagel junkies, though connoisseurs may be disappointed.

The West End section, just below the southwest corner of Dupont Circle, borders both Georgetown and Foggy Bottom. Apartments in the West End are mostly luxury residences. Residents shop at the **Townhouse Safeway** (2060 L St., N.W.; 202/659-8784) or **Federal Market** (1215 23rd St., N.W.; 202/293-0014), which has a thriving noontime sandwich business for its terrific sandwiches. Characteristic of grocery stores in urban settings, these stores promise cramped aisles and high prices.

Commute to Downtown Five minutes by foot

Post Office Temple Heights Station, 1921 Florida Ave., N.W. (202/232-7613); Farragut Station, 1145 19th St., N.W. (202/523-2506)

Library West End Branch, 1101 24th St., N.W. (202/727-1397)

Police Station 1624 V St., N.W. (202/673-6930)

Recreational Facilities Rock Creek Park has numerous trails for running and biking. A 1.5-mile exercise trail, with eighteen workout stations, begins near the Taft Memorial Bridge. Be careful running or walking through the park when others are not around.

Connecticut Avenue Neighborhoods

Woodley Park is the first in a series of residential neighborhoods (Woodley Park, Cleveland Park and Van Ness) lining the upper part of Connecticut Ave. all the way to the Maryland border at Chevy Chase Circle. These convenient and somewhat quieter neighborhoods prove desirable to many newcomers. All three neighborhoods are on the Red line. The L2 and L4 buses also pass through these areas.

■ Woodley Park

When you spot the large mural of Marilyn Monroe painted on the side of a Connecticut Ave. townhouse, you will know that you have reached Woodley Park, just over the Taft Memorial Bridge from the Kalorama Triangle area. This Connecticut Ave. neighborhood is home to many young professionals, some students and hundreds of kindred species at the National Zoo. Older high-rise apartment buildings dominate this neighborhood. Many of their apartments are boxy and small, but have a wonderful old-fashioned charm lacking in the suburbs. The area's popularity stems from its safety as well as its proximity to Adams Morgan and Downtown. Many residents attribute its safety to the presence of several embassies in the area possessing their own security forces. If you are looking for a group house, you should continue up to Cleveland Park. Street parking is

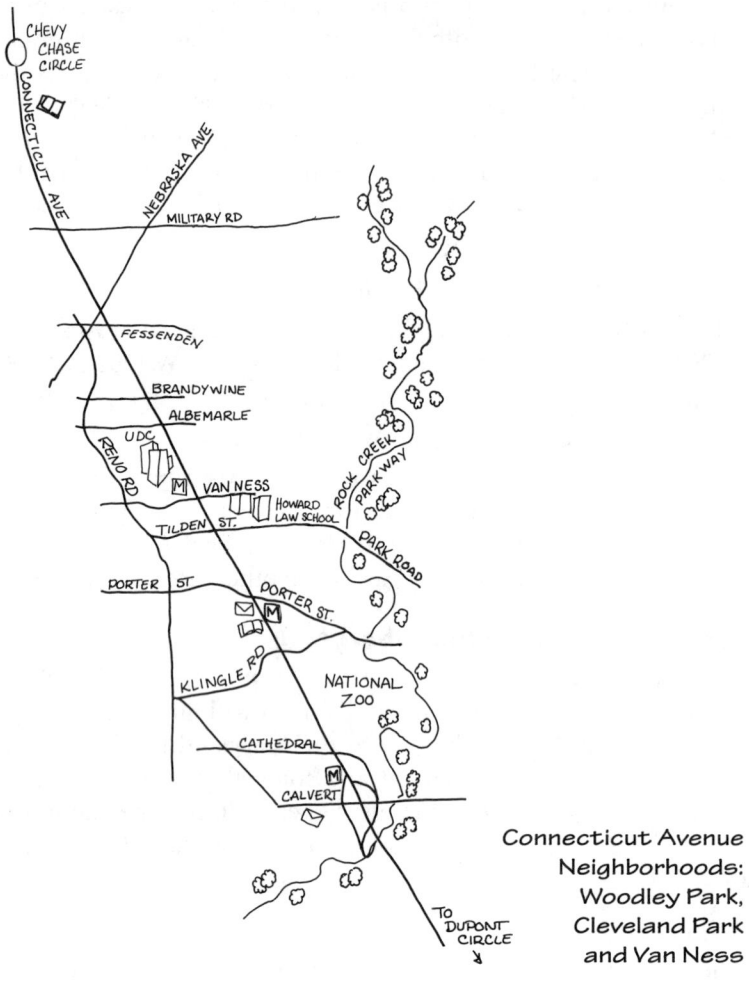

Connecticut Avenue
Neighborhoods:
Woodley Park,
Cleveland Park
and Van Ness

generally not a problem; just make sure that you have your residential parking stickers.

Woodley Park's commercial strip spans a three-block area right around the Metro stop on Connecticut Ave. This stretch includes some of Washington's best ethnic restaurants including **Cafe Paradiso** (202/265-8955), **Saigon Gourmet** (202/265-1360) and the **Lebanese Taverna** (202/265-8681). You can also find **People's Drug** (202/265-6818) and the **Washington Park Gourmet** (202/462-5566). There is, however, no major supermarket. Serious grocery shopping requires a trip to one of the bordering neighborhoods—Adams Morgan's **Safeway** (202/667-0774) or Cleveland Park's **Brookville Supermarket**(202/244-9114).

Commute to Downtown   Ten minutes by Metro
Post Office   A mini post office is located in the basement of Sheraton Hotel (2660 Woodley Rd.). The entrance is on Calvert St. (202/328-2000).
Library   Connecticut Ave. and Macomb St., N.W. (202/727-1345)
Police Station   3320 Idaho Ave., N.W. (202/282-0070)
Recreational Facilities   Running and biking paths are easily accessible at Rock Creek Park. A 1.5-mile exercise trail, with eighteen workout stations, begins just below the Taft Memorial Bridge.

■ Cleveland Park

Historically, Cleveland Park was the first neighborhood developed outside of Capitol Hill and Georgetown. In the late nineteenth century, wealthy merchants began building mansions on Piedmont Plateau. At the time, the only access to the neighborhood was through Georgetown. President Grover Cleveland sought refuge from the heat of the White House in the 1880s by purchasing a country house in this neighborhood, where the temperature was approximately fifteen degrees cooler than at 1600 Pennsylvania Ave. Only when the Taft Memorial Bridge opened at the beginning of this century did this neighborhood really begin to develop. Today, Cleveland Park offers a growing number of amenities as well as easy access to Downtown and the Hill.

As in Woodley Park, most of Cleveland Park's commercial activity takes place within a three-block radius of its Red line Metro stop (Cleveland Park). **The Uptown Theatre** (3426 Connecticut Ave., N.W.; 202/966-5400), one of Washington's best movie houses, sits in the middle of this activity. Besides **Brookville Supermarket**(3427 Connecticut Ave., N.W.; 202/244-9114), the neighborhood has more than its share of small gourmet stores, including **Vace** (202/363-1999), **Uptown Bakers** (202/362-6262), **Quartermaine Coffee Roasters** (202/244-2676), **Starbucks** (202/966-8118) and **Yes! Natural Gourmet** (202/363-1559). If you want to go to Giant or Safeway, you will have to make a trip up Connecticut Ave. to Van Ness. On the east side of the 3500 block of Connecticut Ave., N.W., sits a small strip mall, Park and Shop. This remnant of a 1920s shopping mall, reputed to be the first strip mall, was renovated in 1992. Although some traditionalists may blanch at the glitzy new site, this new mall has brought even more amenities to the neighborhood, with a bagel bakery, **Whatsa Bagel** (202/966-8990), **The Wiz** (202/364-7007), the District's first **Kenny Rogers Roasters** (202/244-8008) and **Pizzeria Uno** (202/966-3225).

House hunters can choose from a wide range of apartment buildings lining Connecticut Ave. or individual houses and many more apartment buildings tucked away on the quieter side streets. Most of the apartment buildings cater to professionals or students and offer efficiencies, one-bedroom and two-bedroom apartments. Those searching for a group house will find lots of large, older, bungalow-style homes. These group houses are relatively inexpensive. Monthly rent for an entire house (five or six bedrooms) begins around $1800. Street parking can be found easily on side streets on the western side of Connecticut Ave.

> **Commute to Downtown** Twelve to fifteen minutes by Metro
> **Post Office** 3430 Connecticut Ave., N.W. (202/523-2395)
> **Library** Connecticut Ave. and Macomb St., N.W. (202/727-1345)
> **Police Station** 3320 Idaho Ave., N.W. (202/282-0070)
> **Recreational Facilities** The Cleveland Park Club (3433 33rd Place, N.W.; 202/363-0756) has a small swimming pool and offers classes in aerobics. Tennis courts at 45th and Van Ness St., N.W., are not far away.

■ Van Ness

In the high-rise apartment landscape of Connecticut Ave., Van Ness forms an island of commercial activity between Cleveland Park and the rest of Upper Connecticut Ave. The presence of Howard University Law School and the University of the District of Columbia define much of the neighborhood's college-town character. Modern apartment buildings provide the bulk of available housing in the form of efficiencies, one-bedroom and two-bedroom apartments. But once off Connecticut Ave., Van Ness is transformed into a suburban neighborhood of pricy, single-family homes.

Many conveniences surround the Metro station. Two supermarkets, **Giant** (202/364-8250) and **Safeway** (202/244-4390), and a wide variety of other stores reside within a three-block radius of the Metro station. As befitting a "college town," Van Ness can also boast more than its fair share of fast-food outlets, including **Taco Bell, Burger King, Pizza Hut** and **Roy Rogers**. Giant offers free underground parking in the garage under the GHA building. The entrance is on Veazey Terrace. On-street parking in Van Ness is limited, especially when the two universities are in session, but there are several underground parking garages. Most apartment buildings offer parking at about $75 per month.

Above Van Ness, blocks of apartment buildings alternate along Connecticut Ave. with several pockets of commercial activity. A small shopping area with several restaurants, gas stations and a drugstore, **Higger's Drugs** (202/966-1815), does business near the intersection of Connecticut and Nebraska. The original **Marvelous Market** (202/686-4040), one of Washington's most notable bakeries, resides here. Further up Connecticut Ave. by Chevy Chase Circle, you will find several more restaurants, another **Safeway** (202/244-6097), **Magruder's Supermarket** (202/244-7800) and the gourmet bakery **Bread and Chocolate** (202/966-7413).

Commute to Downtown   Fifteen minutes by Metro
Post Office   Friendship Station, 4005 Wisconsin Ave., N.W. (202/523-2401)
Library   Connecticut Ave. and Macomb St., N.W. (202/727-1345)
Police Station   3320 Idaho Ave., N.W. (202/282-0070)
Recreational Facilities   UDC has three public tennis courts just behind the Safeway; UDC students and faculty have first priority.

Foggy Bottom

In the last century, Foggy Bottom has switched from being the home of thousands of middle-class workers to a neighborhood of students and bureaucrats. There are several theories as to the origin of the rather unusual name for this neighborhood. Some say that the neighborhood was built on top of a swamp. Others claim that the State Department's murky politics gave rise to the name. Regardless, its proximity to George Washington University, the State Department, the World Bank, the International Monetary Fund (IMF) and the Kennedy Center make it an attractive neighborhood for students and those in the foreign service.

A mix of moderate and luxury apartments checker Foggy Bottom's residential streets—the most expensive being the Watergate (it was a ritzy establishment long before it was a synonym for Washington corruption). Apartments at the Watergate sell for millions and cost thousands to rent. More economical housing can be found to the north of Virginia Ave. Buildings closest to the George Washington campus tend to offer the most reasonable rents. You should be able to find a wide range of apartment types. Getting the best deals will require some legwork.

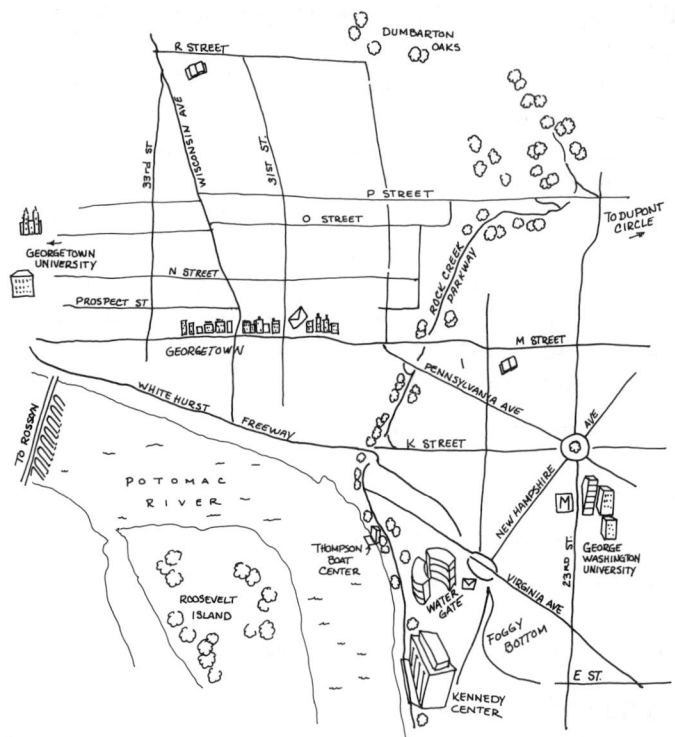

Foggy Bottom and Georgetown

Residents buy groceries at the **Townhouse Safeway** (202/659-8784) at 2060 L St., N.W. or another **Safeway** (202/338-3628) in the basement of the Watergate Complex. The Watergate Complex also houses a small, rather exclusive shopping mall, comprised of a small post office, a **People's Drug** (202/333-5031) and the fabulous **Watergate Pastry Shop** (202/342-1777). Take the elevator down to the shops from the entrance on Virginia Ave. In addition, several small mom-and-pop grocery stores catering to students' late-night eating habits dot the area.

Music fans can get their fix at the 2000 Pennsylvania Shopping Mall. **Tower Records** (202/331-2400) occupies one end of the mall and **Tower Video** (202/223-3900) anchors the other end. In the middle, you will find **One Stop News** (202/872-1577), the **Cone E. Island** ice cream shop (202/822-8460) and a few restaurants, including **Kinkead's** and **Bertucci's.** Morning coffee, bagels and muffins can be picked up at **Ciao** (202/296-6796)—a favorite among GW students.

Commute to Downtown Five minutes by foot
Post Office 2600 Virginia Ave., N.W., in Watergate Complex (202/965-2730)
Library West End, 1101 24th St., N.W. (202/727-1397)
Police Station 3320 Idaho Ave., N.W. (202/282-0070)
Recreational Facilities The Mall, with its vast playing fields, is just a few blocks south of the Metro stop. The Federal Reserve has several tennis courts that are open to the public. To reserve one, you can call 202/452-3357.

Georgetown

Georgetown, right on the banks of the Potomac River, started out as a commercial port and remained so until the latter half of the last century. This helps explain the layout of this historic quarter. To the west of Wisconsin Ave. you will find some of the neighborhood's nicest homes where the wealthy merchants used to live. Less successful merchants and workers resided to the east of Wisconsin in a mix of two-story Victorian and "clapboard" houses. You would hardly be able to guess the humble origins of much of Georgetown, since it now attracts a predominantly well-to-do crowd.

As Washington's oldest and choicest neighborhood, Georgetown offers its residents urban elegance mixed with an active night life. The intersection of Wisconsin Ave. and M St. forms the business and entertainment hub of this neighborhood. Upscale restaurants, fashionable clothing stores, popular bars and night spots crowd the area. Moving away from this hub, one finds a beautiful residential neighborhood, full of tree-lined streets and cozy Georgian and Victorian townhouses. Many young professionals and a large portion of Washington's jet-set have found their niche in this neighborhood. In fact, for $6,500 a month you can rent a three-bedroom apartment at Georgetown's exclusive Washington Harbour (yes, they actually spell Harbour with a "u"), constructed right along the banks of the Potomac. While Georgetown does offer a mix of apartments, English basements are probably the most prevalent vacancies in this area for rich students and young professionals. Georgetown's popularity has brought some problems to the neighborhood. Street parking in the area around Wisconsin Ave. and M St. is virtually impossible and it is not much easier to find spaces in the residential areas. To protect their parking spaces, some residents have opted to rope off private parking spaces in front of their homes. Of course, apartment residents have the option to pay for private parking, but like most things in Georgetown, this amounts to a serious expense.

Georgetown's lack of easy access to a Metro station prevents many from choosing this neighborhood. The closest Metro stop to the eastern half of Georgetown, Foggy Bottom (Blue and Orange lines), is a ten to fifteen-minute walk. For those closer to the Georgetown University campus, a walk across Key Bridge to the Rosslyn Metro stop is actually closer. Fortunately, both Wisconsin Ave. and M St. are on major bus routes.

The **"Social" Safeway** (1855 Wisconsin Ave., N.W.; 202/333-3223) is the largest supermarket in the area. As its nickname suggests, this Safeway is a popular spot for singles to check each other out at the checkout. In addition, Georgetown has several smaller gourmet markets: **Neam's Grocery** (3217 P St., N.W.; 202/338-4694) and **The French Market** (1630 Wisconsin Ave., N.W.; 202/338-4828). The most recent addition to the Georgetown food scene is **Dean & DeLuca** in the Old Market House (3276 M St., N.W.; 202/342-2500). Bagel lovers can choose between **Georgetown Bagelry** (3245 M St., N.W.; 202/965-1011) and **Booeymonger** (3265 Prospect St., N.W.; 202/333-4810). By the way, the Georgetown Bagelry is also one of the few places in this metropolitan area where you can get anything approximating a slice of New York pizza.

Commute to Downtown Twenty-five minutes by foot, fifteen minutes by bus

Post Office 1215 31st St., N.W. (202/523-2405)

Library Georgetown Regional, Wisconsin Ave. and R St., N.W. (202/727-1353)

Police Station 3320 Idaho Ave., N.W. (202/282-0070)

Recreational Activities C&O Canal Towpath is great for walking, running, biking and, when weather allows, ice skating. You will find tennis courts at 30th and R Sts., N.W. and 33rd St. and Volta Place, N.W.

Upper Wisconsin Neighborhoods

The neighborhoods on Upper Wisconsin (Glover Park, Cathedral and McLean Gardens) offer quiet community living, safety and close proximity to other parts of the city. Like Georgetown, their biggest drawback is that they are not directly served by the Metrorail system. To commute Downtown, residents must ride the Metrobus. Buses #30, 32, 34 and 36 cruise up and down Wisconsin Ave.

Chapter One | Neighborhoods

■ Glover Park

Glover Park rests just above Georgetown, bounded by Wisconsin Ave. and Glover and Whitehaven Parks. Glover Park contains many large, older homes, making it a popular spot for group houses, especially for Georgetown University students. You should find group houses available on the streets off of Wisconsin Ave. Monthly rents for an entire house average between $1,400 and $1,700. For those who prefer apartment living, there are many older apartment buildings, with a mix of high-rise and garden-style apartments.

For an area so close to the bustle of Georgetown, there is a pleasant small-town feel to much of Glover Park. Apart from the

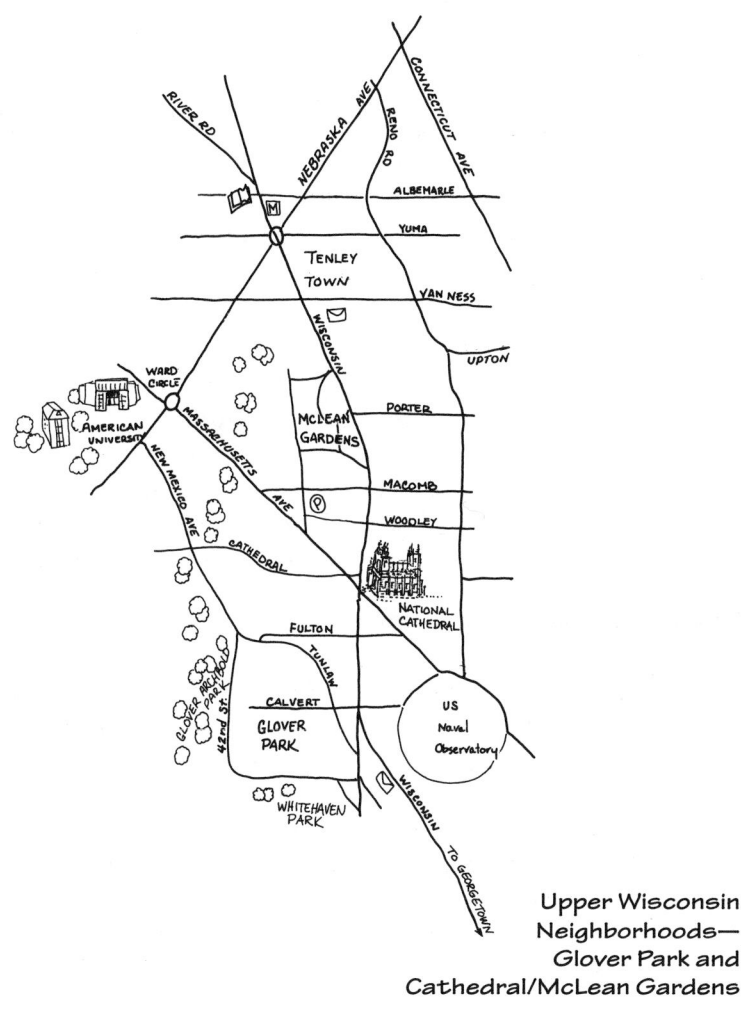

Upper Wisconsin
Neighborhoods—
Glover Park and
Cathedral/McLean Gardens

main retail area on Wisconsin Ave., there are only a few businesses. A cozy Little League baseball park at the intersection of Calvert St. and Wisconsin Ave. is hidden by trees and might otherwise be missed. You can meet your neighbors at **Glover Park Day,** a neighborhood block party in June.

Glover Park's border with Georgetown stirs with commercial activity. Here you will find **G&G Market** (2444 Wisconsin Ave., N.W.; 202/333-5300), **Bob's Famous Homemade Ice Cream** (2416 Wisconsin Ave., N.W.; 202/342-7622), **Plain Old Pearson's Liquor** (2436 Wisconsin Ave., N.W.; 202/333-6666) and the **Glover Park Market** (2411 37th St., N.W.; 202/333-4030). The **"Social" Safeway** at 1855 Wisconsin Ave., N.W. (202/333-3223) is also nearby. On Saturday mornings, a farmer sells organic and market produce at the corner of Calvert and 39th Sts., N.W. An **Amoco** station with some of the highest prices in town sits at the corner of Calvert St. and Wisconsin Ave. Despite these high gasoline prices, having a car in this neighborhood should not be a problem—street parking is plentiful and access to a car makes getting around town much easier.

Commute to Downtown   Fifteen minutes by bus

Post Office   Calvert St. Station, 2336 Wisconsin Ave., N.W. (202/965-8966)

Library   Georgetown Regional, Wisconsin Ave. and R St., N.W. (202/727-1353)

Police   3320 Idaho Ave., N.W. (202/282-0070)

Recreational Activities   A recreation center sponsors art and aerobics classes as well as programs for senior citizens. It is located at 3600 Calvert St., N.W. Several small parks are in the neighborhood and tennis courts are nearby at 33rd St. and Volta Place, N.W.

■ Cathedral and McLean Gardens

Traveling further up Wisconsin Ave., you will reach Cathedral and McLean Gardens. These two relatively small and quiet neighborhoods lie between Georgetown and Tenleytown. Cathedral earns its name from the defining landmark in the area, the National Cathedral, which is visible from points throughout the City and even across the river. Its grounds are a wonderful place to stroll.

The blocks surrounding the Cathedral host a number of older apartment buildings and one-family homes. Generally, apartment buildings line Wisconsin Ave. and the side streets to the west. Single family homes appear on the side streets east of Wisconsin in the shadow of the Cathedral. Many of these homes are actually in the Cleveland Park Historical District.

Further up Wisconsin, the former McLean family estate now houses McLean Gardens. The McLean family, one of D.C.'s wealthier families, suffered many misfortunes often blamed on the curse of the Hope Diamond (a famous 45 1/2 carat blue diamond now on display at the Smithsonian, which so far does not seem to have inherited the curse). In 1941, The McLeans sold their estate to the Federal Government, which used the land to build apartment buildings and dormitories to shelter the swelling population that came to the District to work for the growing War Department. After World War II, private interests took control of the land and turned the buildings into private apartments. Today, McLean Gardens is a large garden apartment and condominium complex.

Most of the commercial activity along Wisconsin Ave. occurs between the two neighborhoods. A 24-hour **Giant** (202/244-5922) and **People's Drug** (202/966-9268) face each other at the corner of Wisconsin and Newark. The first **Starbucks Coffee** (3430 Wisconsin Ave., N.W., 202/537-6879) in Washington recently opened here. Other restaurants range from the venerable **Zebra Room** (3238 Wisconsin Ave., N.W.; 202/362-8307) to the chic **Thai Flavor** (3228 Wisconsin Ave., N.W.; 202/966-0200).

Commute to Downtown Fifteen minutes by bus

Post Office Friendship Station, 4005 Wisconsin Ave., N.W. (202/523-2401)

Library Tenleytown, 4450 Wisconsin Ave., N.W. (202/727-1389)

Police Station 3320 Idaho Ave., N.W. (202/282-0070)

Recreational Activities McLean Gardens maintains its own pools that are open to residents. Three public tennis courts sit near the corner of Newark and 39th Sts. Public gardens are also located at Newark and 39th Sts. To reserve a garden plot, call 202/576-6257.

American University Park and Spring Valley

American University Park and Spring Valley are two of the several neighborhoods that touch the fringes of American University. Massachusetts Ave., a main D.C. thoroughfare, runs through these neighborhoods and up to suburban Maryland. The frequent N bus lines provide residents with the best access to Downtown.

American University Park is a modest neighborhood, containing reasonable housing options. The suburban feel of this area com-

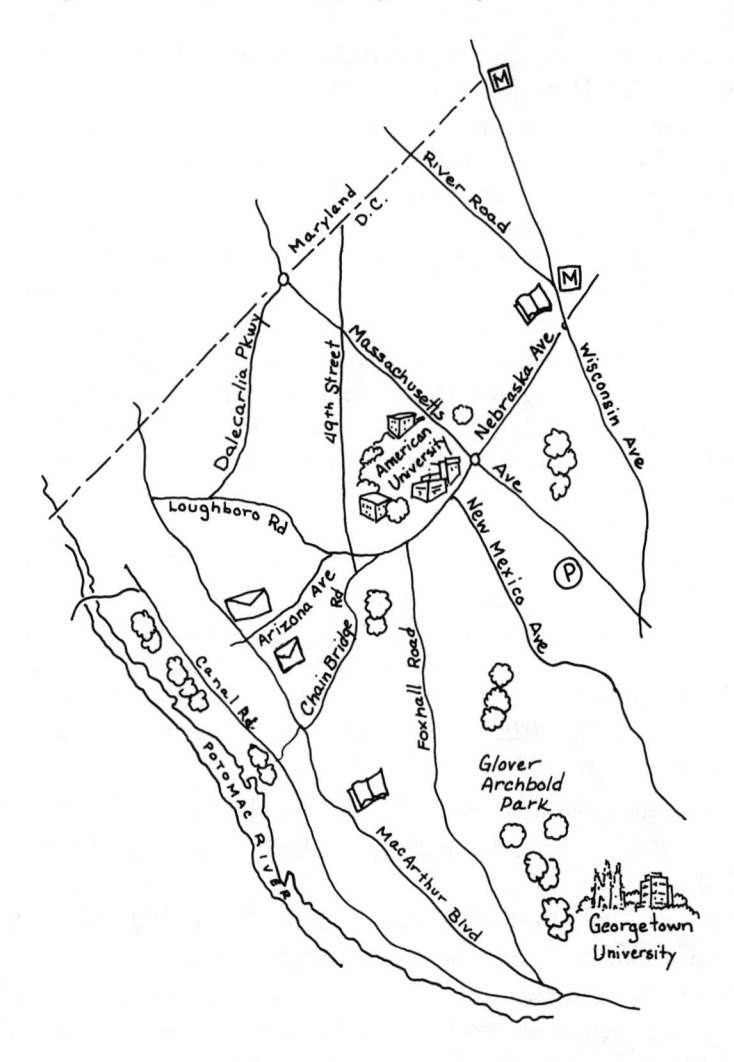

American University Park,
Spring Valley and Friendship Heights

bined with affordable starter homes makes it popular for young families. Apartment housing, although not plentiful, is available. Rents tend to reflect the scarcity, with one-bedrooms in the $800 range. Students favor the mammoth apartment buildings just below campus on Massachusetts and New Mexico Ave.

Spring Valley, one of the most affluent sections in Washington is known for its quiet, tree-lined neighborhood streets full of large, single family homes. Houses in this neighborhood can reach into the seven-figure range, with more moderately priced houses in the high $200,000s. For those just beginning to move into houses, leasing a house may be a more practical option. Rental prices here compare to other Northwest neighborhoods. Available rental housing ranges from attached houses, to cluster homes, to detached, single-family residences. There are few apartment buildings or complexes in this area.

The close proximity to American University offers residents many entertainment options. AU athletic events, performances, movies and museums are open to the public. Information about upcoming events can be obtained from the AU Student Confederation at 202/885-6400. Two popular student hang-outs in the area are **Maggie's** (4237 Wisconsin Ave., N.W.; 202/363-1447) and **Quigley's** (3201 New Mexico Ave., N.W.; 202/966-0500).

Grocery shopping can be done at **Safeway** (4865 MacArthur Blvd. N.W.; 202/337-5649) or just over the Maryland line at **Giant** (5400 West Bard Ave., Bethesda; 301/652-1484). **Sutton Place Gourmet** (3201 New Mexico Ave., N.W.; 202/363-5800) satisfies the neighborhood's need for gourmet. A second, smaller **Sutton Place Gourmet** (202/966-1740) sits at 4872 Massachusetts Ave., N.W.

Commute to Downtown 30 minutes by bus
Post Office Friendship Station, 4005 Wisconsin Ave., N.W. (202/523-2401); Palisades Station, 5136 MacArthur Blvd., N.W. (202/363-2921)
Libraries Palisades, 49th and V Sts., N.W. (202/727-1369); Tenleytown, Wisconsin Ave. and Albemarle St., N.W. (202/727-1389)
Police 3320 Idaho Ave., N.W. (202/282-0070)
Recreational Activities A track and indoor pool at the Wilson Senior High School (Nebraska Ave. and Chesapeake St., N.W.; 202/282-2216) are open to the public. Turtle Park at Van Ness and 45th St., N.W. hosts organized baseball and soccer teams.

Friendship Heights

This tiny, high-rise neighborhood straddles the D.C./Maryland line. Its 32 acres host a variety of upscale stores and mammoth apartment buildings. This neighborhood is famous for its fashionable shopping district that includes Gucci, Gianfranco Ferre, Valentino, Neiman Marcus and Saks Fifth Avenue to name a few. Boston's Filene's Basement recently joined the ranks.

One-bedroom apartments start around $800 a month and all other options are available. If you prefer older or cozier neighborhoods, you should look elsewhere. If you do not mind living in a high-rise and want to be near upscale amenities and the Metro, this just might be the place. Many chose to live here because it has an "urban feel" and Maryland taxes. Most apartment complexes have swimming pools and relatively inexpensive underground parking. The area's close proximity to American University and Downtown via the Red line make it quite convenient. The **Chevy Chase Shopping Center,** on the east side of Wisconsin Ave., has a **Giant** (301/718-6559) and a **People's Drug** (301/652-4959). A free shuttle bus service connects all of the major apartment complexes with this shopping center.

The **Friendship Heights Village Council** (301/656-2797) maintains an office at 4433 South Park Ave. You can call them to receive information about the Village. **The Village Center,** in the same building, provides residents with various recreational, educational, cultural and health services.

Commute to Downtown   25 minutes by Metro
Post Office   5530 Wisconsin Ave. (301/652-1198)
Libraries   Tenley-Friendship Branch, Albermarle St. and Wisconsin Ave., N.W. (202/727-1389); Bethesda Regional, 7400 Arlington Rd. (301/986-4300)
Police Station   7359 Wisconsin Ave. (301/652-9200)
Recreational Facilities   A track and indoor pool at the Wilson Senior High School (Nebraska Ave. and Chesapeake St., N.W.; 202/282-2216) are open to the public. The Hubert Humphrey Friendship Park is within walking distance.

☐ VIRGINIA NEIGHBORHOODS
Arlington
Arlington was originally part of the ten-mile square allocated to the new District of Columbia in 1791. At the request of its residents, Arlington was returned to the Commonwealth of Virginia in 1846. As the Federal Government has grown over the last 50 years, so has Arlington. Today, D.C. has virtually reclaimed its own. True Virginians barely consider Northern Virginia and particularly places like Arlington part of Virginia at all. Once you venture past the Beltway, you will understand why.

Hundreds of government offices now spread across Crystal City, Rosslyn and Ballston. To meet the demands of its swelling population, Arlington's housing and shopping have multiplied exponentially. Many new residential and commercial communities have sprouted up over the last decade along Arlington's Blue, Orange and Yellow Metro lines.

The renting prospects run the gamut from efficiencies to group houses. Condos and houses, small and (some) large, also abound. Prices for many apartments, especially those in luxury buildings, rival those in the District and Bethesda. Further out and away from the Metro, prices drop quickly. Wilson Blvd. above ground and the Orange line underneath link the North Arlington neighborhoods of Rosslyn, Court House, Clarendon and Ballston. The Orange line's quick access to Downtown makes North Arlington quite popular for commuters. South Arlington is dominated by the world's largest office building, the Pentagon. Rents here are slightly lower and the neighborhoods are not quite as nice or as convenient. Metrobus #16 travels up Columbia Pike, starting at the Pentagon and continues to Baileys Crossroads.

■ Rosslyn

When you look across the Potomac River to Virginia, Rosslyn seems like an aberration. High-rise office buildings, forbidden in the District, dominate Rosslyn's skyline. What Rosslyn lacks in aesthetic appeal, though, it makes up in convenience. Rosslyn sits directly across the Key Bridge from Georgetown and across the Roosevelt Bridge from the Mall. The Orange and Blue lines stop here first on their way out to Virginia.

Rosslyn's main thoroughfare, the five-laned Wilson Blvd., climbs up from the Key Bridge. Rosslyn built several sky-walks to accommodate both heavy commuter traffic and pedestrians. In reality, though, these ramps are confusing and many seem to lead nowhere. One Washingtonian said, "It is like a concrete labyrinth. You turn a corner and find yourself facing a brick wall."

During the day, more than 36,000 workers toil in Rosslyn's office towers. At night, though, Rosslyn's streets are deserted. This lack of nighttime activity should not dissuade new residents. According to the Arlington police department, Rosslyn is quite safe.

Despite Rosslyn's appearance, many young professionals and students (especially from George Washington University) find the neighborhood a fine place to live. Rosslyn offers a surprising array of garden and high-rise apartments, some right on the Potomac. Rents are generally slightly below those of the Northwest's most popular neighborhoods. Those looking for group houses should explore the streets north of Wilson Blvd. toward I-66.

Rosslyn has most of the usual conveniences at or around the intersection of Wilson Blvd. and North Lynn St.—several dry cleaners, **People's Drug** (703/243-4993) and **Tivoli Gourmet** (703/524-8904). Residents do their grocery shopping at **Safeway** (703/276-9315) at 1525 Wilson Blvd. A 30-foot-tall sculpture called "Anna and David" marks the spot for this underground Safeway, making it pretty easy to find.

Commute to Downtown Seven minutes by Metro
Post Office 1101 Wilson Blvd. (703/525-4336)
Library Central Library, 1015 North Quincy St. (703/358-5990)
Police Station 2100 North 15th St. (703/558-2222)
Recreational Facilities Two tennis courts are at Lyon Village Park (20th Rd. and North Highland St.).

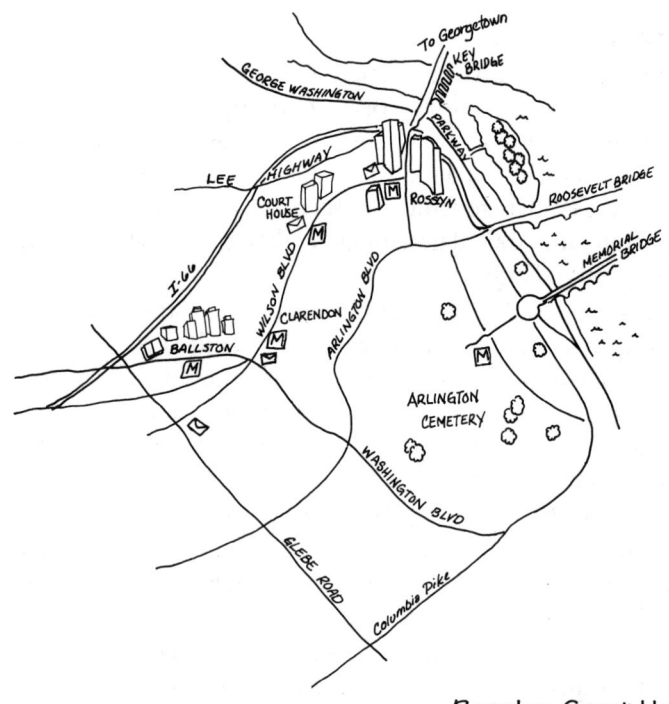

Rosslyn, Court House, Clarendon and Ballston

Chapter One | Neighborhoods

■ Court House

Guess what important landmark is the focal point of this neighborhood? Yes, it is the Arlington County Courthouse. While you may not initially think living near a Courthouse is a plus, it does make handling official business easy.

Developers have been busy recently, erecting large, new luxury apartment buildings and a shopping complex around the Courthouse and along Clarendon Blvd. These buildings offer a selection of one and two-bedroom apartments. Rent for a one-bedroom starts around $800 a month. Older, smaller (and cheaper) apartment buildings inhabit the side streets, supplying an even wider range of apartment options. A number of large-scale developments have also been built south of Clarendon Blvd. toward Route 50.

The plaza adjoining the Courthouse contains a convenience store, **The Metro Market** (703/841-3530), several restaurants, gourmet food shops and an eight-screen AMC movie theater. There are several supermarkets nearby, the **Safeway** in Rosslyn, another **Safeway** about a mile away on Lee Highway (3713 Lee Highway; 703/841-1155) and two **Giants,** one at 3115 Lee Highway (703/527-9453) and another near the Virginia Square Metro stop at 3450 North Washington Blvd. (703/358-9343).

A weekly farmers' market takes place on Saturday mornings from April to October. Farmers sell their fresh produce on 14th St. between North Courthouse and North Veitch Sts., just past the police station near the Courthouse.

Commute to Downtown   Ten minutes by Metro
Post Office   2043 Wilson Blvd. (703/525-4441)
Library   Central Library, 1015 North Quincy St. (703/358-5990)
Police Station   2100 North 15th St. (703/558-2222)
Recreational Facilities   There are two tennis courts at Lyon Village Park at 20th Rd. and North Highland St.

■ Clarendon

Clarendon, just up Wilson Blvd. from Court House, has not yet been subjected to the high-rise building boom enjoyed (or suffered) by its neighbors. It remains a mostly quiet, low-key neighborhood, full of ethnic restaurants and older one-family homes. This abundance of older houses makes Clarendon a great area to get a group house. Rents in the range of $350 to $400 per person in a group house are not out of the question here.

The square around the Clarendon Metro station is the main hub of the neighborhood. The square reflects the changes that are beginning to happen to Clarendon. In the middle of the square stands a World War I monument. On Clarendon Blvd., a sleek, modern high-rise building dominates the block. Across the street on Wilson Blvd., older beat-up storefronts full of small shops and restaurants still cover the block. Washington's best Vietnamese restaurants occupy this side of the square.

If you are planning on living here, I suggest that you have a car or live with someone who does. Most conveniences are not easily accessible by foot. If you have a car, there are several large supermarkets to chose from, including the **Safeways** and **Giants** mentioned above.

Commute to Downtown Fifteen minutes by Metro
Post Office 3118 North Washington Blvd. (703/525-4838)
Library Central Library, 1015 North Quincy St. (703/358-5990)
Police Station 2100 North 15th St. (703/558-2222)
Recreational Facilities Washington-Lee High School (1300 North Quincy St.; 703/358-6262) has a swimming pool and a track. Six public tennis courts are across the street at Quincy Park.

■ Ballston

Ballston gives every indication that it will become the next Rosslyn, with too many high-rise buildings crammed cheek to jowl within a few blocks of the Metro station. Even the recession seems barely to have curbed its rapid growth, except for a conspicuously empty, rubble-strewn vacant lot across from the Metro and the foundations of a never-completed apartment complex behind Rio Grande.

Housing can be found in any one of the many apartment buildings or town houses on the side streets off Fairfax Drive, Washington Blvd. and Glebe Rd. High-rise apartment buildings generally offer one, two and three-bedroom apartments, but not many efficiencies.

The blue-capped **IHOP** (International House of Pancakes; 703/522-3118) stands as a landmark on Fairfax Drive, having weathered the changes to the neighborhood. It stays open round the clock and is a great spot for Sunday morning breakfasts. In addition to this remnant of old Ballston, the area has a shopping mall, **Ballston Common** and a few restaurants, including one of Washington's most popular Tex-Mex restaurants, **Rio Grande Cafe** (703/528-3131). **Giant** (703/351-9220) is at the corner of Washington Blvd. and Lincoln, a short walk from the Virginia Square Metro and George Mason Law

School. You will have to do some driving for the rest. If you have a car, you might be inclined to shop at the **Safeway** (703/524-1528) at 5101 Wilson Blvd. past Glebe Rd., the **Super Fresh** (703/237-0331) at the corner of North Harrison and Lee Highway (2425 North Harrison St.) or the **Safeway** across the street at 2500 North Harrison St. (703/538-6700). **Tivoli Gourmet** (703/528-5201), right at the Metro stop, is the neighborhood's only gourmet shop and, unfortunately, not a particularly good one.

Commute to Downtown: 20 minutes by Metro
Post Office Buckingham Station, 235 North Glebe Rd. (703/525-4170)
Library Central Library, 1015 North Quincy St. (703/358-5990)
Police Station 2100 North 15th St. (703/558-2222)
Recreational Facilities Washington-Lee High School (1300 North Quincy St.; 703/358-6262) has a swimming pool and a track. Six public tennis courts are across the street at Quincy Park.

■ Pentagon City

This quiet community, just off of Army-Navy Drive, rests beneath the shadow of the Pentagon. Many one-family houses and several massive apartment buildings crowd the area. Unfortunately, this working class neighborhood lacks many of the suburban amenities that make daily life more convenient. As a result, Pentagon City offers lower rents than nearby, amenity-rich Crystal City or North Arlington. One-bedroom apartments cost approximately $700 a month. A wide selection of group houses occupies the streets behind the Virginia Highlands Park. Rents here can be as low as $350 a month per person. Whether you live in an apartment building or a house, parking never seems to be a problem.

Pentagon City is home to one of Washington's newest malls, the **Fashion Centre at Pentagon City.** Residents particularly enjoy the mall's six-screen movie theater and huge food-court. The Pentagon City Metro (Blue and Yellow) has an exit leading directly into the mall.

The neighborhood does not have a large grocery store, but there is a convenience store in the basement of River House I. For grocery shopping, you can go to the **Safeway** in Crystal City (2129 Crystal Plaza Drive; 703/415-0422), just one Metro stop away. If you have access to a car, you can take advantage of the shopping along Columbia Pike or Glebe Rd. Both **Safeway** (2303 Columbia Pike; 703/920-2909) and **Giant** (2515 Columbia Pike; 703/685-7050 and 1303 South Glebe Rd.; 703/836-0245) are there.

Commute to Downtown 20 to 30 minutes by Metro
Post Office Eads Station, 1720 Eads St. (703/979-2108)
Library Aurora Hills, 735 South 18th St. (703/358-5715)
Police Station 2100 North 15th St. (703/558-2222)
Recreational Activities Six public tennis courts are at Virginia Highlands Park, corner of 17th and South Ives Sts. The Carver Center at 1415 South Queen St. has three tennis courts.

■ Crystal City

If you have ever flown into National Airport, you may have noticed a crowd of skyscrapers towering near the Pentagon. These complexes make up Crystal City, lining both sides of Jefferson Davis Highway (Route 1) with a mix of offices, hotels and apartments. The Office of Patents and Trademarks, USAir, IBM and Booz, Allen & Hamilton all have offices in these buildings. Crystal City was planned and built as a unit. It was all originally owned by one developer and while it may lack charm, it makes up for it in convenience.

This area's gigantic apartment warrens offer a variety of choices. You will easily find everything there from efficiencies to three-bed-

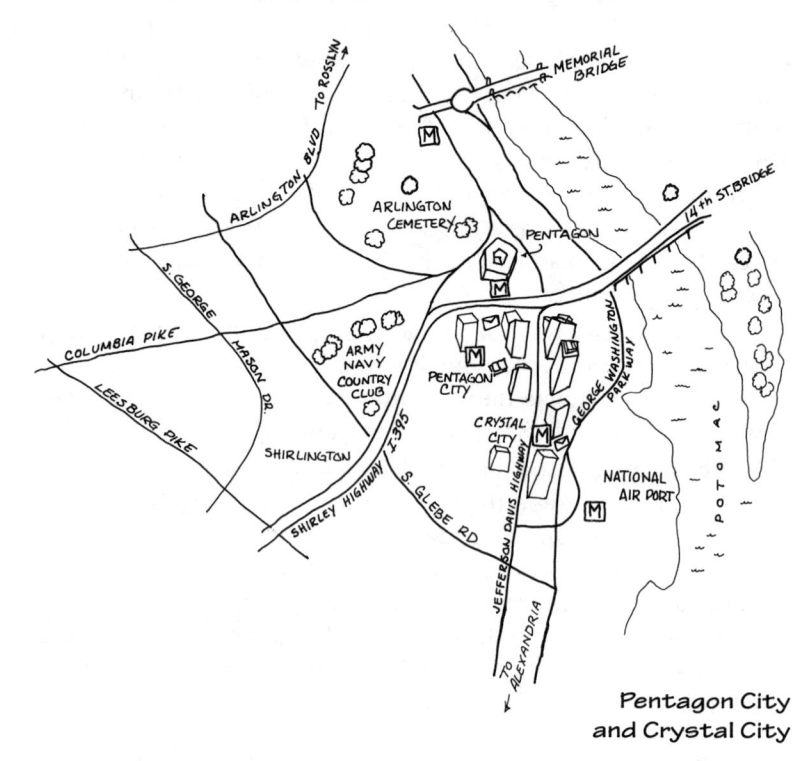

Pentagon City
and Crystal City

rooms at prices lower than those in North Arlington. Some older one-family homes, perfect for group houses, can be found on the west side of Jefferson Davis Highway.

If you opt to live in Crystal City, especially in one of the highrise apartment buildings, chances are you can exist here without ever venturing outside. Most of Crystal City is connected by miles of underground passages, which comprise the Crystal City Underground Shopping Center. This shopping center has every amenity, including a post office, several small gourmet shops, restaurants and a **Safeway** (2129 Crystal Plaza Drive; 703/415-0422). Even the Crystal City Metro (Blue and Yellow) feeds into this underground mall.

A word of caution: because of Crystal City's close proximity to National Airport, airplane traffic can be heard throughout the day. The noise gets especially loud during the early evening hours. Fortunately, National closes around 10:00 p.m. If you are looking for an apartment or house here, be sure to ask your prospective landlord about the noise and then drop by at night or early in the morning to gauge it for yourself. Those renting apartments facing east towards National should be especially wary.

Commute to Downtown 25 minutes by Metro
Post Office 1632 Crystal Drive (703/413-9267)
Library Aurora Hills, 735 South 18th St. (703/358-5715)
Police Station 2100 North 15th St. (703/558-2222)
Recreational Facilities Six public tennis courts at Virginia Highlands Park, corner of 17th and South Ives Sts.

Alexandria

Most newcomers mistakenly associate Alexandria only with Old Town. They do not realize that Alexandria offers a host of other options. Single-family houses and bucolic green lawns abound throughout this sixteen-square-mile city. Four Metro stops, as well as Metrobus and DASH, link Alexandria to the District. DASH runs six bus routes through Alexandria for just 75¢. Frequent air travelers may want to consider living in Alexandria, since it is less than a ten-minute commute to National Airport.

Old Town looks almost too good to be true. Strict zoning regulations protect its freshly-painted Georgian houses, cobblestone streets and clean sidewalks. This historic quarter begins at Washington St. and continues down to the waterfront. Naturally, rents are the highest here. Landlords can demand as much as $1,500 to $2,000

Mastering DC | A Newcomer's Guide to Living in Washington

[Map of Alexandria showing National Airport, Old Town, Potomac River, Woodrow Wilson Bridge, and various streets including King Street, Braddock Rd, Russell Rd, Commonwealth, Mt. Vernon Ave., Jefferson Davis Highway Rt.1, George Washington Memorial Parkway, Powhatan St., Henry St., Patrick St., Queen St., Duke Street, Eisenhower Ave., Capital Beltway I-95, Huntington Ave., Washington St., So. Richmond Highway, Rt. 1, To Mount Vernon]

Alexandria

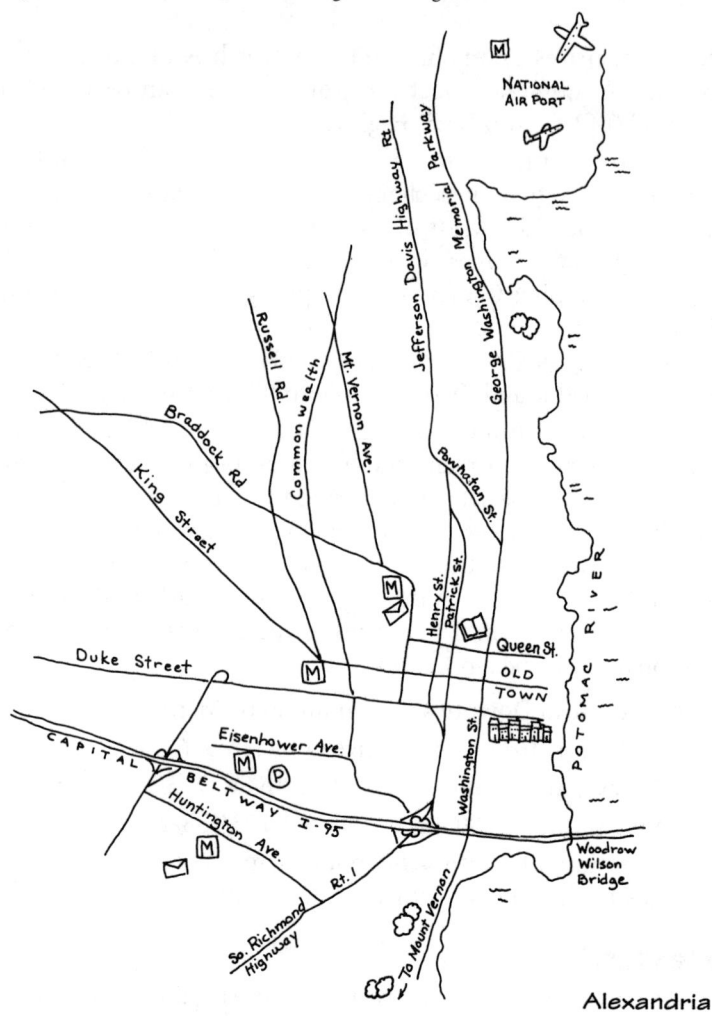

a month for a two-bedroom apartment or small townhouse. Finding lodging in Old Town can be difficult without assistance. With rents like these, local real estate agents will be only too happy to help.

As you leave Old Town and travel south down Washington St. towards Mt. Vernon, you will find several apartment complexes that try to capitalize on their proximity to Old Town. If reasonably priced, these apartments can be quite convenient. Further to the southwest, you will find numerous high-rise and garden-style apartments. Apartment complexes along Route 1 South, Duke St. and areas around the Van Dorn Metro station promise even lower rents. The northwest end of the city, near the Braddock St. Metro and

National Airport, contains a mix of immaculate condos and low-rent housing.

Supermarkets can be found at either end of Old Town. A **Giant** (530 First St.; 703/739-0751) is at the northern end, about seven blocks from the Braddock Rd. Metro station and **Safeway** (500 South Royal St.; 703/836-0380) has a store at the south end. In addition, the Downtown area boasts several gourmet stores, including **Sutton Place Gourmet** (600 Franklin St.; 703/549-6611) and the **King St. Gourmet Cellar** (210 King St.; 703/683-5439).

Since colonial days, lots have been set aside in Alexandria's town square for a farmers' market. Today, the tradition of selling fresh produce, meats and baked goods continues at the weekly Saturday morning market on the south plaza of the City Hall (301 King St.).

Further away from Old Town, you will find shopping along the city's main arteries. Both **Safeway** (703/379-6019) and **Giant** (703/845-0851) have supermarkets in the Bradlee Mall on upper King St., right near the intersection of King St. and Braddock Rd.

Commute to Downtown 30 to 45 minutes by Metro

Post Office Main Branch, 1100 Wythe St. (703/549-4201); George Mason Branch, 126 South Washington St. (703/549-0813); Parkfairfax Station, 3682 King St. (703/379-6017); Trade Center Station, 340 South Pickett St. (703/823-0968); Jefferson Manor Branch, 5834 North King's Highway (703/960-4440)

Libraries Lloyd House, 220 N. Washington St.(703/838-4557); Ellen Coolidge Burke Branch, 4701 Seminary Rd. (703/370-6050); James Duncan Branch, 2501 Commonwealth Ave. (703/838-4566)

Police Station 2003 Mill Rd. (703/838-4444)

Recreational Activities Chinquapin Park (703/931-1127) at 3210 King St. has an indoor pool, fitness room, racquetball courts, tennis courts, picnic areas and a nature trail. Cameron Run Regional Park (4001 Eisenhower Ave.; 703/960-0767) has a wave pool, miniature golf course (a tough one—no windmills and dog houses here) and batting cages.

Fairfax County

Like its neighbor across the Maryland line, Fairfax County is filled with a plethora of green lawns, tree-lined streets and some of the country's best public schools. It is an affluent area, long-settled and quaint. Signs everywhere mark important Civil War sites. The overriding character is suburban, but if you travel further west it begins to become more rural. This area is better for those planning on buying a house and settling down than for those planning on renting short term.

As in all suburbs, residents are heavily dependent on cars to get them around. I-66 runs west through the county while I-495 crosses from north to south. The Orange line shoots out to this area with stops at Falls Church, Dunn Loring and Vienna. The county-run bus service, the Fairfax Connector (703/339-7200), links the southeastern section of the county.

■ Falls Church

The actual City of Falls Church spans only two square miles, but the area Washingtonians refer to as Falls Church is much larger. Much of the area lodged between northern Arlington and the posh community of McLean has a mailing address of Falls Church.

Eastern Falls Church encompasses the area between Arlington Blvd. at the Seven Corners Shopping Center and the East Falls Church Metro. Rents here are particularly low for the Washington metropolitan area. The high-rise and garden apartment complexes located along commercial Leesburg Pike (Route 7) supply an abundance of efficiencies and one-bedroom apartments. In general, locations closer to the East Falls Church Metro are more convenient, although slightly more expensive. Group houses can be found in and around the Washington Blvd. area.

West Falls Church, by contrast, has fewer choices for apartment seekers and more for those looking to buy. There are a few high-rise apartment complexes, though, between the Metro station and Tysons Corner.

Falls Church is a shopper's paradise. The **Seven Corners Shopping Center** houses **Woodie's** and **The Gap** in East Falls Church. West Falls Church sits in the backyard of upscale shopping at **Tysons I** and the **Galleria at Tysons II**. Both malls are packed with the usual mall-suspects, including **Bloomingdale's, Macy's** and **Saks Fifth Avenue**.

The only way to reach one of the best supermarkets in the area, the **Giant** (703/845-0446) at Baileys Crossroads, is by car. This Giant has everything. If you choose to shop here, go during the week. The supermarket and surrounding mall are extremely popular on the weekends and the parking lot is chaotic and often full. Another **Giant** (703/237-9609) is at the corner of West Broad St. and Haycock Rd., within walking distance of the West Falls Church Metro. **Safeways** are located at 6118 Arlington Blvd. (703/241-4131) and at 7397 Lee Highway (703/573-2057). **Magruder's** (703/280-0440) is on Graham Rd. **Fresh Fields** (7501 Leesburg Pike; 703/448-1600) between I-66 and Tysons Corner, offers a large selection of organically-grown produce.

Commute to Downtown   30 to 45 minutes by Metro

Post Office   301 West Broad St. (703/532-8822); 6019 Leesburg Pike (703/671-0221)

Libraries   Thomas Jefferson Branch, 7415 Arlington Blvd. (703/573-1060); Mary Riley Styles Library, 120 North Virginia Ave. (703/241-5030)

Police Station   300 Park Ave. (703/241-5054)

Recreational Activities   The Falls Church Community Center at 223 Little Falls St. (703/241-5077) sponsors a variety of sports activities and offers classes in cooking and dancing. The Washington & Old Dominion bike trail whisks bikers and joggers all the way to the Arlington/Alexandria border and as far west as Purcellville.

■ Fairfax City

Fairfax City dates back to the pre-Revolutionary era and retains some of the charm of its colonial roots. However, the twelve miles separating it from downtown Washington have not shielded it from the rapid growth of the metropolitan area in recent decades. Downtown Fairfax City remains village-like, with small houses and restaurants. Beyond downtown, though, you will find many strip malls and housing developments. "Fairfax" now sprawls beyond its official boundaries and large sections of outlying Fairfax County are considered part of the city, complete with a Fairfax address.

Just across the city line is the Vienna Metro, actually more convenient to Fairfax than to the neighboring city that gives it its name. Fairfax is served by the Metrobus system as well as by Metro. Fairfax also operates its own mini-bus system, called CUE, with four routes, running about every ten minutes covering most of the city proper and the Vienna Metro. Most residents, however, find a car necessary.

Fairfax is home to **George Mason University** (GMU), one of the largest schools in the Virginia state system. GMU students commute from all over the region but Fairfax is not overrun by students. The **Fairfax Symphony Orchestra** and the **Virginia Opera** perform at GMU's **Center for the Arts** (703/993-8888).   For the economy-minded, the **University Mall Theater** (703/273-7111) shows almost-current films for only $3 a ticket. Several bars offer live music. **T.T.**

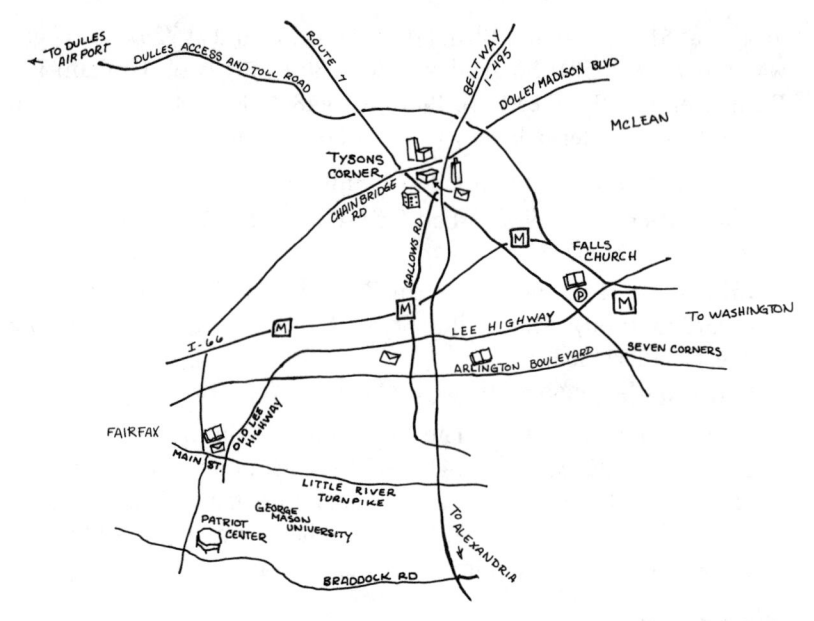

Falls Church and Fairfax City

Reynold's (10414 Main St.; 703/591-9292) has live entertainment every day of the week. **Fat Tuesday's** (703/385-8660) has more of the same, with blues and rock bands playing nearly every day. At **The Legend** (3979 Chain Bridge Rd.; 703/591-1478), you can hear blues, rock, reggae and progressive music.

All types of housing are available for purchase and rental. Apartments and townhouses in the Fairfax Circle area are most convenient to the Metro, some within walking distance of the station. From other areas, rail commuters must use the CUE bus or drive to the Vienna station. Several apartment and townhouse communities are located along Blake Lane going northwest to Fairfax Circle. There are others along Main St. (Route 236) between downtown and Pickett Rd. Rents in Fairfax follow the Washington area rule: the more accessible to D.C., the higher they go. Apartments average $750 to $800, townhouses $1250 to $1500. Detached homes run $1200 and up.

There are numerous smaller shops in downtown Fairfax and convenient shopping centers. But for serious shopping, area residents head for nearby malls. **Fair Oaks** (703/359-8300), at the intersection of Route 50 and Interstate 66, is anchored by **Hecht's, Woodie's, Sears** and **J.C. Penney.**

Chapter One | *Neighborhoods*

Victoria's Cakery (3995 Chain Bridge Rd.; 703/273-0800), tucked away in a funky Victorian house in downtown Fairfax, is guaranteed to satisfy any sweet tooth. **Safeway** has locations at the Courthouse Plaza Shopping Center (703/591-8473) and the Pan Am Shopping Center near Fairfax Circle (3043 Nutley St.; 703/560-6696). **Giant** is at 11054 Lee Highway (703/273-0147), 9570 Main St. (703/323-9108) and 12997 Lee Jackson Memorial Highway (703/803-7732). Fairfax also has its own **Price Club** (4725 West Ox Rd.; 703/802-1223) for buying in bulk.

Commute to Downtown   45 minutes to an hour by Metro

Post Office   Main, 3951 Chain Bridge Rd. (703/273-5571); Turnpike, 3601 Pickett Rd. (703/239-2900); Fairfax Station, 5616 Ox Rd. (703/250-9188); Chantilly Branch Post Office, 4410 Brookfield Corporate Drive (703/968-7272)

Library   Fairfax Regional, 3915 Chain Bridge Rd. (703/246-2741)

Police Station   10600 Page Ave. (703/691-2131)

Recreational Activities   Burke Lake Park (7315 Ox Rd., Fairfax Station; 703/323-6600) has a 18-hole golf course, fishing, hiking, camping and boating. Children will enjoy its carousel and miniature train.

■ Reston

To some, Reston is the "ultimate suburb." To others, this completely planned community in the rolling Virginia countryside has the look of a residential theme park.

The community takes its name from its visionary founder, Robert E. Simon, who willed it into being on farmland near Dulles Airport beginning in the Sixties. Almost half of Reston is park land, or other open space, including a series of four man-made lakes around which the neighborhoods are organized. Each part of town — Hunters Woods, South Lakes, Lake Anne and Tall Oaks — has its own village center, complete with food, banking and other facilities, as well as a community center and a fellowship house for senior citizens. The neighborhoods in Reston are mainly self-contained, screened from major streets and the busy Dulles Toll Rd. by dense groves of trees. In the past few years, Reston and other communities have been home to a blitz of development. Office building after office building went up along the Dulles Toll Rd. to support the high-tech businesses that were relocating to this part of the state. The recession has left a number of these buildings empty or only partly-occupied.

Another relative newcomer to the community is **Reston Town Center** (11911 Freedom Drive; 703/742-6500). This mall and gathering place looms up out of the landscape and is a focal point for the area's nightlife. In the middle of the Town Center is an outdoor pavilion that provides seating for some of the restaurants. Concerts are held here during the summer, and in the winter the pavilion is converted into an ice skating rink. Aside from dozens of shops such as **Ann Taylor, Banana Republic, The Gap, Brentano's Books** and **Sam Goody,** the Town Center houses a number of restaurants and a **National Amusements Multiplex Cinema** (703/318-1800). Georgetown's imports have made their way out to Reston's Town Center: **Clyde's** (703/787-6601) and **Paolo's** (703/318-8920). **Rio Grande Cafe** (703/904-0703) serves delicious fajitas and the **Market Street Bar & Grill** (703/709-6262) offers a good brunch and a bit of culture with live jazz Friday, Saturday and Sunday nights.

Rents in Reston fall between $700 for a one-bedroom apartment to $1,000 for a three-bedroom apartment. Prices along the lakesides are the highest, with single-family homes and townhouses predominating. The **Reston Visitor's Center** (11450 Baron Cameron Avenue; 703/471-7030) provides detailed information and directions to all areas.

Residents get their groceries at Safeway and Giant. **Safeway** has a location at 1120 South Lakes Drive (703/620-2444) and 2369 Hunters Wood Plaza (703/620-6691). **Giant** has a store at 12040 North Shore Drive (703/478-6718) and another at 1450 Reston Parkway (703/435-4100). Reston also has a **People's Drug** (11160 South Lakes Drive; 703/620-6691).

Commute to Downtown   45 minutes to an hour by Metro
Post Office   11110 Sunset Hills Rd. (703/437-6677)
Library   Reston Regional, 11925 Bowman Towne Drive (703/689-2700)
Police Station   12000 Bowman Towne Drive (703/478-0904)
Recreational Activities   Reston has lots of public swimming pools and tennis courts all over town for its residents. In addition, there are footpaths and bike trails that link every part of Reston.

■ Herndon

Herndon, Reston's next door neighbor, is quite different. "Herndon has more pick-up trucks that BMWs," says one resident. Unlike Reston, which was planned start to finish, Herdon was a little village

Chapter One | Neighborhoods

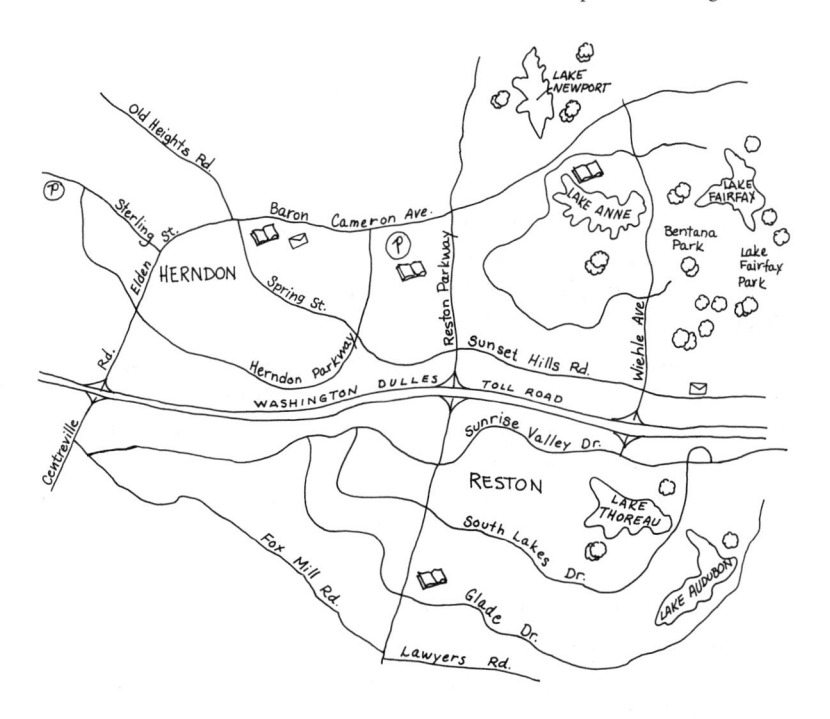

Reston and Herndon

caught up in the regional growth that accompanied the construction of the Dulles Toll Rd. High-tech, defense-oriented and service businesses attracted by the convenience of the airport have created a new commercial nexus called the Dulles Corridor along the combination express and toll road. Herndon has absorbed much of the influx.

Still, you can tell something of Herndon's history as you travel along Elden St. through the somewhat-scruffy, old-fashioned downtown. The town still has the look and feel of the small village railroad stop that Herdon was until very recently. The tiny, old railroad station, which used to be the focal point of Herndon, still sits in the center of town.

Renovating late Victorian houses has become trendy, but recent townhouse and apartment construction has changed the old look elsewhere. Some renovated older homes and townhouses may be available close to the village center. Newer accommodations are more likely to be on the outskirts, although in a town of just over four square miles, that does not require going very far. On average, Herndon's rents for roughly similar housing are well below Reston's.

Downtown is home to the **Ice House Cafe** (760 Elden St.; 703/471-4256). This small, dark jazz club has been an institution in Herndon for years. This area also features the ubiquitous **Champion's Sports Bar** (208 Elden St.; 703/306-8600), **Hard Times Cafe** (394 Elden St.; 703/318-8941) and a discount movie theater showing almost-current flicks. A **Loew's Theater** (703/318-9290) is off the Toll Rd. at Exit 2 in the Worldgate Plaza. This plaza is home to several shops and the **Worldgate Athletic Center** (703/709-9100), a popular health club with great facilities.

Residents do their grocery shopping at a gourmet **Giant Marketplace** (1228 Elden St.; 703/437-3162) or at **Shoppers Food Warehouse** (2425 Centreville Rd.; 703/793-3892). For breads and other baked goods, try **Great Harvest Bakery** (785 Station St.; 703/471-4031). A **People's Drug** (1062 Elden St.; 703/471-9478) and a **Rite Aid** pharmacy (696 Elden St.; 703/787-9830) are in the center of town as well.

Commute to Downtown   45 minutes to an hour by Metro
Post Office   590 Grove St. (703/437-3740)
Library   Herndon Fortnightly Mini, 600 Spring St. (703/437-8855). This library only has current reading.
Police Station   1481 Sterling Rd. (703/435-6846)
Recreational Activities   The Washington & Old Dominion Railroad Regional Park (703/729-0596) has trails for running, bicycling, horseback riding and hiking.

☐ MARYLAND NEIGHBORHOODS

Montgomery County

Montgomery County is one of the wealthiest counties in the country and a premier location for buying real estate. To the west, the county boasts some of greater Washington's most expensive estates. As you make your way eastward, the county approaches an environment more familiar to everyone else. As in all suburbs, residents are heavily dependent on cars to get around. Rockville Pike runs through the heart of the county and provides much of its shopping. The Red line extends out to this area, including stops at Friendship Heights, Bethesda and Silver Spring.

■ Bethesda

Bethesda occupies the southern tip of Montgomery County and is one of the most affluent suburbs in the metropolitan region. Pricy single-family homes predominate, punctuated by a number of important research facilities, including the National Institutes of Health, the Naval Medical Center and the Uniformed Services University of the Health Sciences. Four Red line Metro stops serve Bethesda along the traffic-congested Wisconsin Ave./Rockville Pike corridor: Bethesda, Medical Center, Grosvenor and White Flint.

Downtown Bethesda, centered around the Bethesda Metro, demonstrates the rapid expansion this suburb has undergone. Just 20

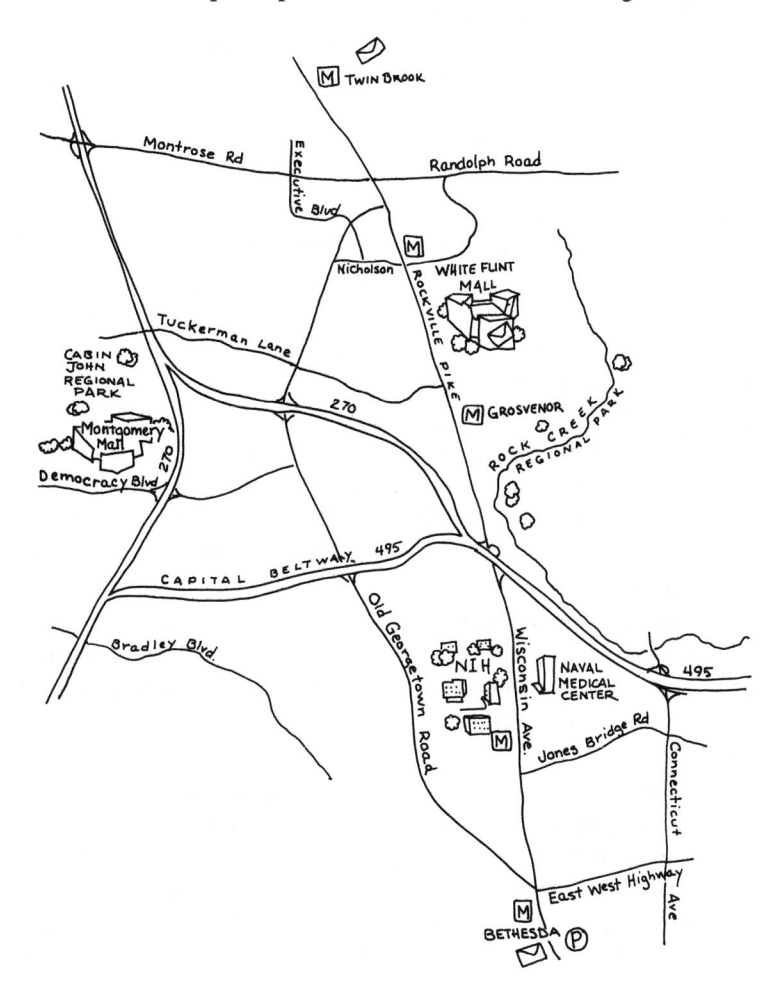

Bethesda

years ago, Bethesda was a sleepy farm town. Development accelerated in the Seventies, spurred on further by the coming of the Metro in 1982. You will find remnants of old Bethesda near the Metro station—a weathered post office and a statue honoring the "Madonna of the Trail," a tribute to Maryland's pioneer women. Next to these, *The Rainbow Forest,* an aluminum-disc sculpture and the recently-built Hyatt Luxury Hotel stand as icons of modern-day Bethesda. During the summer, the courtyard by the Metro station rocks to the beat of outdoor concerts; in the winter, it turns into an ice skating rink.

Beyond the high-rise buildings, to the west of Wisconsin Ave., you will find Woodmont Triangle. Many small shops and some of the area's best ethnic restaurants reside here. Your dining options include **Bacchus, Kabul West, Matuba Japanese Restaurant** and the **Cottonwood Cafe,** just to name a few. **Travel Books & Language Center** (4931 Cordell Ave.; 301/951-8533) offers a huge collection of travel guides and maps from around the world. Even the State Department orders from this store. The city has built numerous unsightly parking garages, so you should not have a problem parking.

Bethesda does not lack rental housing, but it does not come cheaply. The newer luxury apartment buildings near the Metro offer all conceivable amenities at top-notch rental prices. A multitude of older, renovated buildings along Battery Lane, a few blocks away rent for slightly less.

The Medical Center Metro stop further up Rockville Pike was built on the campus of the National Institutes of Health. If you exit the Metro just at the right time, you will hear reveille blown from the Naval Medical Center across the street. These institutions border residential neighborhoods. Several homeowners rent out rooms in their homes or in detached apartments on their property. Group houses are also available. Around the Grosvenor Metro station, you will find more high-rise condominiums and apartments. Some buildings offer discounts to NIH employees; if you qualify, be sure to ask at the rental office.

In this affluent suburb, grocery stores and supermarkets promise no shortage of fully-stocked shelves. Residents can shop at the **Safeway** at 5000 Bradley Blvd. (301/656-8641) or opt for the gourmet **Safeway Marketplace** (301/907-0700) at 7625 Old Georgetown Rd. **Giant,** on its home turf in the suburbs, has a store at Arlington Blvd. and Elm St. (301/718-2470). A Giant pharmacy (301/652-9130) is across the street. **People's Drug** has one store at

4601 East-West Highway (301/986-9144) and a 24-hour store at the corner of Bradley Blvd. and Arlington Rd. (301/656-2522). In addition to large grocery stores, there are several supermarket-size gourmet stores. **Sutton Place Gourmet** (301/564-3100) has a store in the Wildwood Shopping Center off Old Georgetown Rd. Further out, **Fresh Fields** (5225 River Rd.; 301/984-4860) offers its natural foods. On Wednesdays and Saturdays, the **Montgomery Farm Women's Cooperative** hosts a farmers' market selling fruit, flowers and Amish baked goods at 7155 Wisconsin Ave. An outdoor flea market, replete with oriental rugs, furniture and jewelry, takes over this location on Sundays.

Once you have moved into the area, you can pick up free information about Bethesda and Montgomery County at the **Bethesda-Chevy Chase Center** (301/986-4325) at 7815 Woodmont Ave.

Commute to Downtown   30 to 35 minutes by Metro
Post Office   7400 Wisconsin Ave. (301/652-7401)
Library   Bethesda Regional, 7400 Arlington Rd. (301/986-4300)
Police   7359 Wisconsin Ave. (301/652-9200)
Recreational Activities   Cabin John Regional Park (301/299-4555) at 7400 Tuckerman Lane has tennis and handball courts, hiking trails and an ice skating rink. Glen Echo Park, (7500 MacArthur Blvd., Glen Echo; 301/492-6282) the area's gem, is a national park that sponsors hundreds of classes in the arts. Its historic Spanish Ballroom offers a variety of dance classes and four dances per week from April through November. The park also operates a beautiful antique carousel from May through September.

■ Silver Spring

Silver Spring, a sprawling area comprising the easternmost part of Montgomery County, sits atop the northern part of the District's diamond. Since Silver Spring's real estate market has not yet exploded like Bethesda's, you can find some of the most reasonable rents in the Washington area around its three Red line Metro stops: Silver Spring, Forest Glen and Wheaton.

Downtown Silver Spring, the area near the junction of Georgia Ave. and Colesville Rd. (Route 29), boasts a busy Red line Metro stop (Silver Spring) and a number of new high-rise office buildings. The downtown area's last renaissance was in the 1930's and since then most of the larger stores have left for Rockville Pike. This loss of economic vitality offers Silver Spring's residents many advantages. Silver

Spring's Metro stop is accessible by car, even at rush hour, and there is plenty of nearby parking. In addition, rents remain lower than most neighborhoods around Washington. A number of small, ethnic restaurants and shops have filled the vacant storefronts. You will find Italian, Ethiopian, Thai, Indian and Latin-American establishments here. A controversial development project, the Silver Triangle, is being built in an effort to rejuvenate downtown Silver Spring. The first installment, **City Place** (8661 Colesville Rd.; 301/589-1091), opened in 1992. Capped by a ten-screen movie theater, the mall emphasizes outlet stores including **Nordstrom's Rack, Ross** and **Marshall's**.

Single-family houses and clusters of apartment buildings, both high-rise and garden-style, surround each of the three Metro stations. Group houses are available around the Forest Glen and Wheaton Metro stops. For those willing to brave the morning commute down

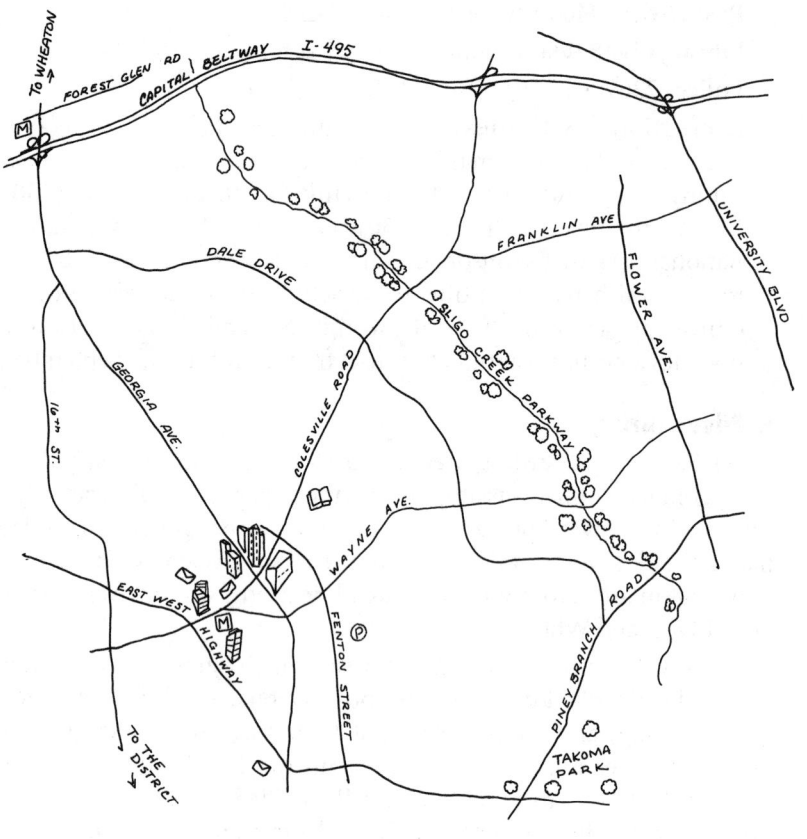

Silver Spring

Route 29, there are even cheaper options out Colesville Rd. at White Oak and beyond.

The area is served by several large grocery stores. **Snider's** (1936 Seminary Rd.; 301/589-3240), a local favorite, has a steady following who rave about its meat and wine selection. The larger chains can be found in downtown Silver Spring, including **Giant** (1280 East-West Highway; 301/585-1670) and **Safeway** (909 Thayer Ave.; 301/565-0686). Another **Giant** (301/949-1458) is in Wheaton Plaza and there is a **Safeway** (301/949-7690) nearby at 11201 Georgia Ave.

To match its varied population, Silver Spring offers a huge variety of ethnic markets and restaurants. Prices are generally better than in other, more upscale neighborhoods. For ethnic groceries, downtown Silver Spring offers **Italia** (8662 Colesville Rd.; 301/588-6999), **Muskan Fine Indian Grocery** (956 Thayer Ave.; 301/588-0331), the **Thai Market** (902 Thayer Ave.; 301/495-2779) and **Las Americas Mercado Latino** (8651 16th St.; 301/588-0882). The **Parkway Deli** (8317 Grubb Rd.; 301/587-1427) has almost everything you could want from a deli.

The area's largest shopping center is **Wheaton Plaza** (301/946-3200), which lies between Veirs Mill Rd. and University Blvd., just west of Georgia Ave. The standard Washington department stores, **Woodie's** and **Hecht's,** anchor this mall.

Commute to Downtown 20 to 30 minutes by Metro

Post Office Main Branch, 8616 Second Ave. (301/588-2926) Silver Spring, 8455 Colesville Rd. (301/588-5086)

Libraries Silver Spring, 8901 Colesville Rd. (301/565-7689) Wheaton Regional, 11701 Georgia Ave. (301/929-5520)

Police Station 801 Sligo Ave. (301/565-7740)

Recreational Activities The area boasts two great parks. Sligo Creek offers a hiker-biker trail as well as numerous playgrounds and playing fields. Wheaton Regional Park has everything: horseback riding, hiking trails, a fishing pond, a playground with carousel and miniature trains and the beautiful Brookside Gardens.

Prince George's County

Prince George's County is a diamond in the rough. While it suffers from a poor image concerning crime, the quality of its school system and even a lack of restaurants and shopping malls, the county has its advantages for residents. First and foremost, living in PG County is less expensive than in other parts of Maryland and Virginia. For both buyers and renters, housing can be quite cheap.

■ Takoma Park

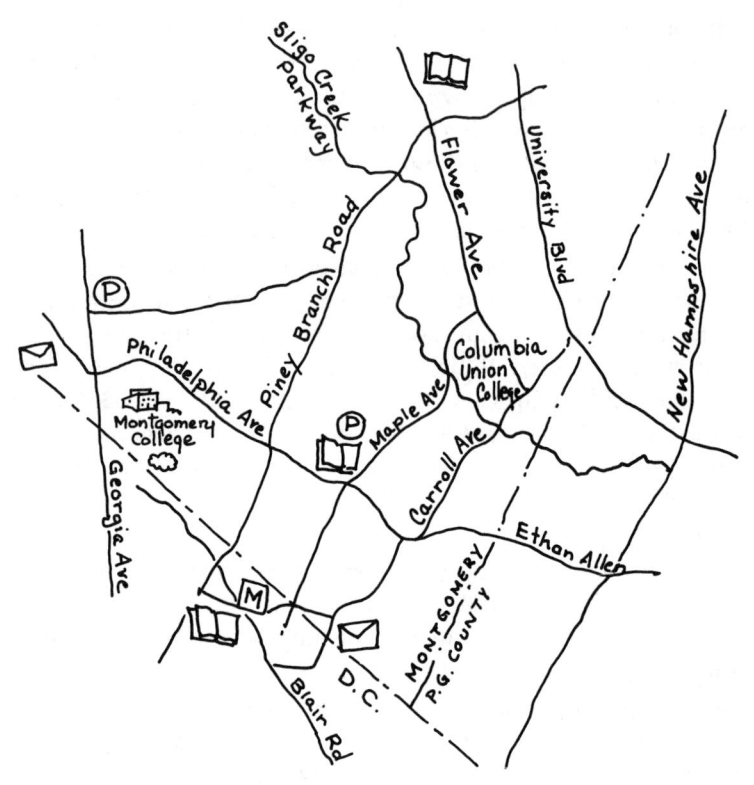

Takoma Park

Takoma Park rests along the upper northeast boundary of D.C. and straddles the border of Montgomery and Prince George's County. Takoma Park is served by the Red line (Takoma Park). A planned suburban community founded in 1833 along a branch of the B&O railroad, Takoma Park was conceived as a healthful clean-water alternative to Washington's malarial swamps. These days, Takoma Park is still conceived of as an offering outside the mainstream. "A lot of people who are looking for an alternative, less-established place to live will end up here," says one long time resident.

A mixture of religion and politics has given shape to the community. From 1904 to 1989, Takoma Park was world headquarters of the Seventh-Day Adventist Church, whose institutions (Washington Adventist Hospital, Columbia Union College) remain and traditions of family, vegetarianism and temperance endure. In recent years, signs of the church's waning influence have appeared, including a small bar near the center of town.

Takoma Park is also famous for its leftist politics and latter-day hippie lifestyle, causing some to call it the "Peoples Republic of Takoma Park." Contributing to this impression are progressive measures such as a declaration of a nuclear-free zone, legal recognition of non-marital partnerships and a (thus far unsuccessful) movement to ban gas-powered lawn mowers.

Takoma Park is a family-oriented place where neighbors are still neighborly and stick together to build speed bumps and oppose crime. Takoma Park's politically active population is also comprised of an enviably diverse racial mix.

If you are looking to buy a house, Takoma Park may be a good place to start. Single-family, three bedroom homes range from $140,000 to $160,000. The grand Victorians near Old Town will cost much more, as will anything that can be described with a straight face as "Walk to Metro."

Rental housing is scarce. Most of Takoma Park's apartments are located on or around Maple Ave., a ten-minute walk from the Metro. Two-bedroom apartments rent for upwards of $600 a month and rent stabilization is in effect.

Old Town Takoma Park, around the intersection of Carroll and Laurel Aves., offers a quixotic mix of small, locally-owned specialty shops. For food, there is **Everyday Gourmet** (6923 Laurel Ave.; 301/270-2270) for take-out or eat-in pastries, sandwiches and other prepared items; **Mark's Kitchen** (7006 Carroll Ave.; 301/270-1884), a cappuccino-serving, semi-vegetarian, Korean luncheonette; and the **Middle East Market** (7006 Carroll Ave.; 301/270-5154) for exotic breads, coffee and spices.

From the end of April until the weekend before Thanksgiving, there is a farmers' market every Sunday in the center of town at the intersection of Laurel and Carroll Aves. While not as big as other markets, the Takoma Park farmers' market has a loyal following among residents, who consider it a major cultural event.

Commute to Downtown   15 minutes by Metro
Post Office   6909 Laurel Ave. (301/270-5606)
Libraries   Takoma Park Library, 101 Philadelphia Ave. (301/270-1717); and Takoma Park Tool Lending Library, 7500 Maple Ave. (behind City Hall; 301/589-8274).
Police Station 7500 Maple Ave. (301/270-1100)

Recreation Takoma Park's best parkland includes hiking trails and playing fields on both sides of Sligo Creek, which runs through the eastern part of town. To accommodate bikers, skateboarders and the like, vehicles are banned from the Takoma Park section of Sligo Creek Parkway on Sundays.

■ Mount Rainier

Mount Rainier is a 1.2-square-mile, early 20th century "streetcar suburb" situated along Washington's northeast border at the gateway to Prince George's County. Mount Rainer is described by its city manager as a "working-class bedroom suburb" and by *The Washington Post* real estate section as a "place waiting to happen." Mount Rainer is located along the Route One Corridor (Rhode Island Ave.), barely five miles from the center of D.C. The recent opening of the Metro's Green Line (West Hyattsville) has made it even more convenient. Mount Rainer is also one of the last places inside the Beltway where

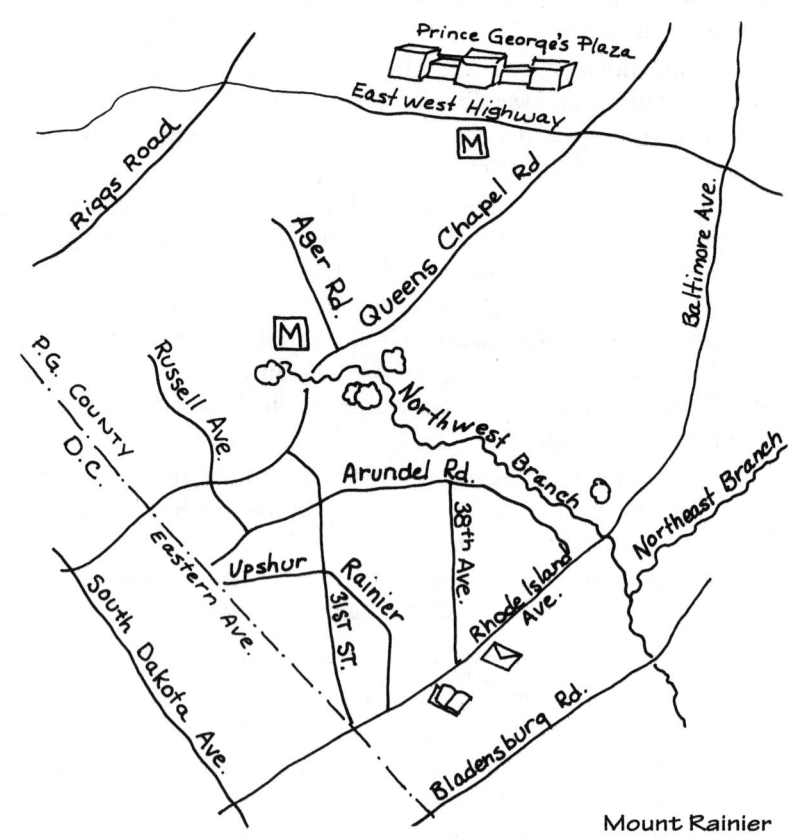

Mount Rainier

you can still find single-family detached houses selling for five figures. Finally, Mount Rainer is reputed to have one of the area's most compatible racial-ethnic mixtures.

Mount Rainier is primarily residential, most of the housing stock consists of small, owner-occupied, prewar bungalows and other house styles. The city has numerous Thirties-era Sears mail-order homes with spacious rooms and hardwood floors. A few larger Victorians can be found in the blocks just north of Rhode Island Ave. A number of low and high-rise rental apartment buildings line Queens Chapel Rd. on the city's northern edge, close to the newly-opened West Hyattsville Metro. Apartment rents range upward from $500 for one-bedrooms, $600 for two-bedrooms.

Downtown Mount Rainier shopping can be characterized as serviceable at best. The main draw is the **Glut Food Co-op** (4005 34th St.; 301/779-1978), the Washington area's oldest surviving food co-op and a great place to stock up on inexpensive grains, spices, whole wheat bread, fresh fruit and vegetables. One other notable downtown store is discount-minded **Party Times Liquors** (3307 Rhode Island Ave.; 301/927-3037). The nearest major grocery store is the **Giant** (301/699-0501) in Queens Chillum Shopping Center.

> **Commute to Downtown** 20 to 30 minutes by Metro (West Hyattsville Station) or take Metrobus to the Red line Metro station at Rhode Island Ave.
>
> **Post Office** 3709 Rhode Island Ave. (301/699-8855)
>
> **Library** 3409 Rhode Island Ave. (301/864-8937)
>
> **Police Station** 3409 Rhode Island Ave. (301/985-6565)
>
> **Recreation** Mount Rainier has a number of neighborhood parks scattered throughout the town, including a Nature Center (301/927-2163) on 30th St. near Arundel Rd.

■ Greenbelt

This suburban Maryland town was one of three planned communities created in the mid-Thirties by the Federal Government as part of the New Deal. These towns not only provided needed jobs for the area during the Depression, but also gave people an inexpensive place to live. Much effort was made at the start to make Greenbelt a 'green' city, and most of the original landscaping, although growing sparser by the day, is still intact. You will find many paths, parks and quiet areas here. Today, the city has a high concentration of academics, scientists and

Mastering DC | A Newcomer's Guide to Living in Washington

Greenbelt

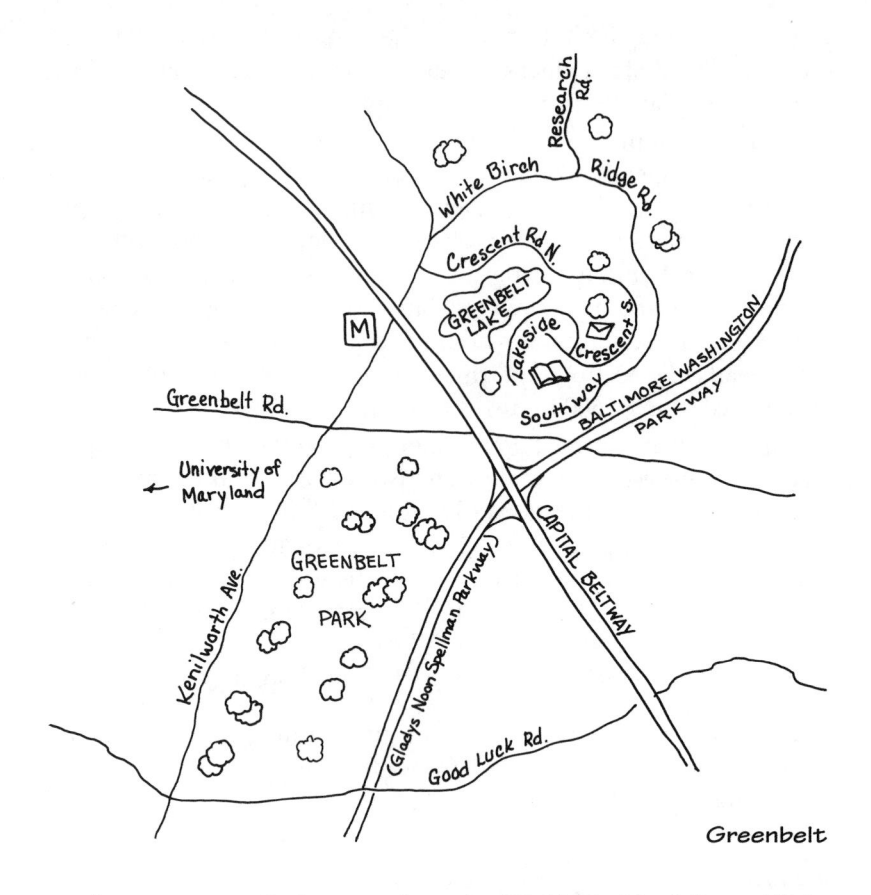

engineers, many of whom work at the NASA/Goddard Space Flight Center or the University of Maryland in nearby College Park.

The town of Greenbelt sits at the intersection of five major roads, making it ideal for people commuting in all directions. The Baltimore-Washington Parkway, the Capital Beltway, I-95, Kenilworth Avenue, and Route 1 all go in or around Greenbelt. Downtown D.C. is about 15 miles away, while Baltimore is only 25. This community's place on the commuter's map was forever secured in late 1993, when the Greenbelt Metro (Green line) was opened.

Greenbelt is really two communities in one. The original section, known as "Old Greenbelt," follows the original city plan. Old Greenbelt is essentially the same as it was in 1938, when it was first opened. Long, white-washed apartment buildings are obviously products of the 1930's, with art-deco accents and utilitarian lines.

Some single-family homes managed to work their way into the community plan and line several quiet streets in the western part of town.

The newer parts of Greenbelt sprawl in either direction along Route 193 (Greenbelt Road) and are not as neatly laid out. The "new" section of Greenbelt is typical of the hodgepodge suburban development seen in the metropolitan area, with modern town house communities taking up most of the real estate. Average home prices are $160,000 and two-bedroom townhouses are available for under $80,000. For renters, Greenbelt is home to one of the largest apartment complexes on the East Coast, Springhill Lake (301/474-1600). This complex has almost 3,000 units. Rents for one-bedroom apartments in the area average $685/month.

All of the town's amenities, including **The Greenbelt Library** and **The Co-op Supermarket Pharmacy** (121 Centerway; 301/474-0522) are located within a hundred yards of each other in the middle of Old Greenbelt. Further out, you will find a **Giant** (6000 Greenbelt Road; 301/982-2359) and **Safeway** (7595 Greenbelt Road; 301/345-0150).

The main event of the year in Greenbelt is the **Labor Day Festival & Parade,** a three-day celebration full of pageants, carnivals, parades and a variety of other entertainment.

Commute to Downtown 30 minutes by Metro
Post Office 119 Centerway (301/345-1721)
Police Station 550 Crescent Road (301/474-7200)
Library 11 Crescent Road (301/345-5800). Greenbelt has a wonderful library that serves equally well as a community center.
Recreation Greenbelt Park (6565 Greenbelt Rd.; 301/344-3948) has walking trails, camping and picnicking. The entire northern edge of Old Greenbelt is bordered by the Federal Department of Agriculture's Beltsville Research Center, a huge tract of government farmland criss-crossed with little-trafficked two lane country roads, that is great for biking and running.

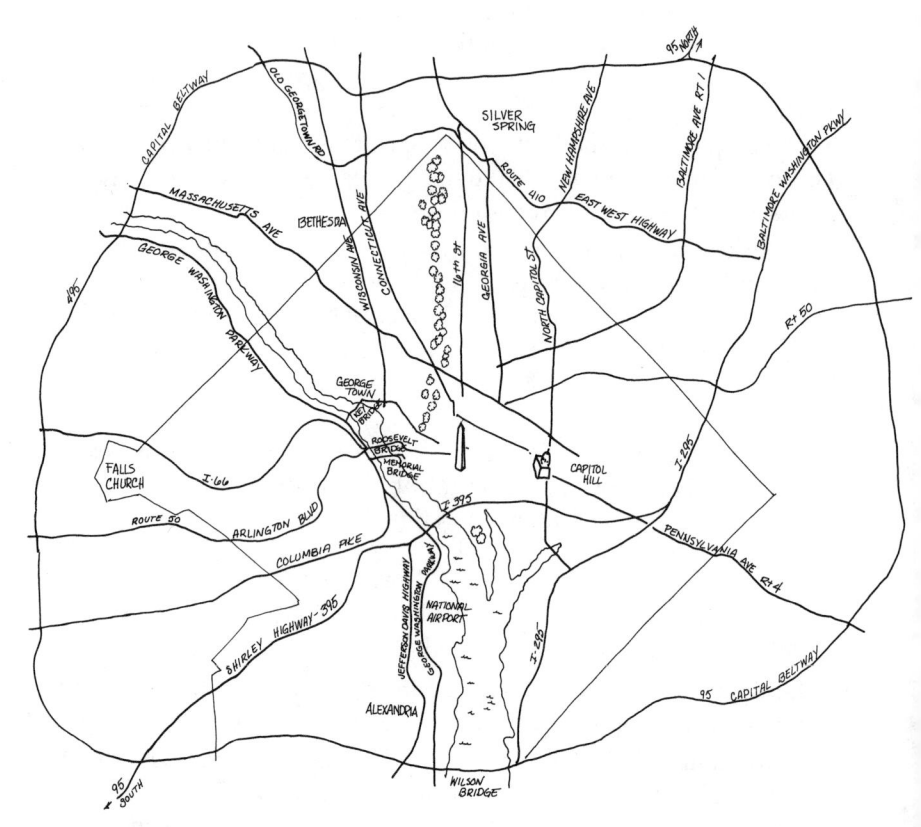

Washington Thoroughfares

Chapter 2
Getting Around

At first, getting around Washington can be frustrating. I remember trying to get to a softball game during my first month in town. I was looking for Sixth and F—and found it easily enough—but was befuddled by the obvious absence of a ballfield. I drove around for half an hour trying to find the field. I did eventually discover it at Sixth and F, a different Sixth and F, and learned a valuable lesson about D.C.'s division into quadrants and its quaint habit of repeating identical street designations in different parts of town.

Learning your way around will be challenging, requiring lots of patience and a little help from others. With a good map and a few tips, Washington is relatively easy to master. One tip, many Washingtonians will assure you that the city's grid-like layout is simple to learn. You should take this with a grain of salt. In truth, the most useful and important thoroughfares (Rock Creek Park and the streets named after states, for example) do not follow this pattern at all.

Maps

As an essential first step to familiarizing yourself with the area, you will need a good, detailed map. The Alexandria Drafting Company (ADC), puts out a comprehensive series of maps (atlases, really) for both D.C. and the surrounding counties. You can find them at virtually all bookstores, card shops, drugstores and supermarkets. **The Map Store** (1636 Eye St., N.W.; 202/628-2608) highly recommends *Station Masters: A Comprehensive Pocket Guide to Metrorail Station Neighborhoods* and *The Travel Vision Map of Washington*. Free maps are available from the Virginia Department of Tourism (202/659-5523), the D.C. Department of Tourism (202/727-4511) and the Maryland Department of Tourism (410/333-6611).

Driving
■ The District: Streets and Roads

"The first time I drove home from the Safeway in Georgetown to my apartment in Woodley Park, I ended up in Virginia," laughed one

Washingtonian as she recounted her early experiences of getting around the city. Stories like this are common but not entirely reassuring when you are new to Washington's roads. Unfortunately, road signs in the metropolitan area can be few and far between. As much as possible, you should try to drive during the day until you have a good feel for the roads.

To understand Washington's streets, you have to understand their history. In 1791, Major Pierre Charles L'Enfant was commissioned to draw up plans to build the nation's capital. Much still survives of his neat urban grid of streets intersected by diagonal boulevards. L'Enfant divided Washington into four quadrants, Northwest, Northeast, Southeast and Southwest, with the Capitol at its center. The streets radiating due north, south and east from the Capitol are called North, South and East Capitol Streets. The Mall is what would have been West Capitol St.

Lettered streets—A, B, C, D...W run east to west heading away from the Capitol. No matter how hard you look, though, you will not find J street. The official explanation is that "J" was eliminated from the plans to avoid confusion with I St. since the Roman letter "I" was once written identically. Another, more colorful, explanation holds that the letter "J" was not included because L'Enfant hated Chief Justice John Jay and deliberately left out J St. to slight him. You will find I St. commonly spelled "Eye" to avoid possible confusion with 1st St. (there goes the first J St. theory). Unfortunately, no official explanation exists for the absence of streets X, Y and Z. One possibility is that W St. was the border of the original settled area and there was no need to go further.

After the lettered streets, east-west streets in the District are labeled with two-syllable words in alphabetical order, then three-syllable words also in alphabetical order, then names of trees and flowers—after that you are probably out of the District and on your own again. Beginning on each side of North and South Capitol Sts., streets running north and south are numbered. So 3rd and D Sts., S.E., is four blocks south and three blocks east of the Capitol.

Addresses are logically arranged within the grid system in hundreds, so addresses on K St. between 17th and 18th, for example, form the 1700 block of K St.

Here is where it gets confusing. The quickest way to get across town often tends to be one of the avenues named after the 50 states. Massachusetts Ave. is the perfect example. It is the most convenient and most confusing street in Washington. It is the quickest way to go from the Hill to Dupont Circle and then on to the Cathedral. However, it does not follow a straight line and the unwary driver can quickly get sidetracked around several traffic circles. The proximity of each avenue to the Capitol is based on when its state entered the Union, with New Jersey, Delaware and Pennsylvania Avenues intersecting the Capitol grounds and Alaska and Hawaii Avenues practically in Maryland. Washington Ave. was missing for awhile (mostly to avoid confusion), but finally those other Washingtonians were given a small stretch of concrete near the Capitol.

During evening rush hour, if you are going north to Bethesda, Chevy Chase or Rockville, the quickest route is Connecticut Ave. Coming from Georgetown, you can also use Wisconsin Ave. to go north to Chevy Chase and Bethesda. Running roughly parallel to Sixteenth St., Georgia Ave. travels out to Silver Spring through the commercial heart of the African-American community. Stately Pennsylvania Ave. begins in Georgetown, passes the White House and the Capitol and continues east through the District and out into Prince George's County, Maryland.

Most importantly, you should try to familiarize yourself with Rock Creek Parkway. This eccentric parkway winds through Northwest D.C. with only one light to slow the flow of traffic, making it an excellent north-south route. The most difficult aspect of learning

D.C. Taxicabs

D.C. taxis do not have meters. Instead, Washington employs a complicated zone system designed to keep legislators' fares cheap and bamboozle the unwary into paying too much. Get to know the zone map (usually displayed behind the driver's seat). Eventually, you will become familiar with D.C.'s geography and learn that sometimes a two- or three-block walk can shave a dollar off your fare.

The District is divided into five zones and each zone has as many as eight subzones. The price of your ride is determined by the number of zones you travel through. Cleverly designed by Congress, the zone system is based on concentric circles radiating out from the Capitol. Any time you are traveling to or from the Capitol area, taxicabs will seem like a bargain. A one-dollar surcharge is added to all trips originating in the District during the weekday evening rush hour (4:00 to 6:30 p.m.). If D.C.-licensed cabs are taking you out of the District, they determine fares by using their odometers: $2 for the first mile and 70 cents for each additional half-mile.

Rock Creek Parkway is memorizing the entrances and exits and how to get to them. K St. near the Kennedy Center, P St. in Georgetown and Massachusetts Ave. are some of the more important ones to know. From Foggy Bottom to Calvert St., Rock Creek Parkway has no dividers to separate the two lanes of traffic traveling in each direction. This can be disconcerting, even dangerous. Driving there at night, particularly on weekends, can be harrowing.

■ ...and the Circles

The problem with traffic circles is once you get on, it is difficult to get off. The circles were originally a way of compensating for the intersection of grid streets and diagonal avenues while providing public space in the middle (if you can reach them through the traffic). Often you have to be in a specific lane of the circle to exit on a particular street. Unfortunately, these lanes are not always marked. Among the worst and most-dreaded is Washington Circle, near George Washington University, which has six intersecting spokes, including K St., 23rd St., Pennsylvania Ave. and New Hampshire Ave. Traffic circle worries are occasionally alleviated by major roads passing beneath the circles. At Dupont Circle, for example, if you want to continue on Connecticut Ave., you can just follow the ramp beneath the circle. The same is true of K St. below Washington Circle.

■ Parking and Parking Tickets

Drivers face a dual challenge when it comes to parking in the city: first, finding a space and, second, making sure it is legal. Do not take this task lightly; Washington traffic officers generally issue over two million parking tickets a year.

If you do find a bright-pink ticket prominently displayed on your windshield, it is best to respond within fifteen calendar days (even if you are a foreign diplomat and think that you are exempt—which you are not). Many Washingtonians have discovered that leaving tickets unpaid will eventually come back to haunt them. If you think out-of-state plates will protect you, think again. I thought so when I first arrived and nonchalantly started piling up tickets —until I got a call from my parents in New York that a sizable bill from New York State Motor Vehicles had come in the mail.

Downtown/Dupont Circle, Georgetown, Adams Morgan and Capitol Hill are some of the most difficult areas to find a parking space. Most meters accept *only* quarters. If you are going to be Downtown for an entire weekday, you may seriously want to consider taking the Metro. Otherwise, you can park your car in an all-day parking garage for around $12 a day. Parking downtown is illegal in all but a few places during rush hour, no matter how many quarters you have.

If your car is going to be a permanent fixture on your neighborhood street, you should register it (see Chapter 4) and get a Residential Parking Permit.

■ Surviving Rush Hour

If you are coming here from Los Angeles, rush hour traffic will not only look familiar, it may be worse. D.C. grew more quickly in the 1980's than the road system could readily accommodate. To compensate, some traffic rules change on several well-traveled streets to handle rush hour better. From Woodley Park to the Maryland border, Connecticut Ave. switches from three lanes in each direction to four in the dominant direction. Changing altogether, Rock Creek Parkway becomes one-way during rush hour, a disconcerting sight the first time you try it. Seventeenth St. (in the morning) and Fifteenth St. (in the evening), each between Massachusetts and Eye St. become one-way streets during rush hour as does Canal Road (running parallel to the Potomac). 16th St. has altered traffic patterns during rush hour all the way from the Maryland border to Adams Morgan.

Washingtonians are pretty good about sharing their commuting time and expenses with others. **Ride-Finders** (800/745-RIDE) helps arrange carpools all over the metropolitan area. An informal car-pooling system has developed in northern Virginia to beat the traffic jams and use the I-395 High Occupancy Vehicle (HOV) lanes. Waiting commuters head to the Springfield Plaza parking lot to meet up with drivers willing to take on passengers. At the end of the day, many of these same commuters can be found lined up along 14th St. at the Mall looking to help drivers meet the southbound HOV restrictions.

And finally, if you are braving the commute by car, WTOP (1500 AM) is the best radio station for traffic reports.

■ Highways—Inside the Beltway

Washington's most famous highway, the Beltway (I-495/I-95), takes 67 miles to circumnavigate the metropolitan region. Radio rush hour traffic reports constantly refer to the Beltway's "inner loop" and "outer loop." This would lead one to believe there are two concentric highways around Washington, as is true of Routes 128 and 495 outside Boston. Actually, all they mean by this is that the "inner loop" is the clockwise inner portion of the highway and that the opposite direction runs counterclockwise outside it.

The Woodrow Wilson Bridge connects Prince George's County, Maryland with Alexandria, Virginia on I-95. One word sums up the problem with this route: drawbridge. To accommodate rush hour traffic, the Coast Guard prohibits openings from 4:00 to 9:00 a.m. and 2:00 to 7:00 p.m. The bridge does open, on average, once a day, causing lengthy traffic delays and occasional serious accidents. Most radio stations keep listeners apprised of when bridge openings are scheduled.

Route 270, one of Montgomery County's main highways, shoots off to the north of the Beltway a few miles from the American Legion Bridge, the border between Virginia and Maryland.

Interstate 66 is one of the area's newest highways. I-66 is often Virginia commuters' first choice since the highway stretches from Arlington west all the way to Front Royal. During morning rush hour, cars traveling eastbound between the Beltway and the District must have at least three passengers in them, and vice-versa during the evening rush hour. Beyond Fairfax, the speed limit changes from 55 to 65 m.p.h. Pay attention to the signs and stay within the speed limit, since this area is a favorite for police looking to fulfill their speeding ticket quotas.

The Shirley Highway (I-395) runs through Arlington County from the Potomac to I-95, providing one of the most direct routes from the District to Crystal City, Alexandria and southern Virginia. Three lanes travel in each direction, with a two-laned HOV road down the center changing direction to accommodate the prevalent traffic flow.

■ Virginia: Street and Roads

Newcomers are lucky they do not have to master the pre-1934 Arlington street plan. Residents then had to find their way around a hodgepodge of streets, many with identical names. There were, for example, ten different Arlington streets and eleven Washington streets. Today, Arlington's streets and roads are still somewhat confusing, but much easier. Arlington's main east-west thoroughfares are Lee Highway, I-66, Wilson Blvd., Arlington Blvd. (US 50), Columbia Pike and I-395. Lee Highway runs roughly parallel to I-66 all the way out to Falls Church where the two cross. Lee Highway turns into Washington St. in Falls Church before it heads out to western Virginia.

Wilson Blvd. begins in Rosslyn and travels west through North Arlington. Wilson becomes one-way (heading west) for about two miles through the Court House and Clarendon sections of Arlington. During this stretch, Clarendon Blvd. provides a parallel route in the eastward direction.

During rush hour, four-laned Columbia Pike switches some of its lanes to accommodate the flow of traffic. In the morning, three lanes carry traffic towards the District and in the afternoon, three lanes help transport cars away from D.C.

The scenic George Washington Parkway runs along the Potomac River from Mount Vernon towards the Beltway and the Maryland border. Glebe Rd. is the main thoroughfare in western Arlington. Jefferson Davis Highway splits off of I-395 at the Pentagon and carries traffic through Crystal City into Alexandria.

In Arlington, named streets, as opposed to numbered streets, are ordered alphabetically, run north to south, beginning at the Potomac River and extending westward. Street names start with one-syllable names: Ball St. to Wayne St. and progress to two-, three- and four-syllable names. Arizona St. is the only four-syllable name. Numbered streets and boulevards named after historic figures run parallel to Arlington Blvd. (US 50) in an east-west direction.

One of the largest and worst traffic circles in the area lurks on the Virginia side of the Arlington Memorial Bridge. This circle links up several major highways in a seemingly random and confusing pattern. To make matters worse, cars travel around it quite fast. Look for the small signs to direct you and do not get frustrated if you end up on the wrong road. This one takes a while to learn.

The major thoroughfare in Alexandria is Washington St. This street runs parallel to the Potomac River, north to the District and south to Mount Vernon. King St. and Duke St. are popular east-west routes. These three streets comprise Old Town's main streets, forming a neat backbone for the grid pattern of downtown Alexandria.

Route 1 cuts through Alexandria and splits into two one-way streets in downtown Alexandria: Patrick St. (Route 1 North) and Henry St. (Route 1 South). During morning rush hour, Patrick St.'s three lanes become gridlocked. One lane is set aside from 6:30 to 9:00 a.m. as a two-person HOV lane. HOV violations are expensive, up to $85. Henry St. supports the homebound commuter traffic. A two-person HOV lane is in effect from 3:00 to 7:00 p.m. Southbound Route 1 provides access to I-95, while northbound Route 1 branches off to I-395 and Glebe Road.

■ Maryland: Streets and Roads

Wisconsin Ave. (which becomes Rockville Pike north of Bethesda) and Old Georgetown Rd. traverse Montgomery County from north to south. East-West Highway (Route 410) connects Bethesda to Riverdale via Silver Spring and Takoma Park. This road begins at Wisconsin Ave. and runs east, eventually intersecting the Baltimore-Washington Parkway.

Georgia Ave., which starts in the District, bisects Silver Spring on its way north to Wheaton. Colesville Rd. (Route 29) heads north to Baltimore, passing through Columbia along the way. Like the District's Connecticut Ave., Colesville Rd. and Georgia Ave. change from three lanes in each direction to four lanes going in the direction of commuter traffic and two the other way.

Metrorail

At the heart of Washington's public transportation system, Metrorail or simply "the Metro," serves as a model to other subway systems. It is safe, clean and convenient. It is also a little pricy.

Five Metrorail lines, each marked with its own color, connect Northern Virginia, the District and Maryland. The Red line links Rockville, Bethesda and Silver Spring to Downtown D.C. The Blue line runs from Alexandria through Downtown and out to Addison Road in Prince George's County. The Orange line parallels the Blue line through the District with end points in Vienna, Virginia, and New Carrollton, Maryland. The Yellow line travels through Alexandria and Chinatown to Mt. Vernon Square and the University of the District of Columbia's downtown campus. The Green line, the newest line, now reaches from Anacostia up to Greenbelt in Prince George's County. The Green line will not be completed in the District until 1999, so the Maryland stations will not have direct access to Downtown for several years. Instead, riders have to transfer to the Red line at Fort Trotten.

There are several central transfer points to switch lines. The Red, Blue and Orange lines all converge at Metro Center, the system's busiest station. Blue and Orange trains are on the lower level and the Red line is on the upper level. In addition, Blue, Orange, Green and Yellow lines meet at L'Enfant Plaza.

While the Metro is convenient, it is not user friendly. Few hints are given as to which track is the right one for your destination and the routes down from the street tend to throw off your sense of direc-

Chapter Two | Getting Around

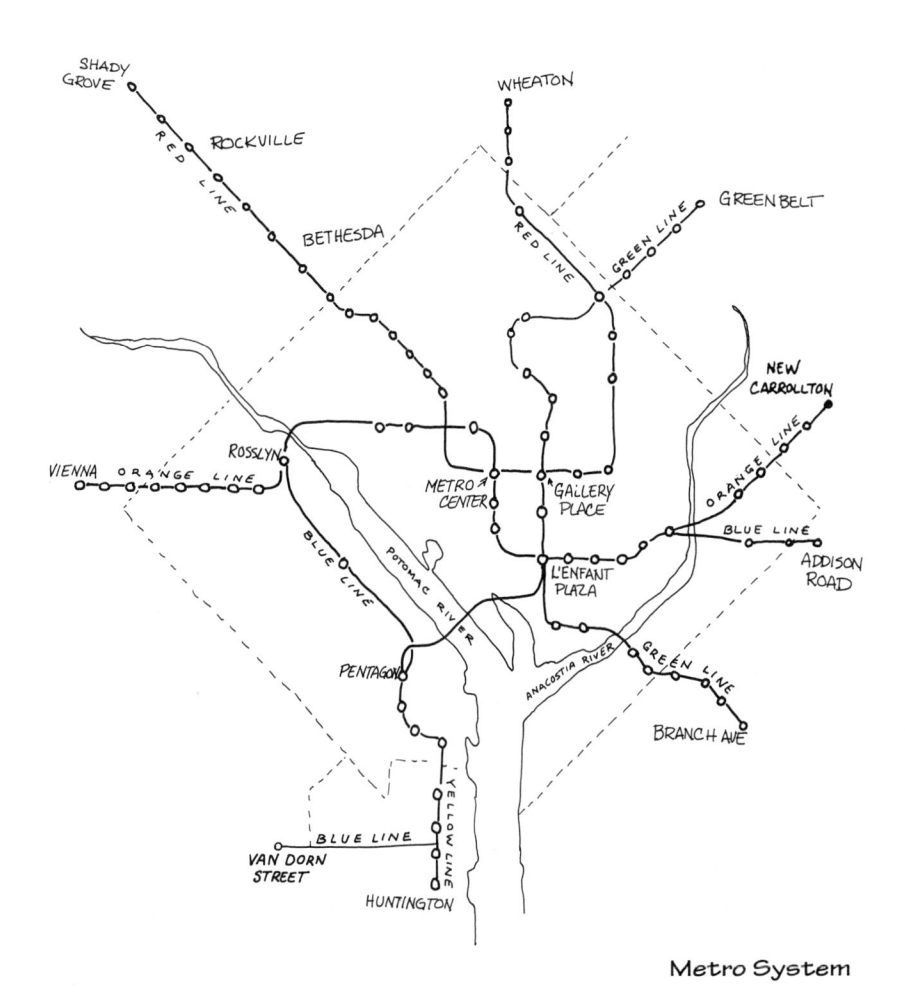

Metro System

tion. Over time, you will recognize the end points of the lines, but at first the Metro's cavernous and virtually identical and featureless stations will be disorienting. At the street level, bronze pylons capped with the letter M mark entrances to the Metro. The pylons are horizontally striped near the top with the color of the trains that stop at the station beneath. For aesthetic reasons, maps of the Metro system are not allowed on the street level. If you get confused, just go down to the station and check the maps there or ask the station attendant at the kiosk. Since all stations look alike, it can be hard to tell which platform you should stand on. Almost everybody has gotten on trains leading the wrong way at some point. If you get confused, look for the posts on the platform indicating the routes followed by the arriving trains. Also, make sure when the train arrives that it is the right color, since different lines pull up to the same platforms in many stations.

Many of the Metro stations are equipped with elevators for use by the physically disabled or those with baby strollers. In addition, the Metro system has some buses that are wheelchair accessible. If you are in need of such buses or want to check on their availability at a particular station, you can call 202/962-1245 or 202/962-1825.

On weekdays, Metro starts operating at 5:30 a.m. On Saturdays and Sundays, trains begin running at 8:00 a.m. One of the biggest complaints about Metrorail is that the trains stop running at midnight. "When I used to live in Silver Spring, I could not go out in the city—my whole life had to be planned around ending an evening at 11:00 p.m.," lamented one Capitol Hill resident. Although midnight is the official closing time, be sure to check at each station for the time the last train passes through. The second biggest complaint about the Metro is how infrequently it runs on the weekends. On Saturdays and Sundays, you can expect to wait on the train platforms an additional ten to fifteen minutes. And if you are planning on transferring from the subway to a bus on weekends, be sure to consult a schedule (or call 202/637-7000 for Metro information) because many of these buses run every hour or, in some cases, every two hours.

■ Farecards

Metro planners knew their economics; fares are based on the time of day (peak or off-peak hours) and distance traveled. One-way fares during peak weekday hours (5:30 to 9:30 a.m. and 3:00 to 7:00 p.m.) range from $1.00 to $3.15, compared with non-peak fares of $1.00 to $2.50.

Points of Interest	Metro Stop	Color
American University	Tenleytown-AU	Red
Arena Stage	Waterfront	Green
Capitol Building	Capitol South	Orange, Blue
Catholic University	Brookland-CUA	Red
Chinatown	Gallery Place	Red, Yellow, Green
City Place	Silver Spring	Red
Convention Center	Metro Center	Red, Orange, Blue
Corcoran Gallery	Farragut West	Orange, Blue
Fashion Centre Mall/Pentagon City	Pentagon City	Yellow, Blue
Folger Shakespeare Library	Capitol South	Blue, Orange
Ford's Theatre	Metro Center	Red, Orange, Blue
George Washington University	Foggy Bottom-GWU	Orange, Blue
Goddard Space Flight Center	Greenbelt	Green
Kennedy Center/American Film Institute	Foggy Bottom-GWU	Orange, Blue
Library of Congress	Capitol South	Orange, Blue
The Mall	Smithsonian	Orange, Blue
Mazza Gallerie	Friendship Heights	Red
National Air and Space Museum	L'Enfant Plaza	Yellow, Green
National Gallery of Art	Archives	Yellow, Green
National Theatre	Metro Center	Red, Orange, Blue
National Zoo	Woodley Park-Zoo	Red
Old Town	Alexandria King Street	Yellow, Blue
Post Office Pavilion	Federal Triangle	Orange, Blue
RFK Stadium	Stadium-Armory	Orange, Blue
Shakespeare Theatre at the Lansburgh	Archives	Yellow, Green
Smithsonian Institution Castle	Smithsonian	Orange, Blue
University of D.C.	UDC/Van Ness	Red
University of Maryland	College Park/U. of Maryland	Green
Washington Monument	Smithsonian	Orange, Blue
Wheaton Mall	Wheaton	Red
White House	McPherson Square	Orange, Blue
White Flint Mall	White Flint	Red

Farecards, the admission tickets in and out of the Metro system, are sold through machines on the mezzanine or street level at every station. Unless you are buying a higher value farecard for several trips, you will first need to check the fare chart by the kiosk for the fare to your destination.

To purchase a farecard, simply put your bills or coins into the appropriate slot in the farecard machine. As you deposit your money, you will see the value of the farecard displayed under "FARECARD VALUE." To reach the desired value of the farecard, use the "–" or "+" buttons. Once you have chosen your fare, press the "PUSH FOR FARECARD" button to receive the farecard and your change.

While farecards may be purchased for as little as one dollar, daily riders coming in from the suburbs can take advantage of $10, $20 or $30 farecards. Metro offers a paltry five percent bonus with farecard purchases of $10 or more. Of course, if you lose your flimsy paper farecard, you are out of luck.

A note of warning about farecard machine change. It will all be returned in quarters and nickels—regardless of how much money you are putting in. Unless you need change for the laundry, you will have to break your large bills somewhere else beforehand. The Metro has no bill changers on the platform nor will the attendants supply change.

Farecard machines can be quite finicky. Veteran rail riders know never to go to the machine closest to the entrance. It always gets the most use and its bill sensors will have the most wear and tear. Luckily, Metro has recently replaced many of the older machines with newer ones that are a good deal more willing to take any bill regardless of how ragged it may be.

To gain access to the train platforms, put your farecard into the pass-through slot with the magnetic strip facing upward and the arrow on the card pointing forward. When you reach your destination, you must insert your card and go through the gates again to exit the system. As you pass through these exit gates, the machine will automatically discount the cost of the ride and print the remaining value, if any, on your card. Often the printed value is illegible, so be sure to keep track of it yourself. Once the card is used up the machine keeps the old card.

If you were able to use your card to take the train but do not have enough money on your card for your destination, the system will not let you out until you put enough money onto the card. The

ADDFARE machines near the exit gates will do the trick. Insert your card in ADDFARE and plug in the change the machine tells you.

Rarely will you use up a farecard exactly. This can quickly result in a drawer full of low-value cards. To get around this problem, the farecard machines (not the ADDFARE machines) have a slot where you can insert your old card and add money to it. The machine will then give you a new farecard with the original amount plus whatever you added. Unfortunately, you cannot take that drawerful of old cards and add them together. The farecard machines allow you to add money to only one card at a time. If you want to cash in several farecards, obtain an envelope at a station kiosk and mail the farecards into Metro headquarters for a refund. At some stations, the kiosk attendant will give you this envelope and you can mail it in yourself, but at others they may mail it in for you.

■ Special Features and Transfers

Many Metro stations, especially those in the suburbs, have Kiss & Ride. Cars can drive up to the Metro stations, drop off their passengers and, well, you get the idea. Another special feature at many of the suburban stations where land for parking abounds is Park & Ride.

Bus transfers are free at Metrorail stations. You can extract them from machines usually placed next to the escalators or stairs leading to the train platforms. You must get your transfer at the station where you entered the system for your transfer to be valid. There are no transfers from Metrobuses to Metrorail.

Metrobus

The Metrobus system complements Metrorail well, extending into the far reaches of the area's neighborhoods with almost 400 routes and some 13,000 bus stops. The buses also link parts of the city not served by the rail system. Like Metrorail fares, Metrobus fares are determined by time of day and length of trip (number of zones crossed). The base fare is $1 and buses accept only exact change. Regular Metrobus users will want to get a Bus/Rail Flash Pass. These cards, good for two-week periods, allow you to pay a single fee for unlimited bus rides within certain zones or some combination of zones. Depending on the Flash Pass, there is a variable amount of Metrorail value. Commuters make only a small amount of money on the deal (the convenience is the big advantage), but for those who also use the bus for other reasons, the Flash Pass savings really pile

Major Through Streets	Bus Lines
Pennsylvania Avenue	30, 32, 34, 36
Massachusetts Avenue	N2, N4
Connecticut Avenue	L2, L4
16th Street	S2, S4
Arlington Boulevard	4
Columbia Pike	16
Old Georgetown Road	C8, J2, J3
Georgia Avenue	70, 71, 73
Wisconsin Avenue	30, 32, 34, 36

up. Flash Passes can be purchased from the Metro kiosk at the Metro Center station and at many area banks.

To find out about Metrobus routes, call 202/637-7000.

Other Commuter Lines

To ease the commute from the furthest suburbs, several counties and the State of Maryland sponsor special commuter bus and train lines to and from the District. **MARC** (800/325-7245) shuttles passengers from as far north as Baltimore and as far west as Harpers Ferry, West Virginia. **Montgomery County's Ride-On** (301/217-RIDE) bus service drops passengers off at MARC, Metrobus and Metrorail stops. **The Fairfax Connector** (703/339-7200) operates in the regions between Springfield Plaza and Mt. Vernon, dropping passengers off either at the Huntington or Pentagon Metro stations. Alexandria's **DASH** (703/370-DASH) connects passengers with Metrobus, Metrorail and the Fairfax Connector. These alternative modes of transportation are a valuable resource for commuters and fares are more than reasonable (most are less than $1). All of these commuter lines offer discounted weekly or monthly passes.

The Virginia Railway Express (703/497-7777) ferries passengers from Manassas and Fredericksburg to Union Station with four trains in the morning and four returning in the evening. Fares vary with the top one-way from Fredericksburg to Union Station costing $6.15. Ten-trip or monthly tickets can be purchased at a reduced price (15% off of a ten-trip and 30% off of a monthly pass).

Airports

Washingtonians love to complain about **National Airport.** Despite its small size and substantial distance between terminals, National Airport is a blessing for District residents and Northern Virginians. Opened for business in 1941, National serves as a "short-haul" airport. It offers non-stop service only to destinations within 1250 miles from Washington. For any destination further away, travelers must book connecting flights. National is just 15 minutes from most locations in the District, Arlington and Alexandria. Frequent travelers often try to see how late they can leave their offices and still make their flights. Rumor has it that one harried K St. attorney hailed a cab at 7:17 p.m. and made a 7:30 p.m. shuttle.

Both the Yellow and Blue Metro lines will take you to National Airport. A shuttle bus connects the Metro station to the airport terminals. The quickest way from the District by car is to take 14th St. (south) over the 14th St. Bridge and then follow the National Airport signs. The George Washington Memorial Parkway is the best option from McLean, Arlington or Alexandria. Travelers from Montgomery County can either cut through the District and take 14th St. or take the Beltway to the George Washington Parkway. From Downtown, cabs to National cost approximately $9 to $12.

For cross-country flights, a better option is **Dulles International Airport** in northern Virginia. Dulles was all the rage during the mid-1960's, with its Eero Saarinen design. Much larger than National and much further from D.C. (26 miles from Downtown), Dulles offers non-stop flights to a multitude of domestic cities and foreign destinations.

Because Dulles is so far from most of the metropolitan region, taxis in either direction can cost a small fortune—upwards of $40. The Washington Flyer offers taxi and shuttle bus service from many of the big Downtown hotels at relatively inexpensive rates. One-way fares originating at 1517 K St., N.W., cost $16. It takes approximately an hour to get to the airport. You can also take the Orange line to the West Falls Church stop. From there, the Washington Flyer Dulles Express bus provides direct service to the airport every half hour for an additional $8. For more information, call 703/685-1400. If you are driving, take I-66 west to the 17-mile Dulles Access Road. No matter how you get there, you should budget extra time, since Dulles has a peculiar shuttle bus system out to the airline gates. This adds another 10 to 15 minutes before you reach the gate.

Washingtonians often overlook **BWI (Baltimore-Washington International) Airport.** Twenty-eight miles from Downtown, BWI has long been considered the area's number three airport. BWI has recently undergone massive renovations: extending runways, enlarging concourses, adding passenger gates and building a new parking garage. If you are driving, take I-95 or the Baltimore-Washington Parkway to I-195 and follow the signs to BWI. While the Metro system has no direct service to BWI, Amtrak and MARC provide travelers with access to and from the airport through Union Station. There is a free shuttle bus from the train station to the airport. In addition, Airport Connection (301/261-1091) runs a shuttle between BWI and Downtown every 90 minutes from 7:00 a.m. to 8:30 p.m. One-way fares cost $14.

Walking

Transportation in D.C. does not depend on having a car, train, bus or plane. If you live in the District or just across the Potomac River in Northern Virginia (Rosslyn, Crystal City or Pentagon City), you can walk or take the Metro to almost any location. In these areas, all types of shopping, especially grocery shopping, can easily be done on foot. Because of a scarcity of affordable parking, the benefits of having a car in many D.C. neighborhoods can often be more costly and aggravating than it is worth. Further out in Virginia and suburban Maryland,

> *"As a new member of Congress who travels home to California just about every weekend, it has been hard to find time to indulge in many of the attractions which draw tourists to this city from around the world. For me, getting to appreciate Washington has meant enjoying its simple pleasures. Having been raised in the East, I like having the four seasons back in my life. There is not a better way to enjoy them in D.C. than taking a leisurely drive on scenic Rock Creek Parkway. I love looking at the Capitol building softly lit at night, as well as taking walks through its stately halls — good exercise, but not easy if you are wearing heels. These things aside, I have found that there are three essential elements to thriving in Washington: a good dry cleaner, a good hairdresser and a good cabby. Once you find those, you have got it made."*
>
> REP. ANNA G. ESHOO (D-14, CA)

getting around without a car becomes increasingly difficult, even if you live close to a Metro station or bus line. While it remains easy to travel into the District by Metro, grocery stores and other necessities are not designed to be convenient to pedestrians or Metro riders.

Bicycling

480 miles of marked bike routes and 670 miles of paved, off-road bike paths to explore make Washington a cyclist's dream. Knowledge of several basic routes will help you take advantage of this network. Rock Creek Parkway gives cyclists a quick route from the Connecticut Ave. neighborhoods to Downtown. The C&O Canal bike path provides an excellent car-free route in from Maryland towns like Potomac. To get across the Potomac from Virginia, both the Key Bridge and the 14th St. Bridge have wide sidewalks that also make for great bike paths.

During rush hour, you should avoid the avenues that cut through the Downtown area, particularly North Capitol St., and Massachusetts, Pennsylvania, Connecticut and Wisconsin Aves. Anxious commuters tend to exceed the speed limit and bikers can easily find themselves in gutters. Beach Drive should also be avoided during commuter hours. During the weekends, though, certain sections of Beach Drive in the northernmost part of Rock Creek Park are closed off to cars so bikers can ride freely.

If the weather suddenly turns bad or exhaustion sets in, riders just hop on the Metrorail system. Metrorail sells bike passes that allow passengers to bring bicycles on the trains. These passes are good for evenings after 7:00 p.m., on weekends and holidays. Applications for a Metro Bike-on-Rail permit must be made in person at Metro headquarters, 600 Fifth St., N.W., during designated times. Call 202/962-1116 for information. To obtain a permit, you must complete a written test about transporting bicycles on Metrorail. Bicycles are not permitted on Metrobuses.

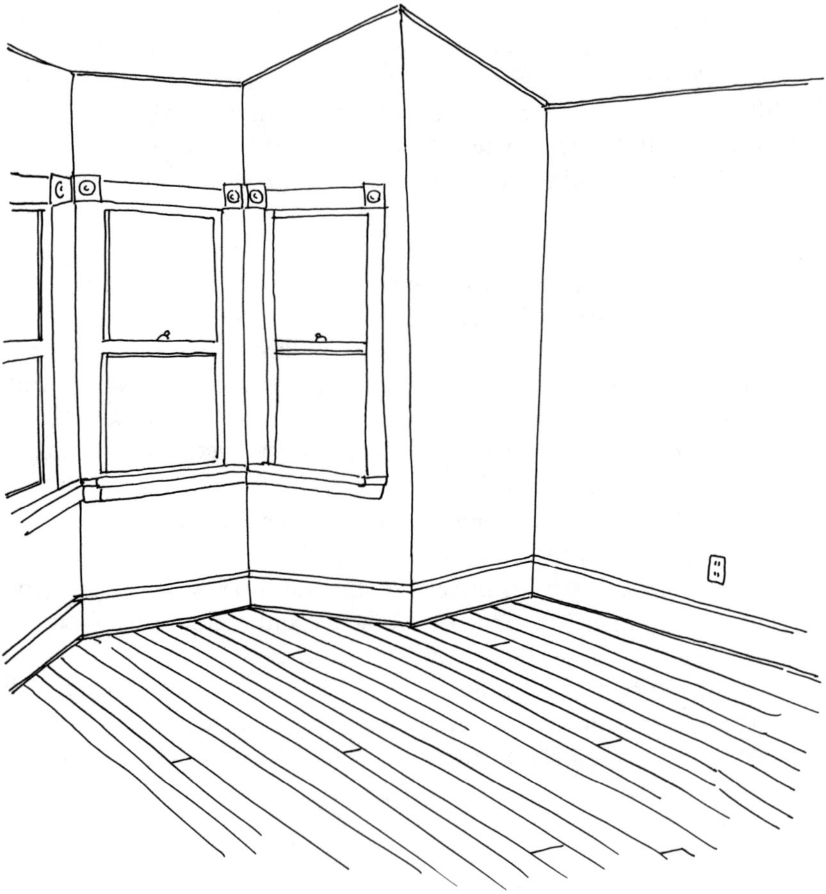

Chapter 3
Settling In

Typically, the first piece of advice newcomers receive when they move here is to make a pilgrimage to **Potomac Mills** (800/VA-MILLS). If you have little time to set yourself up before you start work or school, Potomac Mills is the perfect place to go. It is easy to find even if you are not familiar with the area and has everything you could possibly need to set up your new home.

Viewed by many as the mecca of shopping malls, Potomac Mills is on Interstate 95 (Exit 156-Dale City), about 27 miles south of D.C. on the way to Richmond (look for the tall circular sign right before the Dale City exit). Potomac Mills boasts over 230 stores and outlets, making it the largest discount mall in the region.

Potomac Mills is also extremely popular. When you go, start out early. The parking lot is huge but fills up quickly, especially during the holiday season. It can take half an hour to park and then almost as long to walk to the mall from your parking space. You may also want to bring a friend or roommate to help lug your purchases back to the car.

If you have time, Potomac Mills need not be your only destination to furnish your home. The greater metropolitan area offers many opportunities to furnish your dwelling. In fact, the further afield you go, the more interesting the options.

Furniture

Most everyone will recommend you tackle warehouse-sized **Ikea** (Potomac Mills; 703/494-4532) first. Ikea sells a wide range of home furnishings (lamps, dishes, pots, pans, wallpaper, paint, tools and bedding) but is best known for its put-it-together-yourself, Scandinavian-style furniture. The furniture is relatively simple to assemble and can make for a fun weekend project. If you want to get an idea of the furniture Ikea sells, call and ask them to send you a catalog.

Ikea receives accolades for prices, not quality or service. Compared to other stores, Ikea undoubtedly offers lower prices, certainly against traditional furniture stores like Ethan Allen, where furniture prices quickly run into the thousands instead of the hundreds charged by Ikea. Ikea's plastic and presswood construction does guarantee, however, that the furniture will not stand the test of time. Long-term durability may not be a concern for you, but if you have the time, other inexpensive options are available. Once you shop around, you will quickly realize that with a little creativity, you can get nicer furniture for the same amount or less elsewhere, particularly if you like antiques (discussed later). Nonetheless, Ikea bookcases, shelves and other simple items are worthwhile. If you live in the Maryland suburbs, a more convenient Ikea location for you may be in suburban Baltimore at the White Marsh Mall (410/931-5400). To get there, take I-95 north past Baltimore to exit 67B.

The Door Store also competes in this market. Its prices and selection are similar to Ikea's: beds, bookcases, tables and chairs. The Georgetown (3140 M St., N.W.; 202/333-7737) and Baileys Crossroads (5520 Leesburg Pike; 703/820-3262) stores have the largest inventory. Furniture shoppers without wheels will find their new stores in Dupont Circle (1718 Connecticut Ave., N.W.; 202/232-1322) and Friendship Heights (5225 Wisconsin Ave., N.W.; 202/244-0104) convenient. If you are looking for bargains, try The Door Store Outlet (202/333-3351)—it's at the corner of K St. and Wisconsin Ave., N.W., just under the Whitehurst Freeway.

Conran's Habitat has two local stores—one in Georgetown (Georgetown Park Mall; 202/298-8300) and the other in Bethesda (10400 Old Georgetown Rd.; 301/564-9590). Both stores sell furniture, kitchenware and some knick knacks (tablecloths, placemats, picture frames, lamps and woven rugs). Conran's does not have Ikea's wide variety, but its two stores are more convenient, especially if you do not own a car. The Georgetown store caters to city-dwellers with a trendier selection than the Bethesda store and is easier to get to without a car.

Scan International has the reputation of being an upscale Ikea. Scan sells some assembly-required furniture at prices competitive with Ikea's, but most of its furniture is well-made, pre-assembled and pricy. Scan's largest store is in Loehmann's Plaza on Route 50 (7311 Arlington Blvd.; 703/573-0100) just beyond Baileys Crossroads. Scan also has a store in Springfield (703/644-0500) and Maryland stores in Columbia (301/596-1060), Silver Spring (301/942-0600) and Greenbelt (301/474-8880).

For those who want to buy furniture already assembled, many traditional stores can meet your needs. Naturally, major department stores have furniture departments, where you can expect to find quality furniture at higher prices. Unless you come across a good sale, though, bargains can be few and far between. If you can afford the time, shop around and watch the newspapers and Sunday circulars for specials. Many large department stores will probably sound familiar to you: **Macy's, Nordstrom, Lord & Taylor, Neiman Marcus, Saks Fifth Avenue** and **Bloomingdale's**. **Woodward & Lothrop,** (commonly referred to as Woodie's) and **Hecht's** are Washington's two indigenous chains. Both have maintained downtown flagship stores since the end of the Nineteenth century. Today's stores are within walking distance of Metro Center (Hecht's 202/628-6661; Woodie's 202/347-5300). Most, but not all, of their suburban stores also carry furniture. You can call the main numbers listed above to find appropriate locations.

Marlo boasts that it sells more furniture in the area than anyone else. Marlo stores are organized so that bedroom and dining room furniture are sold in one half, living room furniture in the other. Marlo simplifies its maze-like showroom by organizing each aisle according to style (traditional, contemporary, Italian, etc.). Beware of their expensive delivery and set-up charges—seven percent of the total cost of the furniture, before tax. The District (901 Seventh St., N.W.; 202/842-0100) store is within walking distance of the Chinatown Metro. Suburban Maryland Marlo stores are located in Laurel (13450 Baltimore Ave.; 301/419-3400) and Forestville (7801 Marlboro Pike; 301/735-2000); the Virginia store is in Alexandria (Edsall Rd. and I-395; 703/941-0800).

The Hub (430 Hungerford Dr., Rockville; 301/762-6164) has a string of nineteen stores along the Washington-Baltimore corridor. These furniture centers carry contemporary and traditional styles for the living, dining and bedroom areas. Call to find the store nearest you, or check *The Washington Post* for their advertisements.

Antique Stores

Antiques are one of the hidden treasures of the area. Antiques collected from all over the Mid-Atlantic states and the Carolinas sell in local shops. The best buys are traditional, early American style furniture and 1930's and 1940's mahogany pieces. For items like bureaus, tables and desks, you can get solid oak, cherry or mahogany pieces which have already withstood the test of time. Even better, they will cost about the same price or a little more than what you would pay at Ikea.

Getting the best deals requires time and effort. Antique stores in the District and Old Town Alexandria tend to be markedly more expensive than shops in the Maryland or Virginia country. The farther out you travel, the better the deal. If you can get down to some small town in North Carolina or West Virginia, you stand an even better chance of getting a good piece of furniture at an excellent price. That is where the antique merchants go. One note, always negotiate and turn down the first offer.

Antique stores inhabit several areas in or near the District, including 18th St. in Adams Morgan, M St. and Wisconsin Ave. in Georgetown, Howard Ave. in Kensington, Maryland and King St. in Old Town Alexandria.

A good place to begin your antique hunt is **Laws Antique World** (2900 Clarendon Blvd.; 703/525-8300) between the Court House and Clarendon Metro stops in Arlington. This converted supermarket houses 50 antique shops selling furniture, vintage clothes and jewelry. Laws also hosts several auctions each month. For more information, call the store or check in *The Washington Post* classified ads (under antiques) for the next auction. Laws has another, much larger store (actually it's a complex of several buildings) in Manassas at 7209 Centreville Rd. (703/631-0590). Auctions at this Laws are held Monday and Friday nights and admission is free.

Fairfax County and points west and south have plenty of small antique shops; just stop off in any small town. Many of these mom-and-pop antique stores can seem deceptively small at first. If you cannot find what you want, just ask. Antique stores generally have storage facilities not readily visible at first (a garage, a basement or a back room). Antiques can also be obtained through estate or house sales. Check *The Washington Post* Home section on Thursdays or the classified section daily.

Thrift Shops

Thrift stores are another great alternative for the truly budget-minded furniture shopper. Keep in mind that the selection can be somewhat erratic. Consequently, it may take time to find the right bargains. It helps to have a car on these shopping expeditions, because many of these shops do not deliver. Since so many people move in and out of the Washington area, the market for used furniture is large and constantly replenished. Thrift shops near military bases can be a particularly good starting point.

Below are some thrift shops that regularly stock furniture items.

AMVETS	301/953-0090
9880 Washington Blvd., Laurel	
Columbia Pike Thrift Shop	703/521-3110
4101 Columbia Pike, Arlington	
Fort Myer Thrift Shop	703/527-0664
224 Forest Circle, Arlington	
Prevention of Blindness Thrift Shop	703/683-2558
900 King St., Alexandria	
Salvation Army	703/642-9270
6528 Little River Turnpike, Alexandria	
Salvation Army	202/396-0916
1375 H St., N.E., Washington	
St. Coletta Thrift Store	703/486-2362
2919 Columbia Pike, Arlington	

Clearance Centers

Clearance centers provide another option, especially for those on tight budgets. Clearance centers sell discontinued furniture and housewares. **Hecht's Clearance Center** (703/354-1900) in Landmark Plaza (I-395 to Duke St. West), sells furniture, TVs and stereos on the first floor; mattresses, bedding, lamps, dishes, pots, pans and luggage in the basement. All prices are twenty to fifty percent below retail. Hecht's has an automatic price reduction policy where prices are reduced five percent every thirty days.

Woodie's (703/750-1600) has a similar outlet on Industrial Dr. in Springfield (I-395 to Edsall Rd. West). This store sells only furniture and rugs, but the Woodie's outlet (703/490-4994) in Potomac Mills (Neighborhood #1, right next to Waccamaw) sells discounted clothing, towels, sheets and other home decor items.

You can purchase used rental furniture at various clearance centers in the suburbs. Of them, you will find the best buys at **CORT's Clearance Centers** at 3137 Pennsy Dr. in Landover, Maryland (301/773-3369) or at 14130 Sullyfield Circle in Chantilly, Virginia (off Route 50; 703/818-2678).

Renting Furniture

If you know that your stay in Washington will be brief, you may want to consider renting your furniture rather than buying it. Renting prevents many hassles, including what to do with your furniture when you move on. Most furniture rental stores have showrooms Downtown. Their salespeople can show you samples and discuss the details (prices, length of lease, delivery and insurance). Renting furniture creates a pile of paperwork, including a credit application, a lease and insurance papers. Most rental companies require one month's rent for a security deposit and will deliver your furniture within three to five business days. Many places offer student discounts.

Although renting furniture can be enticing, be aware of the pitfalls. Get a quote for the entire price. Unlike rent for an apartment or house, furniture rentals are subject to tax. In addition to this, rental companies often charge for a fire damage waiver. Be sure to include these extras in your budget. If you already have renters' insurance, you do not need to pay the damage waiver fee—just ask your insurance agent to supply you with a certificate of coverage for the full value of the furniture.

All of the rental stores listed below are relatively inexpensive, except for Cort Furniture Rental, which can be costly.

AAA Furniture Rentals	703/671-8905
2784 South Arlington Mill Dr., Arlington	
Aaron Rents Furniture	703/941-7195
5720 General Washington Dr., Alexandria	
Cort Furniture Rental	202/223-9241
1100 New York Ave., N.W.	
Furniture Renters of America	202/293-9400
2101 L St., N.W.	
General Furniture Leasing	202/296-6555
1129 20th St., N.W.	

Beds and Futons

Its many outlets and aggressive advertising make **Mattress Discounters** easy to find. This local chain gained its prominence not just through advertising, but from its relatively low prices. They offset their $30 delivery charges by including a free frame with each purchase of a mattress and box spring. You can call (800/666-2344) to find the store nearest you.

> **Package Deals Available**
>
> Some rental companies offer package deals to provide all of the basics for various apartment configurations. Prices vary, but to give you an idea of what to expect, here is a package that was available at **Furniture Renters of America** (2101 L St., N.W.; 202/293-9400) for $85/month: a "one-bedroom" package included a sofa, matching chair, cocktail and end tables, dining table with four chairs, bed (box spring, mattress and frame), chest, night table and two lamps.

Several stores have the same prices as Mattress Discounters, but since they cannot afford the large advertising budgets they often get overlooked. Salespeople at these stores are always willing to make a deal. **The Market** (3229 M St., N.W.; 202/333-1234), a block west of Georgetown's hub, sells mattresses, futons and carpeting. In Arlington, **Brass Beds & Bedding** (2811 Columbia Pike; 703/486-0204) does the same. **The Bed Store** (1100 King St.; 703/549-8005) provides an excellent alternative for Alexandria residents.

Getting a futon rather than a bed can add much-needed room to your place, particularly if you have moved into an efficiency. Futons come in all sizes and you can purchase the mattresses alone or with a variety of adjustable wooden frames. Washington has several futon dealers with very competitive prices. The two most popular are **Atlantic Futon** (703/893-9125) in Tysons Corner and **Futons by Shonin** in both Arlington (6015 Wilson Blvd.; 703/538-4603) and Takoma Park (6915 Laurel Ave.; 301/270-1036).

Other futon dealers include **Dezzenio Futon** in both Georgetown Park (202/337-2331) and in Falls Church (5151 Leesburg Pike; 703/820-9190) and **Ginza** in Dupont Circle (1721 Connecticut Ave.; N.W., 202/331-7991). Ginza's prices tend to be slightly higher than the rest, but they do run frequent sales and have the advantage of being in the District close to a Metro stop.

Discount Department Stores

Montgomery Ward offers a wide selection of name-brand electronics and furniture (including beds, lamps, shades and bedding) at reasonable prices. Montgomery Ward does not have a store in the District, but does maintain a branch in Falls Church at 6100 Arlington Blvd. (703/241-8700) and another in Wheaton at 11160 Veirs Mill Rd. (301/468-5300).

Wal-Mart made its grand entrance into the Washington area in 1992. Since the opening of the first Wal-Mart in Easton, Maryland (410/819-0140), stores have opened in Fairfax (703/222-3927), Manassas (703/330-5253), Waldorf (301/705-7070), Hagerstown (301/714-1373), Leesburg (703/779-0102) and Woodbridge (703/ 497-2590).

Pots, Pans and Dishes

Waccamaw Pottery (703/494-7999) at Potomac Mills (Neighborhood #1) is an excellent place to start. Supermarket-sized Waccamaw fills its shelves with a wide selection of dishes, pots, pans, silverware, glassware (some for less than a dollar), linens, various small appliances and thousands of Rubbermaid items. China lovers should walk over to **Fitz & Floyd Factory Outlet** (Neighborhood #2; 703/494-1282).

Bed, Bath & Beyond (5716 Columbia Pike, Falls Church; 703/578-3374) sells everything you could want for your kitchen, bathroom and bedroom at reasonable prices. The quality of their merchandise is also superb. The Metro does not stop anywhere nearby, so you can get there by car or Metrobus #16. Marylanders can shop at BB&B's location at 12270 Rockville Pike (301/231-7637).

If you need to do all of your shopping by Metro, try the **Kitchen Bazaar:** two of its stores are right near Metro stops. You can easily reach their Van Ness location at 4401 Connecticut Ave., N.W. (202/244-1550) by the Red line or their store at The Fashion Centre at Pentagon City (703/415-5545) on the Blue or Yellow lines. Every store offers cooking classes and you can pick up a course catalog at any store.

Appliances

For the best prices, head out to the suburbs and seek out the catalog discount stores. National chains, **Best** and **Evans** have low prices on a huge array of brand name items. Best has stores in Arlington (2800 South Randolph St.; 703/578-4600), Fairfax (11001 Lee Highway; 703/385-2929) and Rockville (12345 Parklawn Dr.; 301/881-8422). **Evans** has locations in Arlington (Arlington Blvd. and Glebe Rd.; 703/892-2800), Alexandria (6200 Little River Turnpike; 703/256-6700), and Rockville (5060 Nicholson Lane; 301/770-6400). If you do not want to leave the District, you can head downtown — both **Hecht's** and **Woodie's** at Metro Center provide appliance shopping.

Hardware Stores

A trip to the hardware store is often the first step (after moving in your furniture) to making your house or apartment more livable. For a large selection and one-stop shopping, try **Hechinger's**. Its massive blue and white hardware stores throughout the area contain virtually everything: lumber yards, electrical supplies, cleaning supplies, garbage cans, file cabinets, fans, door mats, humidifiers, contact paper, paint—you get the idea. The Tenleytown store on Wisconsin Ave. (202/244-0650) sits within blocks of the Metro station. A second District location is in Northeast (Hechinger Mall, 17th St. and Benning Rd., N.E.; 202/398-7100). Suburbanites can avail themselves to Hechinger's other locations: Baileys Crossroads (5516 Leesburg Pike; 703/379-0200), Alexandria (3131 Duke St., 703/370-5810), Bethesda (Montgomery Mall; 301/469-6620), and Wheaton (Randolph Rd. and Georgia Ave.; 301/942-8200).

    Candey Hardware in Dupont Circle (1210 18th St., N.W.; 202/659-5650) has been dispensing its goods since the beginning of the Twentieth century and retains the musty charm to prove it. This store's location is ideal for those working Downtown. **Frager's Hardware,** (1115 Pennsylvania Ave., S.E.; 202/543-6157) serves Hill residents' needs.

    Residents of Arlington can visit their own **Virginia Hardware** (2915 Wilson Blvd.; 703/522-3366). This hardware store is within sight of the Clarendon Metro. Alexandria's **Smitty's Servistar** (8457 Richmond Highway; 703/780-7800) houses a huge lumber yard and will deliver.

    In Bethesda, **Strosnider's Hardware** (6930 Arlington Rd.; 301/654-5688) offers all the usual items, from lawn and garden to electrical to housewares. There is also a **Strosnider's Kemp Mill Paint and Hardware** in Silver Spring (1386 Lamberton Dr.; 301/593-5353), but it is unrelated to the one in Bethesda. Aside from stocking the usual, they will also perform small repairs to anything but appliances. **Zimmerman and Sons Hardware** (8860 Brookville Rd.; 301/585-5200) also serves Silver Spring.

Wiring In

■ Phone Service

To set up phone service, call your local Bell Atlantic office. If you do not have a credit history you will be asked to tender a deposit. The phone company will generally connect your service within a few business days.

Service numbers in the District correspond to the first letter in your last name.

District of Columbia:		Maryland:
A-K	202/346-1000	301/954-6260
L-Z	202/346-1110	

Virginia:
703/876-7000

■ Cable TV

Alexandria	Jones Intercable	703/823-3000
Arlington	Cable TV Arlington	703/841-7700
District	District Cablevision	202/797-2877
Fairfax	Media General	703/378-8411
Montgomery	Cable TV Montgomery	301/424-4400
Prince George's	Metro Vision	301/499-1980
	Multivision	301/731-5560

■ Natural Gas

If your apartment or house needs gas service, you can call **Washington Gas** at 703/750-1000.

■ Electricity

To turn on the electricity, residents in the District and Maryland should call **Potomac Electric Company (PEPCO)** at 202/833-7500. Northern Virginia residents can contact **Virginia Power** (703/934-9670).

Newspapers

■ The Washington Post

Home delivery: 202/334-6100

The Washington Post is the area's major newspaper and one of the best in the country. It offers its readers a broad perspective on current events both inside and outside the Beltway. Its Federal Page keeps political junkies in touch with the latest news or scandal from the Hill. Many rely on Friday's Weekend section for its listings of the city's social and cultural events. While the Post has a well-deserved reputation for national and political coverage, its neighborhood reporting is not as comprehensive. You many want to consider a local daily or weekly to keep tabs on your community. Subscription rates for the Post run approximately $9 a month.

Chapter Three | Settling In

■ The Washington Times

Home delivery: 202/636-3333

The Reverend Sun Myung Moon's Unification Church funds this newspaper, although most people feel that the paper reflects extreme political conservatism rather than Rev. Moon's theology. Its layout is flashier and more colorful than its better-known rival and it offers good coverage of local politics and sports, particularly if you prefer a paper with a monolithic conservative bent. Subscription rates are about a dollar a week.

■ Specialty Newspapers

Washington's weekly *City Paper* does an excellent job covering local news and cultural events, particularly the arts. Well-known for its candid features on Washington phenomena and personalities, the *City Paper* has a steady following. You can pick up the latest *City Paper* on Thursdays at Metro stations and many District stores and restaurants. Best of all, it is free!

On the Hill, *Roll Call* (202/289-4900) helps congressional staffers keep up with latest news. This biweekly newspaper covers Congress on much the same level as other community papers cover their neighborhoods. A year's subscription (96 issues) costs $210.

The Washington Blade, another free weekly, is the newspaper of Washington's gay and lesbian community. This paper is especially helpful to interested newcomers with its directory of gay professionals and community resources.

There are many free neighborhood newspapers to keep residents in touch with community news and issues. Examples include *The Georgetowner, Cleveland Park 20008, Hill Rag, The InTowner, Washington Citizen, McLean Providence Journal* (703/356-3320) and *Arlington Courier* (703/356-3320).

Many specialty papers cater to Washington's various ethnic and religious groups. The *Washington Afro-American* (202/332-0080) and *Washington Informer* (202/561-4100) cover news and topics of interest to the African-American community. Washington's sizable Hispanic community is chronicled in the pages of *Tiempo Latino* (202/986-0511) and *El Prognero* (301/853-4504). *The Washington Jewish Week* (301/230-2222) follows the area's Jewish community. *The Korean Times* (202/722-5400) provides news to Washington's growing Korean population.

The monthly *Sports Focus* covers amateur and professional sports in the D.C. area. In addition to several feature articles, the paper includes listings and phone numbers for all area sports organizations and clubs. You can pick up a copy at Metro stations near the Orange and Red lines.

Recreation News is a monthly recreation publication devoted to providing government employees with the facts on Washington weekend entertainment and road trips. Copies are available at any government building.

Local Magazines

Washingtonian Magazine (202/331-0715), a glossy monthly magazine, contains in-depth interviews with Washington's movers and shakers, restaurant reviews, Washington trivia, the occasional exposé and a gossip column. *Washingtonian* is known for its frequent lists of the area's best restaurants and entertainment.

Newsstands

It is ironic that in a city full of diplomats, Hill staffers and foreign embassies, newsstands with a wide range of domestic and international papers seem invisible. **The Newsroom,** (1753 Connecticut Ave., N.W.; 202/332-1489) the best of its kind, is at the corner of Connecticut Ave. and S St., N.W., just north of Dupont Circle. The Newsroom offers an array of national and international newspapers as well as magazines, scholarly journals and bilingual dictionaries. For national and international papers, Downtown must depend on the **American International Newsstand** at 1825 Eye St., N.W. (202/223-2526), and **One Stop News** (202/872-1577) at the corner of Pennsylvania Ave. and 20th Sts., N.W. On the Hill, **Trover Books** (221 Pennsylvania Ave., S.E.; 202/547-2665) carries a wide selection of domestic newspapers.

Bookstores

For me, settling in requires getting to know an area's bookstores. Although national bookstore chains, **Waldenbooks** and **B. Dalton's** have numerous locations throughout the area, the largest chain locally is **Crown Books.** Crown Books offers readers discounts on all of its books. Hard cover best sellers are 40% off list price, with succeeding tiers of discounts down to a simple 10% for paperbacks. As the name implies, the **Super Crown** stores offer an even greater selection. The newest Super Crown (11 Dupont Circle, N.W.; 202/319-1374) has a Ferrara coffee and espresso bar inside.

Borders Books attracts the serious reader, with a tremendous selection of more esoteric titles, while still providing all the entertaining books found elsewhere. Borders shops also have cafes in which to sit and enjoy your recent purchases. Their Downtown store recently opened at 1800 L St., N.W. (202/466-4999). The Rockville store (301/816-1067) has just moved into the White Flint Mall and added an array of videos and compact discs. Another location at 8311 Leesburg Pike (703/556-7766) conveniently serves Northern Virginia residents.

Olsson's Books and Records, a smaller local chain, sells books and music side by side in each store. Olssons has six locations: Georgetown (1239 Wisconsin Ave., N.W.; 202/338-9544), Dupont Circle (1307 19th St., N.W.; 202/785-1133), Downtown (1200 F St., N.W.; 202/347-3686 and 418 7th St., N.W.; 202/638-7610), Bethesda (7647 Old Georgetown Rd.; 301/652-3336) and Old Town Alexandria (106 S. Union St.; 703/684-0077). They also have a mail order department (202/337-8084).

On Capitol Hill, **Trover Books** (221 Pennsylvania Ave., S.E.; 202/547-2665) carries a complete line of Penguin titles and a terrific variety of magazines.

Chapters Literary Bookstore (1512 K St., N.W. 202/347-5495) emphasizes personal service to the serious reader. They will order any book you want and have become one of the main stops for visiting authors, with readings several times each week.

One of Washington's bookstore institutions is **Sidney Kramer Books** (1825 Eye St., N.W.; 202/293-2685). At its new home at the street level of the International Square Mall, Sidney Kramer has an outstanding selection of nonfiction works. Sidney Kramer is justifiably proud of its foreign affairs and political science departments. The political-minded will also want to check out **Politics and Prose** (5015 Connecticut Ave., N.W.; 202/364-1919). In addition to both the politics and prose, there is also a coffee house and a staff that could certainly hold its own in any political discussion you may wish to start.

Dupont Circle's top book stop is **Kramerbooks & Afterwords** (1517 Connecticut Ave., N.W.; 202/387-1400). Kramerbooks is a good, all-purpose bookstore with strong selections in the current and paperback fiction sections. Just as attractive is the two-tier cafe located in the rear. Offering everything from coffee, tea and drinks to sandwiches to full dinners, Kramer's sunny atrium seating area provides a relaxed setting to start your books. A second location recently opened in Arlington at 4201 Wilson Blvd. (703/524-3200).

Lambda Rising (1625 Connecticut Ave., N.W.; 202/462-6969) specializes in gay books and literature. **Lammas** (1426 21st St., N.W.; 202/775-8218) focuses on feminist and lesbian literature.

Bethesda's **Travel Books and Language Center** (4931 Cordell Ave.; 301/951-8533) fills its shelves with thousands of language books, guidebooks, atlases and history books for the well-informed traveler. Downtown, **The Map Store** (1636 Eye St., N.W.; 202/628-2608) stocks up on maps and also has a sizable selection of travel and guidebooks.

Mystery lovers will not want to miss the **Mystery Bookshop** (7700 Old Georgetown Rd., Bethesda; 301/657-2665) and **Mystery Books** (1715 Connecticut Ave., N.W.; 202/483-1600). These stores have books on tape, games and other mystery-related items for the aficionado.

Used Books

Cheap books and a broad selection mark **The Lantern Bryn Mawr Bookshop** (3160 O St., N.W.; 202/333-3222). Several features make this store unique and less expensive than most other used bookstores. Most of the books are donated and the store is run entirely by volunteers. The Lantern is a great place to browse and you can always justify all those book purchases as charity: net proceeds go to scholarships at Bryn Mawr College.

Capitol Hill Books (657 C St., S.E.; 202/544-1621) and **Yesterday's Books** (4702 Wisconsin Ave., N.W.; 202/363-0581) are two of the area's best used bookstores. **The Second Story** (2000 P St., N.W., 202/659/8884; 4836 Bethesda Ave., Bethesda, 301/656-0170; and 12160 Parklawn Dr., Rockville, 301/770-0477) feature antiques, international art and used records, cassettes and CDs in addition to used books.

In Maryland, **Bonifant Books** (11240 Georgia Ave., Wheaton; 301/946-1526) is a good, general stock, used bookstore. An added benefit for bookworms without wheels, they are near the Wheaton Metro stop.

The Washington Antiquarian Booksellers Association (301/460-3700) lists more than 60 member shops. You can pick up one of their directories at any of the above used bookstores.

Food Markets and Gourmet Stores
■ Giant
Giant, one of the two largest grocery chains serving the area, caters mostly to suburbanites. Some outlets, known as "Gourmet Giants," offer a somewhat greater number of specialty items. Do not be misled, though; "gourmet" generally means bigger, not better, to Giant. Only Giant's "Someplace Special" in McLean (1445 Chain Bridge Rd.; 703/448-0800) is entirely gourmet. Every Giant maintains a salad bar and an ATM. Most of the newer stores also have in-store bakeries, pharmacies and seafood departments. Giant's "Special Discounts" aisles offer bulk items at low prices.

■ Safeway
If you live in the District, you will probably frequent a Safeway. Safeway runs twenty stores in the District and many more in the suburbs. Two Townhouse Safeways provide service to the District: one in Dupont Circle at 20th and S Streets, N.W. (202/483-3908) and the other in the West End at 21st and L Streets, N.W. (202/659-8784). Georgetown's Safeway (1855 Wisconsin Ave., N.W.; 202/333-3223) is known as the "Social Safeway." The "Secret Safeway" hides away off upper Wisconsin Ave. at 4203 Davenport St., N.W. (202/364-0290). Like Giant, all stores offer check cashing and ATMs.

■ Dean & DeLuca
The New York institution, Dean & DeLuca, has migrated south to Washington. Its flagship location is the Georgetown Market House (3276 M St., N.W.; 202/342-2500), a star-crossed, historically pre-

> **Where to Buy the Freshest Fish**
>
> Instead of buying your fish at Safeway or Giant, you should go down to the waterfront to the Maine Avenue Wharf (1100 Maine Ave., S.W.). You can stroll around the market and view the dozens of different fish literally at your feet — most of the stalls are built into large boats on the water and the trays of fish float just a few inches above the sidewalk. At night, this fish market resembles a carnival or small fair, with bright lights illuminating the rows of open stalls as groups of people walk about and workers call out to get their attention. The wharf is open everyday from 7:30 a.m. to 9:30 p.m.

served building that has endured several failed incarnations in recent years. Its overwhelming popularity should ensure that D&D will make a little history of its own, with its great selection of gourmet meats and cheeses, fresh vegetables and bakery items. The free parking offered to any customer making over $10 in purchases (not a difficult task) makes D&D especially appreciated in parking-scarce Georgetown. D&D has opened another cafe in D.C. in the Warner Theatre building (1299 Pennsylvania Ave., N.W.; 202/628-8155).

■ Fresh Fields

One of the area's fastest growing chains, Fresh Fields' supermarkets sell "good-for-you foods." The good-for-you list includes organic produce as well as meat, seafood, dairy products, gourmet and vegetarian prepared foods, natural health care products and environmentally-friendly household goods. Prices lower than other gourmet supermarkets will also please your wallet. Fresh Fields has opened stores in Rockville (11503 Rockville Pike; 301/984-4880), Bethesda (5225 River Rd.; 301/984-4860) and Tysons Corner (7501 Leesburg Pike; 703/448-1600).

■ Marvelous Market

In addition to twelve different types of bread, Marvelous Market sells cheeses, sausages, pastas, homemade jams and other gourmet carryout items. On busy Sunday mornings, be prepared to wait in line. Locations:

5035 Connecticut Ave., N.W.	202/686-4040
1514 Connecticut Ave., N.W.	202/986-2222
Union Station, Food Court level	202/371-9524
9889 Georgetown Pike, Great Falls	703/759-5666
4832 Bethesda Ave., Bethesda	301/986-0555
222 North Lee St., Alexandria	703/519-7777

■ Sutton Place Gourmet

Sutton Place Gourmet specializes in the exotic and esoteric. This chain flies in produce daily from all over the world. Its managers boast that "Sutton Place is the only place you will be able to find fresh, hand-picked raspberries during a snow storm." While only the very well off can afford to buy all of their groceries here, Sutton Place is great for picking up special ingredients, coffees, cheeses, meats and fish. Sutton Place has two stores in Northwest Washington, at 3201 New Mexico Ave. (202/363-5800) and 4872 Massachusetts Ave. (202/966-1740); one in Bethesda (10323 Old Georgetown Rd.; 301/

Washington's Best Ethnic Food Stores
BY JIM LAWSON

Americana Grocery (Latin American)
1813 Columbia Rd., N.W. (Adams Morgan), 202/265-7455
8541 Piney Branch Rd., Silver Spring, 301/495-0864
6128-30 Columbia Pike, Falls Church, 703/671-9625

Caribbean Market (West Indian)
11238 Triangle Lane, Wheaton, 301/949-4423

Eden Supermarket (Vietnamese)
6763 Wilson Blvd., Falls Church, 703/532-4950

Heidelberg Pastry Shop (German)
2150 North Culpepper St., Arlington, 703/527-8394

Litteri's Italian Grocery
517 Morse Rd., N.E., 202/544-0183

Lotte Oriental Supermarket (Korean)
11790 Parklawn Dr., Rockville, 301/881-3355

Maxim (Chinese)
460 Hungerford Dr., Rockville, 301/279-0110

Mediterranean Bakery (Lebanese)
374 Pickett St., Alexandria, 703/751-1702

Merkato Market (Ethiopian)
2116 18th St., N.W. (Adams Morgan), 202/483-9499

Muskan (Indian)
956 Thayer Ave., Silver Spring, 301/588-0331

Phil-Fancies
739 Cady Dr., Fort Washington, 301/248-2944

Thai Market
902 Thayer Ave., Silver Spring, 301/495-2779

Yekta (Iranian)
1488-A Rockville Pike, Rockville, 301/984-1190

Jim Lawson's *Washington Ethnic Food Store Guide* (Second Edition) and *Washington Ethnic Bakery Book* are available at local book stores or you can order from Ardmore Publications, P.O. Box 21051, Washington, DC 20009 ($9.95 plus $1.50 shipping and 60¢ tax for D.C. residents).

564-3100) and another in Old Town Alexandria (600 Franklin St.; 703/ 549-6611).

Membership Clubs

In the past few years, super discount membership clubs, Price Club and Sam's Club have proliferated throughout the suburbs. While these stores are ideal for large families or groups living together, even the single dweller will find irresistible bargains. A word of advice, the bulk prices have led many first-time shoppers to overestimate their consumption.

All clubs require that you join to shop there. While membership is specifically aimed at business owners, credit union members and hospital and government workers, most everyone is able qualify for the membership card. Membership usually costs $25.

■ Price Club
Route 1 and Powder Mill Rd., Beltsville (301/595-3400)
4501 Auth Place, Marlow Heights (301/423-6303)
880 Russell Ave., Gaithersburg (301/417-1520)
7373 Austin Blvd., Springfield (703/912-1200)
4725 West Ox Rd., Fairfax (703/802-0372)
21398 Price Cascades Plaza, Sterling (703/406-7000)

■ Sam's Club
610 North Frederick Ave., Gaithersburg (301/216-2550)
8511 Landover Rd., Landover (301/386-5577)
2365 Route 301, Waldorf (301/645-7711)
14045 Worth Ave., Woodbridge (703/491-2662)

Bakeries

■ Breads Unlimited

The owner of **Breads Unlimited** in Bethesda (6914 Arlington Rd.; 301/656-2340) oversees the making of his sourdough bread like a brew master caring for his beers. In addition, all the two dozen different breads baked there are fat and cholesterol free. A second location, called the **New Yorker Bakery** (8313 Grubb Rd., Silver Spring; 301/585-8585), makes its fresh bagels in front of an appreciative audience.

Chapter Three | Settling In

■ Reeves

You only need to know two words about **Reeves** bakery: strawberry pie. This Downtown bakery (1306 G St., N.W.; 202/628-6350) has been in operation for more than a century and is justly famous. If you get around to it, Reeves also offers a selection of pastries and other baked goods as well as a two-floor restaurant offering sandwiches and other light fare.

■ Firehook Bakery and Coffee House

In keeping with the Old Town neighborhood, the **Firehook Bakery and Coffee House** (106 North Lee St., Alexandria; 703/519-8020) bakes its breads in a 17-foot diameter wood-burning oven. The bread is baked with a thick crust much like bread was made 100 years ago. Other special features include twice-monthly poetry readings and complete breakfasts on weekends with quiche, French toast, fresh juice and Italian sodas.

■ Uptown Bakers

Lucky Cleveland Park residents have this bread bakery right in their neighborhood. From its prolific ovens, the **Uptown Bakers** (3313 Connecticut Ave., N.W.; 202/362-6262) offers seventeen types of bread, including sourdough ficelle, killer toast (perfect for breakfast) and olive bread.

Food Co-ops—"Food for People, Not for Profit"

Co-ops are cooperatively owned food stores. In theory, they are owned by their customers, thereby taking away the incentive for profit. Few co-ops today are truly cooperatively owned. Generally, however, these stores do offer lower prices on organic products and bulk foods (nuts, grain, pasta and flour).

■ Bethesda Co-op

The **Bethesda Co-op** (6500 Seven Locks Rd.; 301/320-2530) sells organic and commercial produce, bulk foods, shampoos and household cleaners. Six hours of work at the co-op each month entitles you to a 20 percent discount. To get there by Metro, take the Red line to Bethesda and then hop on the Ride-On bus #32.

■ Takoma Park Silver Spring Co-op

Takoma Park Silver Spring Co-op (623 Sligo Ave., Silver Spring; 301/588-6093) packs plenty of products into a small space. Discounts are available in exchange for volunteer work. You should ask the management for details. This co-op can be reached by taking the Red line to Silver Spring and from there, the Ride-On bus #16.

■ Glut Food Co-op

For over 20 years the **Glut Food Co-op** (4005 34th St., Mt. Rainer; 301/779-1978) has been providing natural food in a not-for-profit setting. On most days, Glut offers fresh-baked breads. Glut opens each day at 10:00 a.m. and closes at 7:00 p.m. On Thursday and Friday evenings they remain open for an extra hour and close at 5 p.m. on Sundays.

■ Uncommon Market/The Arlington Co-op

The Uncommon Market (1041 South Edgewood St., Arlington; 703/920-6855), a co-op in the true sense of the word, is owned by 2,400 members. You can also become a part-owner for an investment of $30 (three shares). Owners receive a five percent discount on their groceries. If you work at the co-op, you can get a further discount: three hours a month translates into an additional 15 percent off.

■ Women's Community Bakery

The Women's Community Bakery (736 7th St., S.E.; 202/546-7944), sells breads, muffins, cookies, rolls and granola. All are baked by women. Specific days are set aside for baking certain items. On Tuesday, it is cookies. They bake fresh bread and rolls every Monday, Wednesday and Friday. Retail hours are between 12:00 and 7:00 p.m. on weekdays and 10:00 a.m. to 2:00 p.m. on Saturdays.

Shopping Malls

If malls are your scene, you will find solace in the suburbs. Just barely within the District are **Mazza Gallerie** (202/966-6114) and **Chevy Chase Pavilion** (202/686-5335) which are on the Red line at the Friendship Heights Metro station on Wisconsin Ave. These two complexes cover all the bases, with Filene's Basement, Lord & Taylor, Saks Fifth Avenue and Woodie's. Parking is generally not a problem; the first two hours are free with a validated ticket.

The glitzy **White Flint Mall** (301/468-5777) on Rockville Pike in Rockville hosts Bloomingdale's and Lord & Taylor. White Flint used to be the prestige mall in suburban Maryland but has fallen on hard times lately. If you are going by Metro, take the Red line towards Shady Grove to White Flint. From there you can either walk or take a free shuttle bus to the mall.

As the fortunes of White Flint have sunk, those of its nearby neighbor, **Montgomery Mall,** (7101 Democracy Blvd.; 301/469-6000) have risen. Nordstrom, Hecht's, Woodies and Sears have stores in this mall. Unfortunately for the mass transit bound, this recently renovated mall in Bethesda is not on the Metro line.

Capped by a top-floor, ten-screen movie theater, one of the area's newest malls, **City Place** in Silver Spring (8661 Colesville Rd.; 301/589-1091), specializes in outlet stores. You will find Nordstrom's Rack, Ross and Marshall's here. The Metro's Red line Silver Spring station is a three-block walk away.

You can take the Yellow or Blue line across the Potomac directly to the **Fashion Centre at Pentagon City** (703/415-2400). Both Macy's and Nordstrom anchor this mid-size and well-designed mall. Walking through **Ballston Common** (703/243-8088) in north Arlington, one has the feeling that this mall has been hurt by its larger and nicer competitors nearby, Pentagon City and Tysons Corner. Few shoppers mill around this three-story mall, but with J.C. Penney, Hecht's and a location just a block from the Ballston Metro, it is hard to pass this mall by, especially if you do not have a car.

The huge **Tysons I** (703/893-9400) and **The Galleria at Tysons II** (703/827-7700) lie further out in Virginia, just beyond the Beltway. The phenomenal success of Tysons I encouraged real estate developers to build another large mall (The Galleria at Tysons II) just across the street. Cars are the best means of travel to this huge shopper's oasis. Almost all of America's usual mall suspects, including Bloomingdale's, Hecht's, Lord & Taylor, Nordstrom and Woodie's (in Tysons I) and Macy's, Saks Fifth Avenue and Neiman Marcus (in The Galleria) live here.

Landmark Center (703/941-2582) in Alexandria includes a Sears, Hecht's and Woodie's under its roof. Landmark is not near a Metro line, but you can get there using public transportation. Take the Blue line to Van Dorn station and then hop on DASH bus #7. Driving is much quicker; take I-395 to Duke St. (East).

Filling the Closets

Bargain-hunters can trek to one or all of the three main discount shopping areas: Maryland's Eastern Shore; Woodbridge, Virginia or Martinsburg, West Virginia. To decide which region to approach first, examine what each offers. Maryland's Eastern Shore has several different discount shopping centers and offers reduced-price china, kitchen items, shoes and clothes. To get to the Eastern Shore, get on

Route 50 East and keep driving. Along the way, you will find the **Bay Bridge Market Place** (410/757-9181), **Chesapeake Village** (410/827-8699) and **Kent Narrows Factory Stores** (410/643-5231).

More mainstream bargain-hunters will enjoy strolling through Potomac Mills (703/643-1770) in Woodbridge, Virginia. This huge mall sells furniture, clothes and housewares. Since Potomac Mills is just a 40-minute drive from Downtown, you can easily drive out there for weeknight shopping. Amongst its outlet stores, shoppers will find **Benetton, Britches, Calvin Klein, Eddie Bauer, Laura Ashley, Nordstrom, Sears** and **Woodie's**.

In West Virginia, the **Blue Ridge Outlet Center** (315 West Stephen Street, Martinsburg, WV; 800/445-3993) specializes in discount designer clothing such as **Anne Klein, Van Heusen, Jones New York, Donna Karan, J. Crew** and **London Fog**. From Washington, take 495 to I-270 (North) to I-70 to I-81 South to WV Exit 13 (King St.). Make a right onto Queen St. and another right to Stephen St. Assuming little traffic, the trip to Martinsburg should take you a little over an hour and a half.

Business Clothes

The power-brokering Downtown corridor boasts **Brooks Brothers** (1840 L St., N.W.; 202/659-4650), **Jos. A. Bank Clothiers** (1118 19th St., N.W.; 202/466-2282) and **Britches** (1219 Connecticut Ave., N.W.; 202/347-8994). Big, tall and short men will find their sizes at **Steve Windsor** (1730 K St., N.W.; 202/293-2770).

Washington just received its first **Filene's Basement.** Filene's Basement got its start in 1908 when the famous Filene's department store in Boston started selling excess merchandise at a discount in its basement. The store still sells casual clothes and business attire at a markdown (30% to 60% off) but it is on street level now. There is a Filene's Basement Downtown at the corner of Connecticut and DeSales (1133 Connecticut Ave., N.W.; 202/872-8430) and one on the outskirts of town, at the Mazza Gallerie (5300 Wisconsin Ave., N.W.: 202/966-0208).

Petite women should drive out to **Lord & Taylor** (301/770-9000) in White Flint Mall. This store has a huge petite department with lots of accommodating salespeople.

As you will quickly find out, there is no shortage of discount clothing stores. You will have to travel to the suburbs for some of the best buys. **Today's Man** at 5714 Columbia Pike, Baileys Crossroads, specializes in men's clothing (703/845-1307). Suits at Today's Man range between $250 and $350, with alterations costing an additional $30 to $50.

Women's skirts, blouses and suits can be purchased at **Annie Sez, Loehmann's** and **Sassafras.** Annie Sez has stores in Tysons Corner (7511 Leesburg Pike; 703/734-0033), Falls Church (3512 South Jefferson St.; 703/931-6544) and in Rockville (Federal Plaza on Rockville Pike; 301/816-2100). In addition to a store in Rockville at the corner of Randolph Rd. and Nicholson Lane (301/770-0030), Loehmann's (703/573-1510) anchors a discount mall out on Route 50, appropriately called Loehmann's Plaza. Sassafras, a locally-based chain that just brought itself back from bankruptcy protection, has twenty stores in the area. You will find their stores at 7514 Leesburg Pike (703/821-3440) and at 12145 Rockville Pike (301/468-5550).

Syms sells discounted clothing for both men and women. It has three locations: 11840 Rockville Pike in Rockville (301/984-3335), 1000 East Broad St. in Falls Church (703/241-8500) and Potomac Mills (703/497-7332).

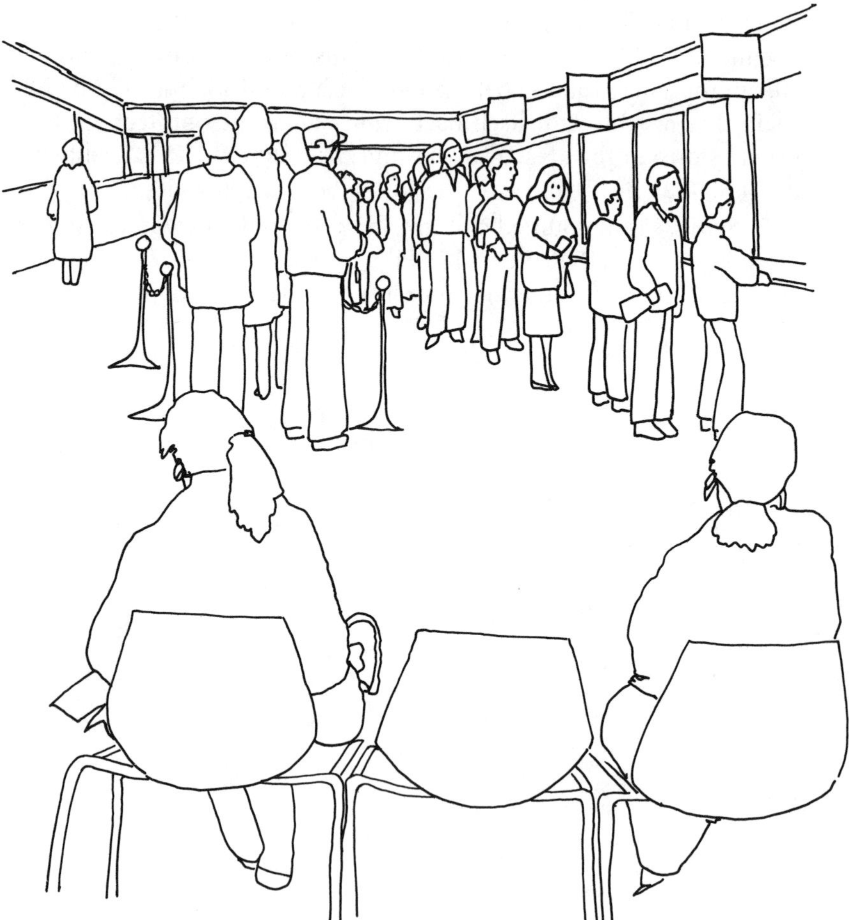

Chapter 4
Dealing with the Bureaucracy

Most newcomers enjoy looking for an apartment, buying furniture and setting up house, but they quickly learn to dread the bureaucratic labyrinth they must navigate to establish residency. Traditionally, the Bureau of Motor Vehicles (BMV) has consumed the most time and inspired the best horror stories. In recent years, though, Mayor Sharon Pratt Kelly has made a concerted effort to make city services more accessible and efficient. While improvements have been made, the District still lags behind the suburban cities and counties.

☐ Drivers' Licenses: Basic Information
Regardless of where you live, bring your checkbook, your current license (if you have one), social security card and one other form of identification bearing your name and birthdate (birth certificates, passports, employer and school IDs are all acceptable— photocopies are not) to the closest full-service BMV office.

Current out-of-state license holders have a 30-day grace period to get a local driver's license and license plates. If you surrender a valid driver's license from another U.S. state or territory, you do not need to take a driving test. Vision tests, though, are mandatory in all jurisdictions. District residents must take a twenty-question written test (a score of 75 percent is passing); Virginia and Maryland both waive written requirements for current license holders.

If you are fresh from the streets of Manhattan and have never gotten a driver's license, you must first apply for a learner's permit and take a written exam. After passing the written exam, you can then sign up for a road test.

Foreign license holders must bring a green card or social security card along with a passport and proof of a foreign license. Without proof of a foreign license, you will be forced to apply for a license from scratch—learner's permit and all. Non-U.S. citizens must pass the vision and written tests. BMV offices decide on an individual basis whether or not a foreign applicant has to take a road test. The vision and written tests are usually given the same day, so come prepared. If you have to take the road test, you will need to make an appointment after you pass the written test.

Driver's License Fees

	Driver's License	Learner's Permit
District	$20	$10
Virginia	$12	$3
Maryland	$18	$30*

*For both learner's permit and license

Registering Your Car

Bring a copy of the title of the car, out-of-state registration (if applicable), proof of auto insurance, proof of address and a blank check.

Where to go
The District

Newcomers to the District have no other choice but to trek down to the BMV's Central Office for licenses and car registration. This drab edifice sits at 301 C St., N.W. If you find yourself lost amidst a series of faceless gray government buildings, you know you are getting closer. Its heavy glass doors creak open weekdays at 8:15 a.m., only to swing shut again at 3:00 p.m. For late-risers, the BMV stays open till 7:00 p.m. every Wednesday. Fittingly, it is much easier to take the Metro to the BMV (Red line to Judiciary Square) than to drive. Parking can be a nightmare.

District residents have been known to spend countless weary hours in the BMV's windowless offices. This past year, though, has brought many changes to D.C.'s BMV. Today, the bureau is much more user-friendly and the average wait has been cut down to only 30 minutes. For quickest results, the BMV suggests visiting during weekday afternoons between 2:00 and 3:00 p.m.

To make things simpler (but not necessarily faster), the BMV has color-coded the offices essential to the registration process. Room 1157 (Blue), the single most important room you need to visit, appears directly in front of you as you enter. In this brightly-lit room,

Washingtonians stand patiently in line, waiting to be shuffled from one window to the next in the quest to register their cars. If you have any questions before you begin, consult either the bulletin board (just behind the chairs in Room 1157) or the person at the information desk.

Once you have filled out your Application for Certificate of Title for a Motor Vehicle or Trailer, secure your place in line at Window One. Following this, you must move on to Window Three to pay the various registration fees you incurred at Window One. Expect to pay $20 for certificate of title, $15 for each recorded lien on your car and a registration fee based on the weight of the car: $65 for small cars (less than 3,500 pounds) and $98 for heavier cars. These two fees already include the $10 inspection fee. The District also charges excise taxes based on the value of the vehicle: six percent of the fair market ("blue book") value for a small car and seven percent of the value of a large car. It will hurt your bank account, but you have to pay the taxes on the spot. Once you have weathered Windows One and Three, you are in good shape and ready to pick up your tags and title at Window Four.

In addition to the main office at Judiciary Square, there is now a BMV adjunct office at 616 H St., N.E., which offers some services (renewals, residential parking permits, driver's license renewals and non-driver identification cards). This office is open from 11:00 a.m. to 7:00 p.m. on weekdays and from 8:15 a.m. to 4:00 p.m. on Saturday.

Residential parking permits are an essential element for survival in the District. "It is peace of mind for just $10. Now you can park your car on your neighborhood street all the time without worrying about the 'boot,'" said one Washingtonian, justifying her place in line. To obtain a parking permit, you must present a valid D.C. vehicle registration, proof of insurance and proof of residence. You can show proof of residence by bringing along a signed lease, a notarized statement from your landlord or a utility bill.

Full-time students, temporary residents (those living in the District fewer than 180 days), congressional staff and military personnel can keep their home state license plates by applying for reciprocity. Students must show proof of full-time status (at least nine credit hours) and residence in the District. If you live on a street that has residential parking, you must still pay the $10 parking permit fee.

If you are seeking a **handicapped parking permit,** you should go to Room 1033 (Green) to file your application. If you are issued handicapped tags, you will not need a residential parking permit.

Once you leave the BMV, your troubles are not yet over—your car still has to be inspected. Safety inspections must be done within 30 days of receipt of your D.C. registration. To complicate things even more, all first-time inspections must be done at one of only two inspection stations operated by the District. Though these two stations may not be convenient, inspections cost only $10 and are relatively quick. In fact, you will already have paid this fee when you registered your car. If the lines are short, your inspection experience can be over in less than 15 minutes. One station is at 1001 Half St., S.W. (between Eye and M Sts.) and the other station is at 1827 West Virginia Ave., N.E. (four blocks south of New York Ave.). Try to avoid visiting these places near the end of the month. These inspections stations are open 6:00 a.m. to 2:00 p.m. during the summer (June 15-September 15) and 7:00 a.m. to 3:00 p.m. the rest of the year.

If you have any questions, you can call the BMV's automated information system (202/727-6680). If the series of recorded messages does not answer your questions, stay on the line and an operator will eventually answer.

For those of you who prefer self-propelled traveling, you will be relieved to know that registering bicycles in the District is much easier than registering a car. Instead of standing in long lines and filling out tedious forms, you can take your bike to any District police or fire station. Registration costs just $1 and proof of ownership is required. For more information, call 202/576-6768.

■ BMV Information

Information   202/727-6680

Central Office   301 C St., N.W.

Hours: Monday, Tuesday, Thursday and Friday: 8:15 a.m. - 3:00 p.m.
Wednesday: 8:15 a.m. - 7:00 p.m.

Virginia

Virginians should be prepared for a scavenger hunt. First, you have to find a state-registered service station to have your car inspected. Your car will have to undergo two inspections: one for safety and another for emissions. The safety inspection is done annually and the emissions inspection is done every other year. Not all places are licensed to perform both tests. Signs at gas stations will indicate which tests can be performed there. See the list below for inspection stations.

With your approved emissions and safety documents in hand, your next stop is a full-service DMV office to register your car (locations listed below). Blue street signs with white DMV letters let you know you are closing in on a DMV office. In return for a $10 titling fee and a $26.50 registration fee (for cars weighing under 4,000 pounds), you will receive a Virginia title, a registration card, license plates and current plate decals. Registration cards and decals are valid for one year. Those who have moved to Virginia for the long haul may want to opt for the two-year registration plan—just double the registration fee.

Unfortunately, you are not quite done. The final stop after getting the safety inspection decal, the registration and the license plates is the local city hall or county courthouses to register for the local personal property tax and to get the license decal for the city or county to indicate registration.

■ Northern Virginia: Local Inspection Stations

Inspection fees total $23.50 (emissions $13.50 and safety $10). Like doctors who examine their patients from head to toe, inspectors check everything. If any part needs to be replaced, be sure to have it done before the inspection. If the car fails inspection, you will not get your money back.

Al & Reese Repair & Service 8413 Lee Highway, Fairfax	703/573-2759
Anderson Sunoco 5501 Lee Highway, Arlington	703/532-0773
Bob Peck Chevrolet & GEO 800 North Glebe Rd., Arlington	703/522-9000
Beach's Automotive Service Center 105 Falls Ave., Falls Church	703/533-1107
Belle Haven Texaco 5905 Richmond Highway, Alexandria	703/329-1780
Boulevard Mobil Service 5905 Richmond Highway, Alexandria	703/573-4438
Commons Shell 1698 Anderson Rd., McLean	703/821-2116
Emission Specialists of Northern Virginia 5601M General Washington Dr., Alexandria	703/256-9282

Gill's Amoco of Fairfax 703/691-9462
11119 Main St., Fairfax
Jerry's Sunoco 703/671-5384
5919 Columbia Pike, Falls Church
Joyce Motors 703/527-2218
3201 North 10th St., Arlington
Mount Vernon Mobil 703/780-0303
8300 Richmond Highway, Alexandria
Springfield Amoco 703/569-2264
6703 Backlick Rd., Springfield

■ DMV Branch Information: Full Service Offices
Information: 703/761-4655
Hours: Monday - Friday: 9:00 a.m.- 6:00 p.m.
       Saturday: 9:00 a.m.- 1:00 p.m.

Alexandria   930 North Henry St.
Arlington   4150 South Four Mile Run Dr.
Fairfax   11215-G Lee Highway
Franconia   6308 Grovedale Dr.
Vienna (Tysons Corner)   1968 Gallows Rd.

■ Arlington County

The Arlington County Courthouse at 2100 Clarendon Blvd. marks the final stop on your bureaucratic journey. Here you can register to vote, register your car in Arlington County and pick up some information about Arlington. Unlike the District, parking should not be a problem. There is a convenient, inexpensive parking garage on site. Alternatively, the Metro can deliver you right there (Orange line-Court House).

    You can register to vote and pick up newcomers' information at the information desk right by the main entrance. The Office of Personal Property Tax, Suite 218 (703/358-3135), waits for you on the second floor. There you file your personal property tax forms and pay the Arlington County processing fee. The county will charge just under five percent of the traded "blue book" value of the car (the tax decreases annually). A wave of relief sweeps over most Arlington residents when they learn that they do not have to pay these taxes on the spot. This tax can amount to a few hundred dollars a year for newer cars. If you register between December 16 and June 15, taxes will be due September 15. For those registering between June 16 and December 15, March 15 will be your deadline.

Bicycles in Arlington must be registered at 2100 North 15th St. (703/358-4252). Bring your serial number and 50¢.

■ Alexandria

Alexandrians must register to pay the personal property tax at Room 1410 in City Hall (301 King St.; 703/838-4560). Lines here, even during lunch hour, are not that long. The registration office is open weekdays from 8:00 a.m. to 5:00 p.m. You will need to bring your driver's license and one of the following: your state vehicle title, state vehicle registration card or bill of sale. The city will bill you in August and expects payment by October 5th. If you register your car in Alexandria after October 5th, you are given a thirty-day grace period to pay your personal property taxes. City stickers, required for on-street parking, cost $25 annually (zoned-area residents must pay an additional $15).

Alexandria cyclists must also register their bikes. Take your bicycle to the Police Department at 2003 Mill Rd. (Eisenhower Station). For 50¢, the police will record your bike's serial number and give you a decal.

■ Fairfax County

Fairfax County residents must bring their Virginia registration card to any county office in order to register a vehicle and purchase county tags. You can call 703/222-8234 to find the county office closest to you.

Fairfax County tags cost $20 for cars under 4,000 pounds and $25 for larger cars. The process for paying personal property tax is simple. Just fill out the proper form and you will be billed in late September. Tax rates are just over four and one-half percent of the current trading value of your car and payment is due by December 5th. Fairfax does prorate its property tax, which is good news if you move to the area halfway through the year.

Fairfax County does not require a bike permit. They do, however, recommend that you etch your social security number on your bike in case of theft.

Maryland

■ Montgomery and Prince George's County

Before you even set foot into a Motor Vehicle Administration (MVA) office, you should go to an authorized service station and have your car inspected. Prices generally range from $30 to $55.

Once your car has passed the safety inspection, you will need to bring your current title, certificate of inspection and all insurance information (company, policy and agent) to a full-service MVA office. For 1994, MVA charges $15 for titling, $70 for registration (good for two years) and $20 to record each lien (if your car is financed). Marylanders must also pay a one-time excise tax amounting to five percent of the fair market value of the car. If you have paid sales tax on your car in another state, bring your bill of sale and the previous tax paid will be credited towards the current tax. For example, a New Yorker who has already paid four percent sales tax when he or she purchased their car must now pay a one percent tax. Maryland requires a minimum payment of $100. Although this one-time tax may seem high, Marylanders should consider themselves lucky not to be hit with the annual personal property taxes charged to Virginians.

Bicycles can be registered for $1 at any police station.

■ Montgomery and Prince George's County: Local Inspection Stations

Aspen Hill Shell	301/460-3414
4001 Aspen Hill Rd., Silver Spring	
Beach's Oak Crest Chevron	301/736-5577
5520 Marlbor Pike, District Heights	
Bethesda-Steuart AGIP Service Center	301/654-3588
4972 Bradley Blvd., Bethesda	
Briggs Chaney Exxon	301/890-9313
3050 Briggs Chaney Rd., Silver Spring	
Butler Automotive Service	301/762-3865
279 Derwood Circle, Rockville	
Chevy Chase Chevrolet and Geo	301/657-4000
7725 Wisconsin Ave., Bethesda	
Colesville Exxon	301/384-1100
13420 New Hampshire Ave., Silver Spring	
College Park Exxon Service Center	301/864-3400
7110 Baltimore Ave., College Park	

Chapter Four | Dealing with the Bureaucracy

Dodson Texaco Service	301/948-2553
15701 Frederick Rd., Rockville	
Euro Motorcars Acura	301/652-9000
4932 Bethesda Ave., Bethesda	
Glen Echo Exxon	301/229-8666
6729 Goldsboro Rd., Bethesda	
Jay's Amoco	301/593-5471
Colesville Rd. & Timberwood Ave., Silver Spring	
Kensington Mobil	301/949-2783
10616 Connecticut Ave., Kensington	
Kensington Texaco	301/949-8529
4100 Randolph Rd., Kensington	
Montgomery Mall Exxon	301/365-0300
Democracy Blvd. & Westlake Dr., Bethesda	
Montgomery Mall Texaco	301/469-9447
Democracy Blvd. & Westlake Dr., Bethesda	
Potomac Amoco Service Station	301/299-8400
10140 River Rd., Potomac	
River Road Texaco	301/986-1221
5151 River Rd., Bethesda	
Rockville Exxon at White Flint	301/231-0756
11433 Rockville Pike	
Route One Shell Service	301/474-0215
10211 Baltimore Ave., College Park	
University Exxon Service Center	301/474-2791
8401 Baltimore Ave., College Park	
Wheaton Plaza Shell Auto Care	301/946-8882
11030 Veirs Mill Rd., Wheaton	
White Oak Shell Auto Care Center	301/593-2893
11150 New Hampshire Ave., White Oak	

■ MVA Branch Information: Full-Service Offices

Information: 301/948-3177
Hours: Monday - Friday: 8:30 a.m. - 4:30 p.m.
        Saturday: 8:30 a.m. - 12:00 p.m. (only driver licensing)

   Gaithersburg   15 Metropolitan Grove Rd. (Off Clopper Rd.)
   Frederick   1601 Bowman's Farm Rd. (Exit 56 off I-70)
   Largo (Upper Marlboro)   10251 Central Ave. (Near Routes 202 & 214)

☐ Obtaining Insurance

Auto Insurance

Car insurance is a necessity, regardless of where you live. Virginians do, however, have the option of paying a $400 uninsured motorist fee instead of purchasing insurance. This is not a particularly smart move, since this fee does not provide the buyer with any insurance coverage.

Insurance rates are determined by factors that are often out of your control: your neighborhood (urbanites pay more), age (older is better than younger), sex (women have lower rates) and marital status (married drivers are preferred). Virginians tend to have the lowest auto insurance rates, but make up for it by paying the annual personal property tax on their cars. City-dwellers (District residents) have the highest annual premiums and Marylanders generally fall somewhere between the two, depending on location.

For buying insurance, you have three options: mail-order, company agents or independent agents. Groups or organizations such as AAA offer insurance by mail. Company agents represent the large insurance companies like Allstate or State Farm. Independent agents sell insurance from various companies and tend to be a little more expensive. In exchange, independents offer more service. If you decide to go with an independent agent, do not count on them to do your comparison shopping. Often, the independent agents tend to have close ties with one or two companies and try to push their products. So make sure you call around to a few independent agents and compare their prices and products. Phone book listings of insurance agents and companies tend to be confusing. When calling, you may want to ask if you are talking to a company agent or an independent agent.

For the best rates, shop around and ask lots of questions, even if you think the answers are obvious. When you are calling insurance agents for price quotes, make sure that you give the same information to each. Do not lie; they have ways of finding the truth.

A large insurer in the area and one with some of the best prices is GEICO (800/841-3000). Short for Government Employees Insurance Company, GEICO was founded to do just that—provide insurance to government workers. Now it offers insurance to everyone. Well, almost everyone. Unfortunately, to qualify for a GEICO policy, your driving record has to be virtually spotless.

Renters' Insurance

If you have an irreplaceable stereo system, computer or a large wardrobe, you should consider buying renters' insurance. Renters' insurance is usually pretty cheap, relative to your stereo and clothes. A $10,000 policy can cost as little as $100 a year. If you opt for renters' insurance, ask your car insurance agent for a quote first. You can often obtain a discount if you buy more than one type of insurance from the same agent.

If you have any general questions about auto or renters' insurance, the Insurance Helpline (800/942-4242) can answer them.

Dealing with Your Income Taxes

District residents take the gold medal (your gold), with the highest income tax rates in the area. Maryland gets the silver and Virginia, the bronze. New Virginia residents accustomed to filing all forms by April 15th will be happy to know that Virginia extends its state income tax deadline until May 1st. District and Maryland residents still have to pay up by April 15th.

Before you begin this dreaded ritual, consult the state instruction booklets for information about filing requirements. Unless you arrived New Year's Day, you should pay special attention to information about part-year residents and non-residents. If you need extra help, each jurisdiction offers some assistance. **Income Tax Help** will answer questions about District taxes (441 4th St., N.W., Room 550; 202/727-6130). This office keeps extended hours during tax season (January to April). In addition to this office, District residents can pick up tax forms at several locations: the lobbies of the District Building (1350 Pennsylvania Ave., N.W.), the Recorder of Deeds Office (515 D St., N.W.), Martin Luther King Library (901 G St., N.W.), the Potomac Building (614 H St., N.W.) or Reeves Center (2000 14th St., N.W.). If you would like tax forms to be mailed to you, call 202/727-6170.

Arlington residents can pick up their state income tax forms on the second floor of the Courthouse (2100 Clarendon Blvd.; 703/358-3055) or at any of the seven public libraries. For Alexandrians, it is off to City Hall (703/838-4570) to get state tax forms. If you would like forms mailed to you, call the Richmond Center at 804/367-8205. Help can be obtained by calling 804/367-8031.

Maryland income tax forms are available weekdays between 8:00 a.m. and 5:00 p.m. at 2730 University Blvd. in Wheaton (301/949-6030) or can be obtained by mail. If you have any questions while you are preparing your return, try talking to someone in the state tax office at 800/638-2937.

In addition, *The Washington Post* prints a tax guide every February summarizing all of the federal and state tax regulations in the area.

Registering to Vote

To receive an application to vote in the District, you should call 202/727-2525 (any time). You will be asked for your name and address. A few days later you will receive an application in the mail. D.C. also has a Motor/Voter program. While you are waiting in line at the BMV, you can fill out the thoughtfully available voter registration form. In addition, public libraries, police stations and fire stations in the District also have voter registration forms.

Virginians can sign up to vote at their courthouses, city halls, public libraries and even some shopping centers (Ballston Common, Pentagon City and Landmark Center). Marylanders can do everything by mail. To receive a voter registration form, just call 301/424-4433 (Montgomery County residents) or 301/627-2814 (Prince George's County residents).

Final Tips and Advice

AAA (703/AAA-JOIN) Potomac membership costs $55 a year for first-time members and $41 to renew. While the membership fee may seem like a lot of money, especially after you have spent up to a few hundred dollars registering your car, AAA can come in extremely handy, especially if your car breaks down or you need your battery restarted. When you join, be sure to ask for the free D.C. area maps.

Quick Phone Numbers
■ District
Bureau of Motor Vehicles	202/727-6680
Income Tax Help	202/727-6130
Voter Registration	202/727-2525

■ Virginia
Department of Motor Vehicles	703/761-4655
Local registration (for personal property tax)	
Arlington County	703/358-3135
Alexandria	703/838-4560
Fairfax County	703/222-8234
Income Tax Help	804/367-8031
Voter Registration	
Arlington County	703/358-3456
Alexandria	703/838-4050
Fairfax County	703/222-0776

■ Maryland
Motor Vehicle Administration	301/948-3177
Income Tax Help	800/638-2937
Voter Registration	
Montgomery County	301/424-4433
Prince George's County	301/627-2814

■ Resources
AAA Potomac	703/AAA-JOIN

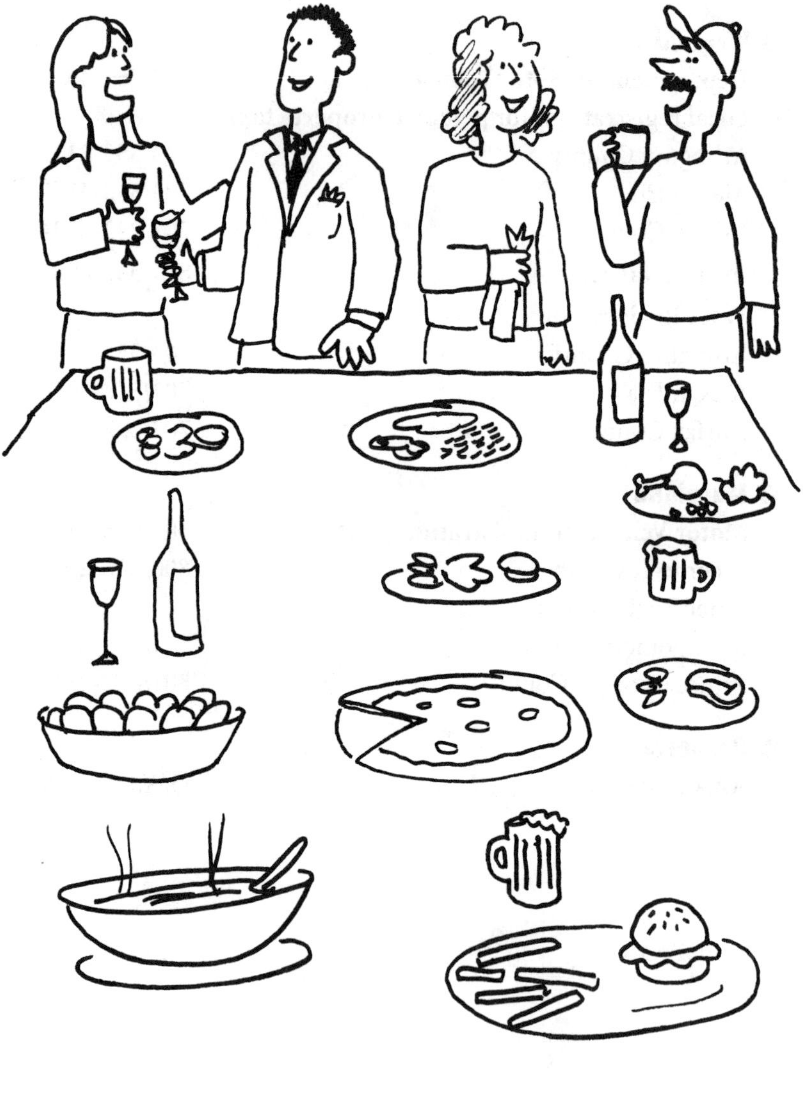

Chapter 5

Food and Fun

As befits an international city filled with workers, visitors and diplomats, Washington offers a stunning diversity of dining options. You will find almost every type of food here: from soft shell crab, ribs and jambalaya to Ethiopian injera, Thai lemon grass soup, Jamaican jerk chicken and Vietnamese Bò-Dun.

This chapter intends to give you a head start—but in the end, it is up to you to explore the tremendous variety of restaurants here. There are more than 1,500 restaurants and bars in the greater metropolitan area to keep you satiated.

The restaurants listed below are classified by type of food but there is no particular order within each section. This selection represents some of the most popular or well-known restaurants in town, some of my favorites, or restaurants mentioned by my friends or interviewees. Since this chapter is intended to be an introduction to dining in D.C., I have avoided many of the national chains (but not all).

☐ RESTAURANTS

American

American food means so many different things nowadays—everything from chili to salads to ribs to burgers. In addition to "American Pubs" (see next section) located all over the city and beyond, there are several notable eateries specializing in "American" food.

The Cheesecake Factory (5345 Wisconsin Ave., N.W.; 202/364-0500) in Friendship Heights is an outpost of a popular L.A. chain. The Cheesecake Factory sports a diverse ten-page menu and huge portions. The crab cakes, nachos, pasta dishes and Chinese Chicken salad are all excellent. Since The Cheesecake Factory does not accept reservations, you can wait for two hours or more on a busy night. Be sure to save room for dessert—there are thirty-four types of cheesecake to choose from, all excellent. This is not a place for dieters.

Downtown dining received a shot in the arm with the spate of building in the area across from the National Archives. One dining addition is **The Peasant** (801 Pennsylvania Ave., N.W.; 202/638-2140), part of an Atlanta-based chain that includes the **Pleasant Peasant** (5300 Wisconsin Ave., N.W.; 202/364-2500) in Friendship Heights. The dining room resembles a chic, comfortable supper club and its menu gives new twists to favorite American dishes such as apple hickory pork chops. The spectacular dessert menu features Mile-High ice cream cake.

Hard Times Cafe (3028 Wilson Blvd., Arlington; 703/528-2233) serves three types of chili (Vegetarian, Cincinnati and Texas) from huge vats behind the bar and a terrific selection of beer. Before you order, ask for a sampler of the different chilis to choose your favorite. If you have never had five-way Cincinnati chili, you are in for a treat. Also, forget your diet and order a plate of the onion rings. The chili oil adds terrific flavor. Hard Times has three other locations: Alexandria (1404 King St.; 703/683-5340), Rockville (1117 Nelson St.; 301/294-9720) and Herndon (394 Elden St.; 703/318-8941).

Lulu's (22nd and M Sts., N.W.; 202/861-LULU) decor reminds me more of Disney World than Bourbon St. but that does not affect the food. You can choose from a variety of po'boys (the catfish po'boy is great!), jambalaya, creole and gumbo. The atmosphere is quieter and cleaner than The Big Easy, at least at lunch time. Since Lulu's is connected to DeJaVu, a popular nightclub and dance spot, their happy hours draw a fairly large crowd. On Fridays, the line can stretch down the street.

American Cafe, a local chain, receives mixed but hardly equivocal reviews—people either really like it or they hate it. Its menu offers non-spectacular soups, sandwiches and salads. Still, its price and generally healthful selection make it a popular restaurant. If you are in a rush, most American Cafes have take-out counters. There are American Cafes in the District at 1211 Wisconsin Ave., N.W. 202/944-9464; 227 Massachusetts Ave., N.E. 202/547-8400; 5252 Wisconsin Ave., N.W. 202/363-5400; 1331 Pennsylvania Ave., N.W. 202/626-0770; 50 Massachusetts Ave., N.E. 202/682-0937; 1200 19th St., N.W. 202/223-2121); and in Virginia at Ballston Common Mall 703/522-2236; Fair Oaks Mall 703/352-0368; and Tysons Corner Mall 703/848-9476.

American Pub Food

Food experts might dispute the existence of "American Pub Food" (APF) as an official classification, but it best describes a type of eating and drinking establishment found all over Washington. APFs are really upscale beer and burger joints and Washington is full of them. While they do not offer much in the way of individuality, APFs do offer the hungry eater a no-surprises, solid meal at generally reasonable prices. The typical APF offers a wide selection of beer and a menu that includes several different types of salads (cobb, spinach and taco) and sandwiches (turkey club, roast beef and now usually grilled chicken) to go along with their variously-topped six- to nine-ounce burgers.

APF establishments are scattered around town and can be found in clusters in Dupont Circle, Georgetown, Capitol Hill and Alexandria. They are great places for meeting friends after work. Most have happy hours. In Dupont Circle, your choices include **The Front Page** (1333 New Hampshire Ave., N.W.; 202/296-6500) and **Timberlake's** (1726 Connecticut Ave., N.W.; 202/483-2266). Not far away sit the **Sign of the Whale** (1825 M St., N.W.; 202/785-1110), **Madhatter** (1831 M St., N.W.; 202/833-1495) and **Hillary's** (1827 M St., N.W.; 202/331-1827). These places are particularly popular happy hour spots. Madhatter has drink specials virtually every night and can be insanely crowded. If you want their food, hang out with the lunch time regulars. **Casey's Bar & Grill** (2524 L St., N.W.; 202/333-1200) on the other side of Washington Circle offers half-price burgers Monday nights.

More APFs reside further down M St. in Georgetown. Burgers and daiquiris have put **Mr. Smith's** (3104 M St., N.W.; 202/333-3104) on the map. **Houston's** (1065 Wisconsin Ave., N.W.; 202/338-7760) has great ribs and **Clyde's** (3236 M St., N.W.; 202/333-9180) is just plain popular. **The Guards** (2915 M St., N.W.; 202/965-2350) looks expensive but is not. Its dark, wood-paneled room and large fireplace makes you feel as if you have been transported to England. Its APF menu swiftly brings you home. **Garrett's** (3003 M St., N.W.; 202/333-1033) has good seafood chowder. **J. Paul's** (3218 M St., N.W.; 202/333-3450) serves the best crab cakes in the District and has its own house beer. **The Tombs** (1226 36th St., N.W.; 202/337-6668), full of crew memorabilia, is a favorite spot for Georgetown students.

Polly's Cafe is a neighborhood bar in the U St. Corridor (1342 U St., N.W.; 202/265-8385) that also has great food. This small restaurant has some cafe seating outside and a casual room with tables and a bar below street level. Aside from the funky jukebox, Polly's offers a selection of sandwiches, burgers, excellent specials and a tasty weekend brunch.

The Old Ebbitt Grill (675 15th St., N.W.; 202/347-4801) attracts the National Theatre crowd and White House staffers. On the Hill, staffers frequent **Slick Willy's** (223 Pennsylvania Ave., S.E.; 202/544-6600) and **Hawk 'n Dove** (329 Pennsylvania Ave., S.E.; 202/543-3300). **Bullfeathers** (410 First St., S.E.; 202/543-5005), a few steps from the Republican National Club, has half-price burgers on Tuesday nights and scads of staffers every night. A second location in Old Town (112 King St., Alexandria; 703/836-8088) caters to more of the preppy but less ideological crowd. Former Redskin Joe Theismann contributes to the APF scene. His namesake Alexandria restaurant, **Joe Theismann's**, is located at 1800 Diagonal Road (703/739-0777). The food is typical of APF's, but the decor makes you feel as if you are eating in a hotel restaurant.

What do you get when you put together three of the biggest names in show business? **Planet Hollywood.** This downtown restaurant (1101 Pennsylvania Ave., N.W.; 202/783-7827) is one of the latest in a galaxy of restaurants started by actors Arnold Schwarzenegger, Bruce Willis and Sylvester Stallone. Positioned near several hotels and across the street from the Post Office Pavilion, this restaurant attracted lots of publicity even before its doors opened in late 1993. Inside, movie memorabilia adorns the walls, including costumes from "Planet of the Apes" and the model of the "Death Star" used in "Return of the Jedi." The food is pretty good, too.

For an opposing view of the planet, try **Planet Fred** (1221 Connecticut Ave., N.W.; 202/466-2336), a restaurant/club that opened in 1994. "It's an everyman's Planet Hollywood," says a manager. Fred features four sections, each offering a differing view of space and the planet, ranging from ancient man's conception of the sky to Stanley Kubrick's vision of space. The restaurant part gives way to a nightclub at the end of the week, with world beat, reggae and progressive music.

Barbecue

Red, Hot & Blue (1600 Wilson Blvd., Arlington; 703/276-7427) is Lee Atwater's only legacy acclaimed on both sides of the political aisle. Its Memphis barbecue is among the best in town. If you do not want to wait in line, you can order from their carry-out store about a mile up Wilson Blvd. Red, Hot & Blue also has locations in Laurel (677 Main

St.; 301/953-1943) and Manassas (8637 Sudley Road; 703/330-4847). **Three Pigs Barbeque** (1394 Chain Bridge Road, McLean; 703/356-1700) cannot boast fancy surroundings. The tables and chairs look like they belong in an elementary school arts and crafts room, but if you are in the mood for hickory-smoked barbecue, this place will do just fine. **Hogs on the Hill** (2001 14th St., N.W.; 202/332-4647) has a herd of other hogs throughout D.C. and Alexandria. Ribs, BBQ sandwiches, "greens" and plenty of everything is what you will get here. Its other locations are at 4525 E. Capitol St., S.E. (202/575-2966), 6209 Georgia Ave., N.W. (202/726-8332) and 3414 Mt. Vernon Road, Alexandria (703/836-6491). At **Old Glory** (3139 M St., N.W.; 202/337-3406) you can choose among seven sauces to season your ribs. Portions (both appetizers and entrees) are large and the frosty-mugged root beer helps wash it down. Old Glory ends its meals with a complimentary tootsie pop.

Just Burgers

George Washington University students would be lost without **Linsey's Bon Apetit** (2040 Pennsylvania Ave., N.W.; 202/452-0055), affectionately called "The Bone." Do not expect to find too many seats here; The Bone prefers you take it somewhere else. Pricy national-chain **Hamburger Hamlet** serves burgers with almost every imaginable topping in its local franchises in Georgetown (3125 M St., N.W.; 202/965-6970) and Friendship Heights (5225 Wisconsin Ave., N.W.; 202/244-2038). Capitol Hill's **Li'l Pub** (655 Pennsylvania Ave., S.E.; 202/543-5526) serves huge burgers (about 11 ounces pre-cooked) for just $3.50. Departing from traditional sit-down burger places, **Five Guys** (4626 King St.; 703/671-1606) in Alexandria sells its bargain burgers ($2.49) and fries (99¢) for carry-out only. These guys have another location at 3235 Columbia Pike in Arlington (703/685-1151).

Chinese

When the Republicans were in the White House, many Washingtonians went to **Peking Gourmet** (6029 Leesburg Pike; 703/671-8088) because it was one of President Bush's favorites. After eating there, it is not hard to see why this restaurant has attained its fame—the food is amazing. Peking Gourmet does not look like much on the outside, but that does not mean the meal will not be expensive. The walls of this brightly-lit restaurant are covered with pictures of Washington's movers and shakers. Democrats should not despair; careful scrutiny will reveal some of their party stalwarts among the lot. Peking Gourmet's specialty is Peking duck. You will never see so many ducks traveling to so many tables in any other restaurant. You should also try their other specialty, garlic sprouts with chicken, shrimp or pork.

Washington is no San Francisco or New York, but strolling through Chinatown can still yield a few treasures. Take the Red or Yellow line to Gallery Place and start walking. **Mr. Yung's** (740 6th St., N.W.; 202/628-1098) presents customers a list of thirty or forty different dim sum to choose from. Close by, the **China Inn** (631 H St., N.W.; 202/842-0909) serves generous Cantonese and Szechuan dishes.

Tony Cheng's Mongolian Restaurant (619 H St., N.W.; 202/842-8669) allows you to concoct your own all-you-can-eat beef entrees. You choose the ingredients and Tony's chefs will prepare your dishes right in front of you. On Sunday mornings, Tony Cheng's offers an extensive dim sum brunch. **Tony Cheng's Seafood Restaurant** (202/371-8669) is upstairs. You can guess its specialty.

City Lights of China (1731 Connecticut Ave., N.W.; 202/265-6688) prepares Dupont Circle's best Chinese food. Because it is located in the basement of a townhouse, passersby can easily miss it. Its crispy beef and spicy eggplant dishes should not be overlooked.

Charlie Chiang's has maintained high quality and prompt service at each of its locations as it has branched out into the suburbs. Its broccoli with garlic sauce is the best I have eaten since I left New York. The location at 4250 Connecticut Ave., N.W. (202/966-1916) has an express lunch counter on the ground floor. Other locations are Downtown (1912 Eye St., N.W.; 202/293-6000), Alexandria (660 South Pickett St.; 703/751-8888) and Shirlington (4060 South 28th St.; 703/671-4900).

The best strategy when going to **Good Fortune** (2646 University Blvd., Wheaton; 301/929-8818) is to bring a group of friends. Its Cantonese menu lists more than 200 dishes that beg to be tried. For $78, you and five friends can feast on an eight-course banquet. If you make it there for lunch, you will be treated to dim sum.

For Chinese food in less than five minutes and for under five bucks, served in unattractive and politically-incorrect styrofoam containers, try any one of the several **China Cafes.** Three popular locations in the District draw big lunch crowds: Dupont Circle (1723 Connecticut Ave. N.W.; 202/234-4053), K St. (2009 K St., N.W.; 202/463-2129) and McPherson Square (1018 Vermont Ave., N.W.; 202/628-1350). Stick to the main courses, especially the daily specials.

For dim sum in Northern Virginia, you have several options. Clarendon's **Hunan Number One** (3033 Wilson Blvd.; 703/528-1177) serves its dim sum daily between 11:00 a.m. and 3:00 p.m. Weekends offer the best selection. If you are up for the drive, **Fortune Chinese Seafood Restaurant** in Baileys Crossroads (5900 Leesburg Pike; 703/998-8888) has a more extensive daily selection. Despite Fortune's supermarket size, you may still have to wait at peak brunch hours.

Ethiopian

Washington is known to have some of the best Ethiopian food in the country. Once you live here, you will quickly discover the best choices reside in Adams Morgan. **Red Sea** (2463 18th St., N.W.; 202/483-5000) and **Meskerem** (2434 18th St., N.W.; 202/462-4100) are right across the street from each other and are rightfully the most popular Ethiopian restaurants in town. For those who have never eaten Ethiopian food, diners eat the spicy stews with their fingers and injera (something like a moist, doughy tortilla). You will risk ridicule if you ask for a fork. It would spoil the experience anyway. In Georgetown, **Zed's** (3318 M St., N.W.; 202/333-4710) serves Ethiopian cuisine almost on a par with Adams Morgan's favorites.

French

Although many French restaurants in Washington are expensive and cater more to expense accounts than to my wallet, you can still find bargains. One of the best French restaurants in the city is **Le Mistral** (223 Pennsylvania Ave., S.E.; 202/543-7747). Its fixed-price menu is a special bargain and on winter nights you would be hard-pressed to find a more romantic spot than Le Mistral's front room, with its roaring fireplace and view of Capitol Hill.

For casual French fare, you can eat at one of these adjoining restaurants in Georgetown, **Au Pied de Cochon** and **Aux Fruits de Mer** (1335 Wisconsin Ave., N.W. 202/333-5440). Au Pied de Cochon is open 24 hours a day and serves salads and crepes. Its next door neighbor, Aux Fruits de Mer, focuses on fish and seafood. Just off M St. towards the Potomac is another Georgetown favorite, **Cafe La Ruche** (1039 31st St., N.W.; 202/965-2684). This small cafe right near the C&O Canal serves lighter fare—soups, salads, sandwiches—and not-so-light desserts. When the weather permits, the tables in the garden can provide a peaceful lunch time interlude from the drudgery of office life.

Le Bistro Francais (3128 M St., N.W.; 202/338-3830) boasts fresh seafood every day and specializes in southern French cuisine. Be sure to ask for a sample of their homemade pates when ordering. The chef at Cleveland Park's **Lavandou Cuisine Provencal** (3321 Connecticut Ave., N.W.; 202/966-3002) serves dishes from just one regional cuisine: Provence. Its soups, appetizers and main dishes are all excellent.

Maison Blanche (1725 F St., N.W.; 202/842-0070) is the very definition of a high-brow French dining experience. Let the staff recommend the day's best or suggest a fine wine. Leaving Maison Blanche without sampling their desserts is a "crime de cuisine." **Dominique's** (1900 Pennsylvania Ave., N.W.; 202/452-1126) has a very expensive and extensive menu. Some items are mouth-watering

My Favorite Restaurants
by Mayor Sharon Pratt Kelly

The Cheesecake Factory
Although my favorite dish is the veal meatloaf topped with layers of mashed potatoes and gravy, the real treat is the post-meal dessert of cheesecake (in any flavor)!

La Fourchette
For authentic French cuisine, La Fourchette can't be beat. The duck is my "usual" entree.

French's
Fantastic, non-greasy "soul food." Although I would recommend anything on the menu, my favorites are the fried chicken, collard greens, candied yams, and of course the cornbread. Simply scrumptious!

Cafe Petitto's
Everything is great. I just ask the waiter for the "special of the day," and pretend I am dining in Italy.

Mr. K's
Authentic Chinese food, all four to six courses of it. You will never leave Mr. K's hungry.

(fresh mussels with white wine sauce) and others are, well, interesting (alligator tail scallopini). For those who cannot make it home for the holidays, Dominique's offers a very reasonable all-you-can-eat Thanksgiving dinner.

Indian

Two Indian restaurants neighbor each other on Connecticut Ave. just across Rock Creek Park from Adams Morgan and Dupont Circle, **Rajaji** (2603 Connecticut Ave., N.W.; 202/265-7344) and **A Taste of India** (2623 Connecticut Ave., N.W.; 202/483-1115). Rajaji will satisfy those who enjoy spicy curries, while A Taste of India caters to those who prefer milder Indian food. **The Bombay Palace** (202/331-4200) at 2020 K St., N.W., features some wonderful vegetarian cuisine. Bombay Palace is a good choice if you are considering dining with a large crowd. It is not terribly cozy, however, for a romantic dinner for two.

Aditi (3299 M St., N.W.; 202/625-6825) receives high praise from Indian-food aficionados. If you cannot choose among its Tandoori specialties, try its sample feast for $13.95. The vegetarian **Madurai** (3318 M St., N.W.; 202/333-0997) offers an all-you-can-eat buffet on Sundays for just $7. Down M St. towards the West End, **Bombay Delight** (2815 M St., N.W.; 202/338-6450), a new cafeteria-style vegetarian restaurant, has reasonably good food that and can be ordered for delivery.

Italian

Arguably the best-valued Italian restaurant in the District, **I Matti** in Adams Morgan (2436 18th St., N.W.; 202/462-8844) prepares fresh bread, gourmet pizza, innovative pasta, roast meat (including rabbit) and seafood in an upscale, trendy atmosphere. I Matti is a more affordable, casual and creative version of the three-star Downtown restaurant, **i Ricchi** (1220 19th St., N.W.; 202/835-0459), a power restaurant that serves authentic and excellent Tuscan cuisine.

A.V. Ristorante (607 New York Ave., N.W.; 202/737-0550) is legendary in Washington. This restaurant has the quintessential neighborhood ambiance Italian restaurants are known for: chianti bottles transformed into candle holders, dark red walls and red-checked tablecloths. Its pizza and pasta dishes are terrific and you will definitely get your money's worth if you opt for a meat platter.

Not only does **Il Radicchio** (1509 17th St., N.W.; 202/986-2627) have excellent pizza but it also has a unique way of serving spaghetti.

After you buy the first bowl ($6), you can refill for free and just buy the sauces. Sauces range from $1 to $4.

Cafe Petitto's (1724 Connecticut Ave., N.W.; 202/462-8771) is famous for their antipasto bar. Nearby, **Odeon Cafe** (1714 Connecticut Ave., N.W.; 202/328-6228), with its chic neon atmosphere, can be good for a light meal or after-dinner drink. The **Italian Kitchen** (1637 17th St., N.W.; 202/328-3222) has cheap and plentiful pasta dishes better for carrying-out than eating-in.

Paolo's (1303 Wisconsin Ave., N.W.; 202/333-7353), a trendy, upscale Italian cafe serves delicious pastas, pizzas and salads. If you would like to avoid the crowds, try late lunches or weekend brunches. Paolo's has other locations in Rockville (1801 Rockville Pike; 301/984-2211) and Reston (Reston Town Center; 703/318-8920).

The budget-minded will enjoy **Adams Morgan Spaghetti Garden** (2317 18th St., N.W.; 202/265-6665) the most when you can sit out on its rooftop on a warm summer evening. Dinner for two, including wine, can easily cost less than $20.

For inexpensive Italian cooking in the suburbs, try any one of the **Pines** restaurants. Each restaurant has a different Italian city attached to its name. Some offer only Southern Italian dishes and some only Northern Italian. Of them, the best are **Pines of Italy** (Southern; 703/524-4969) at 237 North Glebe Road in Arlington and **Pines of Rome** (Northern; 301/657-8775) at 4709 Hampden Lane in Bethesda. Be prepared to wait on weekend nights—these restaurants are popular.

Further out, **Da Domenico Ristorante** (1992 Chain Bridge Road, McLean; 703/790-9000) receives rave reviews. Its pork chops and clams come highly recommended and rumor has it that it has the best martinis around.

Jamaican & Caribbean

Reggae and jerk chicken are only part of the colorful tropical atmosphere of Adams Morgan's **Fish, Wings and Tings** (2418 18th St., N.W.; 202/234-0322). This restaurant is often regarded as D.C.'s best for Jamaican cuisine. This explains the difficulty many have finding a table. Fish, Wings and Tings has only one drawback: it lacks a liquor license. Across the street sits **Montego Bay** (2437 18th St., N.W.; 202/745-1002). Montego Bay is slightly more expensive than its more famous neighbor, but does serve alcohol.

The owners of Fish, Wings and Tings opened a second Caribbean restaurant, **Hibiscus Cafe** (3401 K Street, N.W.; 202/338-0408) in Georgetown. Hint: try the Buffalo Wings.

Japanese

In the West End, upscale Japanese restaurant **Unkai** (1250 24th St., N.W.; 202/466-2299) offers a $6.50 lunch special at its grill which includes salad, soup and a Benihana-style chicken and vegetable stir-fry. Shrimp and beef stir-fry cost slightly more. In the main dining room, you can get some of the best sushi in town, as well as some truly authentic and unusual Japanese dishes, some with gold leaf. As you may guess, this can get very expensive very quickly.   Typical of a restaurant in Adams Morgan, **Perry's** (1811 Columbia Road, N.W.; 202/234-6218) offers its diners lots of atmosphere—high-tech in this case. Its techno sushi, on the other hand, is not much to brag about. During the spring and summer months, though, you can eat your dinner on their rooftop deck overlooking the city.

Tako Grill (7756 Wisconsin Ave., Bethesda; 301/652-7030) departs from the regular sushi and sake restaurants. Diners can feast on robatayaki (grilled fish, meat and vegetables) and other less common dishes, as well as the more typically Japanese staples (sushi, teriyaki, yosenabe and tempura). Tako Grill is a particularly good place for vegetarians.

Yosaku (4712 Wisconsin Ave., N.W.; 202/363-4453) offers the best deal on sushi. Take advantage of their regular sushi assortment; it costs $12.50 and includes 16 pieces of sushi and one California roll.

Pan Asian Noodles (2020 P St., N.W.; 202/872-8889), a cross between a Japanese noodle shop and a Thai restaurant, serves both spicy and mild noodle dishes. My favorite dish is cozy noodles (cold noodles topped with chicken and a spicy peanut sauce).

Kosher

Most of Washington's kosher restaurants are in Rockville or Silver Spring, close to the area's largest Jewish communities. All of the restaurants listed below are under the supervision of the Vaad of Washington.

The **H Street Hideaway** (2300 H St., N.W.; 202/452-1161) caters mostly to G.W. students who are on the Kosher meal plan but is also open to the public. It serves meat and vegetarian dishes. It is open for lunch and dinner (until 8:00 p.m.) on weekdays, except Fridays when only carry-out is available.

Nuthouse (11419 Georgia Ave., Wheaton; 301/942-5900) specializes in pizza, falafel and salads and is open until 1:30 a.m. on Saturday nights.

Both **The Royal Dragon** (4840 Boiling Brook Parkway, Rockville; 301/468-1922) and **Hunan Gourmet** (350 Fortune Terrace, Potomac; 301/424-0191) serve Glatt kosher Chinese food.

Mediterranean

The Lebanese Taverna (2641 Connecticut Ave., N.W.; 202/265-8681) sits among a row of ethnic restaurants across from Woodley Park Metro. This restaurant caters to those with larger budgets; dinner can easily cost $20 a person. Still, it is well worth the occasional splurge, particularly during the summer when you can sit outside and watch the world go by. The food is excellent and the service well-timed. **Bacchus** (1827 Jefferson Place, N.W.; 202/785-0734) also has excellent Lebanese food. This intimate restaurant is neatly tucked away in the basement of a Dupont Circle brownstone. A second, more spacious, restaurant in Bethesda (7945 Norfolk Ave.; 301/657-1722) promises much of the same.

Kabul West in Bethesda (4871 Cordell Ave.; 301/986-8566) serves some of the best Afghan cuisine in the area. To begin, try the aushak—noodles stuffed with scallions and topped with ground meat, yogurt and dried mint. You can follow up this great beginning with one of the kebab dishes. **Kabul Caravan** (1725 Wilson Blvd.; 703/522-8394) serves similar fare in Arlington. Its rather unattractive exterior in a small, run-down strip mall does not hint at its cozy, romantic interior.

The Calvert Cafe (1967 Calvert St., N.W.; 202/232-5431), just over the Calvert St. Bridge in Adams Morgan, looks as if it has gone out of business. Venture in and you will find excellent, inexpensive dishes, succulent desserts and Turkish coffee. Long-time Washingtonians know this restaurant by the name Mama Ayesha's.

Many areas in the District have some form of Middle Eastern or Greek food nearby. Inexpensive gyros and falafel are a lunch time favorite for those working Downtown. In Georgetown, choices include **George's** (corner of M and 28th Sts.; 202/342-2278) and **Fettoosh** (3277 M St., N.W.; 202/342-1199). Both are great for fast and cheap falafel. George's also makes terrific cheese steaks, proclaiming itself "king of cheese steaks." At **Zorba's Cafe** in Dupont Circle (1612

20th St., N.W.; 202/387-8555) you can enjoy eating your gyros outside while listening to Greek music played over a loudspeaker. Union Station's **Pik-a-Pita** (202/842-2438) in the food court serves a wide range of pita sandwiches and salads (hummus, baba ghannouj and fettoosh). Its roast chicken salad with pita croutons is particularly good for dieters. A second Pik-a-Pita (703/415-5630) is in the food court at the Fashion Centre at Pentagon City.

Topkapi Restaurant in Fairfax (3529 Chain Bridge Road; 703/273-4310) is a Turkish restaurant in disguise. Camouflaged among entrees such as tortellini and prime rib, the menu lists a banquet of tasty Turkish dishes. Whatever the reason—whether the owners are trying to appeal to a broader audience or trying to live up the building's past life as a steak house—skip the standard fare and proceed directly to the Turkish selections.

Mexican and Tex-Mex Food

For Mexican food, Washington's best deal is **El Tamarindo** (1785 Florida Ave., N.W.; 202/328-3660). El Tamarindo offers cheap (and good) pitchers of margaritas and solid, no-frills Mexican and Salvadoran dishes. Its primary location is on Florida Ave., just around the corner from 18th St. on the Dupont Circle/Adams Morgan border. El Tamarindo has two other locations: 4910 Wisconsin Ave., N.W. (202/244-8888) and 7331 Georgia Ave., N.W. (202/291-0525). If you are part of a large group, you should go to the Wisconsin Ave. location.

Lauriol Plaza (1801 18th St., N.W.; 202/387-0035) makes for the most romantic of any Mexican meal. Its dimly-lit dining room seems always to be crowded, but I have never had to wait for a table. Lauriol Plaza's prices are much higher than El Tamarindo's—though not extreme for a nice night out—and the food is distinctly superior. Besides excellent fajitas, Lauriol Plaza offers a number of offbeat Spanish and Salvadoran dishes. The same owners manage **Cactus Cantina** near the National Cathedral (3300 Wisconsin Ave., N.W.;

Best margaritas
Austin Grill

Best salsa
Austin Grill

Best fajitas
Rio Grande Cafe

Best (overall)
Lauriol Plaza

Best deal
El Tamarindo

202/686-7222). During warm weather, the tables outside the restaurant are a perfect spot for sipping margaritas and sharing nachos. Cactus Cantina tends to attract a younger and rowdier crowd than Lauriol Plaza.

Austin Grill's bar (2404 Wisconsin Ave., N.W.; 202/337-8080) serves excellent margaritas—the best in town—making it a popular after-work hangout. The menu, like the restaurant space, is somewhat limited. A second restaurant, **South Austin Grill** (801 King St., Alexandria; 703/684-8969) has more space, a more extensive Tex-Mex menu and the margaritas that are as good as in the District.

Georgetown's **Enriqueta's** (2811 M St., N.W.; 202/338-7772) serves authentic Mexican food, as opposed to Tex-Mex. The brightly painted chairs in this restaurant add to its casual and colorful environment. Enriqueta's Chicken Mole is a winner.

Tex-Mex has been made into big business at **Rio Grande Cafe.** Three extremely popular locations (Ballston, Bethesda and Reston) promise long lines, especially on weekends. Take advantage of their fresh chips and salsa while you are waiting. By the time you are seated, you may already be full. In Ballston, Rio Grande is at 4301 North Fairfax Drive (703/528-3131), just down the street from the Ballston Metro station. The Bethesda location is at 4919 Fairmont Ave. (301/656-2981) and the Reston restaurant is at 1827 Library St., Reston Town Center (703/904-0703).

On the Hill not far from the Senate office buildings, garishly-painted **Tortilla Coast** (201 Massachusetts Ave., N.E.; 202/546-6768) offers Tex-Mex dishes in a tropical atmosphere. Naturally, this is a popular spot among Hill staffers and interns. Prices are not as low as you would expect for this crowd; dinner for two can easily hover around $25. Also on the Hill, **La Lomita Dos** (308 Pennsylvania Ave., S.E.; 202/544-0616) serves Mexican food in more typical surroundings. Sombreros and piñatas decorate La Lomita Dos' small white-stucco dining room. Insiders say the original **La Lomita** at 1330 Pennsylvania Ave., S.E. (202/546-3109) serves better food.

Pizza

Over the years, **Armand's** has been recognized as the place to go for pizza. Armand's original pizzeria at 4231 Wisconsin Ave., N.W. (202/686-9450) serves "Chicago-style" pizza (unrecognizable to true denizens of the Windy City) in a casual, family-style atmosphere. The spinach and garlic pizza is particularly good. The salad bar, however, is forgettable, even on a good night. Armand's has now spread throughout the District and the suburbs.

Right next to Armand's original store on upper Wisconsin is rival **Maggie's New York Style Pizzeria** (4237 Wisconsin Ave., N.W.; 202/363-1447). American University students support this New York pizzeria in droves. Again, New Yorkers might not recognize it as being particularly New York. I could never understand how two pizzerias, side-by-side, could survive; I guess the answer is in the crust.

Thin-crust pizza connoisseurs will also enjoy **Faccia Luna** (2400 Wisconsin Ave., N.W.; 202/337-3132) and **Il Forno Pizzeria** (4926 Cordell Ave., Bethesda; 301/652-7757). Faccia Luna tops its pies with interesting items such as tuna, eggplant, spinach and pesto. Faccia Luna opened a second location in Arlington at 2909 Wilson Blvd. (703/276-3099). Il Forno bakes its pizza in a wood-burning oven. This baking method can produce amazing pizza.

Best pizza (overall)
Pizzeria Paradiso

Best pepperoni pizza
Geppetto's

Most exotic
California Pizza Kitchen

Best crust
Pizzeria Paradiso

Thinnest crust
Zebra Room

Best deal
Generous George's

Best atmosphere
Luigi's

The **Zebra Room** (3238 Wisconsin Ave., N.W.; 202/362-8307) wins the prize for the absolutely thinnest crust. Cheap pitchers of beer combined with close proximity to many softball fields make the Zebra Room a favorite summertime team hangout. Pizzas are half-price on Tuesday and Thursday nights.

The best pizza in Washington comes out of the wood-burning stove at **Pizzeria Paradiso** (2029 P St., N.W.; 202/223-1245). The thick, flavorful, chewy crust is paradise particularly when combined with the dozen or so fresh, high quality toppings. On the downside, the small dining room fills up quickly, so be prepared for a long wait for dinner.

Pepperoni pizza? How about tons of pepperoni? **Geppetto's** (2917 M St., N.W.; 202/333-2602) serves the spiciest and best pepperoni in the District and piles it so high that it tends to form a small mountain in the center of the pizza. I usually remove some of the pepperoni so I can actually taste the pizza. The vegetarian pizza, replete with eggplant, provides an excellent alternative. Geppetto's has a second location in Bethesda's Wildwood Shopping Center (10257 Old Georgetown Road; 301/493-9230).

Luigi's (1132 19th St., N.W.; 202/331-7574) is one of the few pizza places in the area that offer a wide range of toppings, including calamari, clam, pineapple and more. Diners can choose to sit indoors or in a glassed-in patio out front. Beware of the blue margarita—one is plenty.

Imported from Beverly Hills, the **California Pizza Kitchen** (Tysons I Lower Level; 703/761-1473) has almost 30 different kinds of Wolfgang Puck-style individual gourmet pizzas. Thai Chicken, Shrimp-Pesto, Barbecue Chicken and Peking Duck are just the beginning of their unthinkable but delicious combinations. CPK also offers terrific salads to start and desserts to finish, if you make it that far. Marylanders will enjoy their second location at nearby Montgomery Mall (7101 Democracy Blvd.; 301/469-5090).

If you prefer quantity, try **Generous George's Positive Pizza and Pasta Place** (3006 Duke St., Alexandria; 703/370-4303). As its name suggests, Generous George's fare includes enormous pizzas, huge salads and gigantic pasta dishes. Quality does not suffer from the excess quantity. **Radio Free Italy** (703/836-2151) sits inside the Torpedo Factory Food Pavilion in Alexandria. "Pizza and pasta with frequency" is their motto and Marconi is their house beer.

While pizza is what put **Julio's** (1604 U St., N.W.; 202/483-8500) on the map, this restaurant is best known for its Sunday brunches and happy hours. Brunches are all-you-can-eat and there is plenty to choose from, including, of course, pizza. Happy hours, from Monday through Thursday, can easily be turned into dinner-they serve free pizza.

Seafood

Since you can now consider yourself a "local," you have to take advantage of Maryland's specialty—soft-shell crabs. It may be a little disconcerting at first to eat a whole crab, shells, claws and all, but it is not to be missed. For the freshest crab, make a trip to Maryland's Eastern Shore during the summer months. Just hop on Route 50 (East) and keep driving. You will know when to stop—when you see corner stands along the highway selling fresh crab and other seafood.

If you want to stay closer to the District, go to the waterfront in Southwest (Metro's Green line to Waterfront). Along Water St., you will see **Phillip's Flagship** (900 Water St.; 202/488-8515), **Hogate's** (9th St. and Maine Ave.; 202/484-6300) and **The Gangplank** (600 Water St.; 202/554-5000). The first two tend to be touristy, but that does not seem to affect the quality of the food.

Tony and Joe's Seafood Place (3000 K St., N.W.; 202/944-4545) is further up the Potomac in Georgetown's Washington Harbour complex. A typical Washington power lunch restaurant, this place delivers good seafood at expensive prices. I prefer its less expensive sister restaurant, **The Dancing Crab** (4611 Wisconsin Ave., N.W.; 202/244-1882), at the corner of Wisconsin and Brandywine, N.W. This restaurant serves all-you-can-eat crab dinners during the summer. During the winter months, the Dancing Crab offers an all-you-can-eat raw bar.

Il Pesce (2016 P St., N.W.; 202/466-3474), a new combination fish market and restaurant, is reported to serve the freshest fish in Washington. It was opened by the same chefs of the four-star restaurants Jean Louis at the Watergate Hotel and Galileo as another outlet for their source of supremely fresh fish. You can either take the fish home and cook it yourself or take advantage of Washington's two finest chefs and have them cook it for you.

Arlington is home to the **Chesapeake Seafood Crab House and An-Loc Landing Vietnamese Restaurant and Pho** (3607 Wilson Boulevard; 703/528-8896). If the name seems like a mouthful, you should see the menu: 15 pages with items ranging from basic seafood to exotic Vietnamese dishes. Despite the incongruity of it all—the menu covers "authentic Vietnamese, Chinese, along with a variety of typically French and American seafood cuisines"—this restaurant pulls it off. The crab and Vietnamese dishes are excellent and plenty of outdoor seating makes the Crab House a must on a summer evening.

Crisfield's (301/589-1306) original location at 8012 Georgia Ave. in Silver Spring is known for its long lines, coffee-shop decor and amazing seafood. Prices tend to be somewhat high. To ease the wait, a second Silver Spring location has opened at 8606 Colesville Road (301/588-1572).

The **Bethesda Crab House** (4958 Bethesda Ave., Bethesda; 301/652-3382) serves up crab on long picnic tables under a sprawling awning. Although the Crab House is slightly pricy, the outdoor seating is nice on a warm evening. If you are with a small group, be prepared, the waiters will move parties from table to table to make way for the larger groups that are constantly arriving.

Fish Market (105 King St., Alexandria; 703/836-5676) has a double personality—upstairs a lively crowd sings along in a pub-like atmosphere, while downstairs a more sedate group concentrates on eating and drinking. The Fish Market's huge 32-ounce "schooners" of beer make it a popular spot on the weekends, particularly for the twentysomething crowd. Up the street, **The Warehouse Bar & Grill** (214 King St.; 703/683-6868) serves seafood with a New Orleans twist. The soups and seafood chowders should not be overlooked. **Blue Point Grill** (600 Franklin St.; 703/739-0404) is a newcomer on the Alexandria seafood scene. The menu starts with more than a dozen varieties of the day's fresh fish.

Thai

One of the newer and more interesting trends in Asian dining is the explosion of restaurants specializing in Thai cuisine. At **Duangrat's** (5878 Leesburg Pike; 703/820-5775), waitresses in beautiful silk gowns serve the area's best Thai food. Glover Park residents can take advantage of Thai-style dim sum on Sundays at **Ploy,** (2218 Wisconsin Ave., N.W.; 202/337-2324) as well as excellent Thai cuisine the rest of the time. The whole fried fish and crying duck come highly recommended at **Bangkok Orchid** (301 Massachusetts Ave., N.E.; 202/546-5901).

Perhaps the best endorsement for Bethesda's **Bangkok Garden** (4906 St. Elmo Ave., 301/951-0670) is that it has two menus: one in English for Americans and one written just in Thai for its many Thai customers. This traditional Thai restaurant, according to a friend who spent a year in Thailand, is as authentic as they come. Try the Som Tum, a hot and sour papaya salad seasoned with dry shrimp and eaten with sticky rice, but be forewarned: the cook often goes easy on the spices for American customers. If you want the hot stuff, you may have to ask for it.

Vegetarian

Dupont Circle's **Food for Thought** (1738 Connecticut Ave., N.W.; 202/797-1095) serves inexpensive vegetarian dishes in a '60s atmosphere to the accompaniment of local musicians. Food for Thought also maintains a huge bulletin board filled with everything from rallies to furniture for sale to rides to San Francisco.

Pat Ferrise's Favorite Cafes (and other eating places)

Tako Grill
I've eaten at this place at least fifty times in the last year, so I think it's safe to call Tako my second home. In my quest for fresh sushi, this place is the best. They also have a warm atmosphere and darn good prices.

Lebanese Taverna
I usually go here for special celebrations (birthdays, bon voyage parties, sock cleaning day) because it's a great place to get together with a lot of people. Order the "meza" and you'll be showered with every appetizer on the menu- from grape leaves to hummus to items from their brick oven. I think you'll want to share so bring lots of friends.

Busara
Especially great in the summer for eating in their outdoor garden. The outside of the restaurant looks kind of like a trendy hair salon, but don't be fooled. It's actually a great Thai place.

Dolce Finale
Okay, I'll probably be sorry I told you this, because only five people can fit in this place, and I really like eating here, but I've already spilled my guts. Dolce Finale has great desserts and a dark old room atmosphere plus lots of hot beverages. It's a great after dinner spot.

The Argentine Grill
Another good place for large gatherings. A lot of pasta cuisine, it is also in Adams Morgan so you are close to a lot of after dinner possibilities.

Tastee Diner
With three locations, one of the oldest diners in the area. I go there a lot after shows for fries and some rude service. I once asked a waitress what was good for dessert and she said, "Honey, it's all bad. You might as well go across the street." I keep coming back.

Pat Ferrise is on WHFS (99.5 FM) from noon to 3 p.m. on weekdays.
He hosts the 'HFS Cafe between noon and 1 p.m.

Health's A Poppin (2020 K St., N.W.; 202/466-6616) is a great alternative for lunch. Its menu bursts with vegetarian sandwiches, salads and frozen yogurt. They have another location on the Hill, just above the Library of Congress at 209 1/2 Pennsylvania Ave., S.E. (202/544-3049).

Tako Grill (7756 Wisconsin Ave., Bethesda; 301/652-7030) offers a great dinner alternative serving robatayaki (grilled vegetables) and other less common dishes, as well as the more typical Japanese staples (sushi and tempura). Upon request, the sushi chef will make vegetarian futomaki providing you get at least two orders.

Several Indian restaurants cater solely to the vegetarian. **Paru's Indian Vegetarian Restaurant** (2010 S St., N.W.; 202/483-5133) serves fast food Southern Indian style. **Siddhartha Vegetarian Restaurant** (1379 K St., N.W.; 202/682-9090) has an all-you-can-eat lunch buffet daily between 11:30 a.m. and 2:00 p.m. for just $6. Georgetown's **Madurai** (3318 M St., N.W.; 202/333-0997) offers an all-you-can-eat buffet on Sundays for just $7.

Nora's (2132 Florida Ave., N.W.; 202/462-5143) is Washington's answer to Chez Pannise, the Berkeley restaurant that started the nouvelle cuisine revolution. From appetizers to desserts, everything is freshly made from organic ingredients. They always have one selection from every part of a meal for vegetarians. The restaurant has a wonderful early-American theme to it but does not come cheap. Be prepared to pay at least $25 to $30 a person.

The **Cheesecake Factory** (5345 Wisconsin Ave., N.W.; 202/364-0500) is a fun alternative if you can stand the wait—up to two hours on a Friday or Saturday night. This restaurant has several interesting pasta dishes and a fabulous warm vegetable pasta salad. Even the nachos can be ordered vegetarian. Make sure you are hungry—the portions are huge.

Vietnamese

If you have never had Vietnamese food, you have been missing something special. Vietnamese food is similar to Thai food, but tends to be sweeter and lighter. Clarendon in Arlington is absolutely the best place to go for Vietnamese cuisine in the area, period. A host of Vietnamese restaurants compete within a several block radius of the Metro station. You can choose among **Cafe Saigon** (1135 North Highland St.; 703/243-6522), **Gourmet Vietnam** (3211 North Washington Blvd.; 703/527-7208), **Nam-Viet** (1127 North Hudson St.;

703/522-7110) and **Queen Bee** (3181 Wilson Blvd.; 703/527-3444). The above restaurants all offer fine cuisine at relatively cheap prices. The best of these restaurants is Nam-Viet, with Queen Bee a close second.

In Georgetown, **Vietnam Georgetown Restaurant** (2934 M St., N.W.; 202/337-4536) and **Viet Huong** (2928 M St., N.W.; 202/337-5588) sit side by side. Word has it that Vietnam Georgetown is the better choice. Eclectic **Germaine's** (2400 Wisconsin Ave., N.W.; 202/965-1185) offers Pan-Asian and Vietnamese dishes. Apparently it is a good restaurant for star-sightings. It is also reputed to be popular among the local press corps.

Etc...

Cities (2424 18th St., N.W.; 202/328-7194) has a unique agenda—every few months, Cities celebrates the cuisine of another city by changing its entire decor and revamping its menu to reflect the new locale. Regional wines are also selected to round out the cultural experience.

Jaleo (480 Seventh St., N.W.; 202/628-7949) recreates the taste, feel and atmosphere of a Spanish tapas restaurant. "Tapas" are small appetizers that customers casually linger over with a glass of one of the fine sherries in Jaleo's extensive selection. With a constant crowd in the bar area, Jaleo makes for an appealing night out.

The quirky decor of **Andalusian Dog** (1344 U St., N.W.; 202/986-6364) should not distract you from its excellent food. This tapas restaurant is yet another establishment in the growing U St. corridor that has been designed by area artists. Winged loaves of bread fly from the painted ceiling in the front room and above the bar. A mixture of painting and relief work creates the illusion of a whirlpool sucking bodies into the gaping mouth of a dog. In contrast, the tapas food is simple and really well done, so do not let the wall of human hands distract you.

If you are a hungry art lover, **Utopia** (1418 U St. N.W.; 202/483-7669) lives up to its name for you. The owner of this new restaurant and bar is a painter and the space does double duty as an art gallery for his work and the works of other local artists. Utopia's high-ceilings (the building used to be a garage) leave ample wall space to be covered with paintings and prints. There is also a full bar with weekday happy hours.

The **State of the Union** (1357 U St., N.W.; 202/588-8810), the former Soviet Union, that is, offers Russian/American cuisine. The menu even lists a shot of Vodka as an appetizer. Make sure you check out their bathrooms. Like many of the other restaurants and bars on U St., the owners have asked local artists to decorate the interior. In this case, they even made the bathrooms into works of art.

At Least Once for Lunch

There are several restaurants that you should go to at least once to round out the "Washington experience." **Sholl's Colonial Cafeteria** (1990 K St., N.W., 202/296-3065 and 1750 Pennsylvania Ave., N.W., 202/737-5293) is a hardy, enduring legacy from Washington's past. In these tough economic times, you will be amazed at how much food your dollar can still buy.

The Well-Dressed Burrito (1220 19th St., N.W.; 202/293-0515), a carry-out-only hole in the wall, operates in the alley between 19th and 20th Sts. in Dupont Circle. It is only open on weekdays from 11:45 a.m. to 2:30 p.m. Its menu is limited, but its dishes create enough aroma to help you find your way there.

Power Meals

With over 40,000 lawyers and lobbyists in the District, it is no wonder D.C. is home to the "power meal." Expensive restaurants, with their fancy awnings and curtained windows, have fallen on hard times in the twilight of the free-spending Reagan era. The heavy-hitters still dine on the K St. corridor. At **Tiberio** (1915 K St., N.W.; 202/452-1915) one can eat needlessly-expensive (but good) Italian food. A bowl of pasta runs $23. **The Prime Rib** (2020 K St., N.W.; 202/466-8811) is K St.'s most impressive meat club. **Mr. K's** (2121 K St., N.W.; 202/331-8868) serves Chinese food in elegant surroundings.

The ultimate power dining experience is had at **Jean-Louis at the Watergate** (2650 Virginia Ave., N.W.; 202/298-4488). Nationally famous, perfection does not come cheap. Expect to pay at least $75 a person.

The Redskins' Super Bowl trophies are on display at **Duke Ziebert's** (1050 Connecticut Ave., N.W.; 202/466-3730). Duke Ziebert's only real appeal is the chance to engage in a little D.C. star-sighting. The food itself is hardly worth the price, but the experience is what you pay for. **The Palm** (1225 19th St., N.W.; 202/293-9091) is for those steak-and-potato eaters from the old boy network. **Morton's of Chicago** (3251 Prospect St., N.W.; 202/342-6258) qualifies as the same. **Le Lion d'Or** (1150 Connecticut Ave., N.W.; 202/296-7972) promises Washington's best traditional French food and generally delivers. **Galileo** (2014 P St., N.W.; 202/293-7191) caters to those who enjoy making deals over some of the finest Italian cuisine anywhere.

The tastes of southwestern cuisine and Santa Fe have galloped into Washington in grand style. With five million dollars spent on its decor, **The Red Sage** (605 14 St., N.W.; 202/638-4444) is a spectacularly fanciful vision of the West. The food may not completely live up to its decor, but the Red Sage has become all the rage.

For wining and dining on the Hill, staffers take to **La Colline** (400 North Capitol St., N.W.; 202/737-0400) or **La Brasserie** (239 Massachusetts Ave., N.E.; 202/546-9154).

Great for Dates

To begin a romantic evening, I suggest stopping by the **Terrace at the Hotel Washington** (515 15th St., N.W.; 202/638-5900) for drinks. The Terrace overlooks the Mall and the White House. When you enter the hotel, take the elevator to the top. If you are looking for something with a dash of Victorian romance for dinner afterwards, try the nearby **Morrison Clark Inn** (1015 L St., N.W.; 202/898-1200).

First dates always bring Italian food to mind for me. Here are some of my favorites: in a chic atmosphere, **I Matti** (2436 18th St., N.W.; 202/462-8844) is the perfect jumping-off spot for a night in Adams Morgan; in Georgetown, **Ristorante Piccolo's** (1068 31st St., N.W. 202/342-7414) intimate candle-lit tables and solid Italian cuisine make for a great meal before wandering around Georgetown.

If you are in the mood for French cuisine, **Le Gaulois Cafe Restaurant** (1106 King St., Alexandria; 703/739-9494) has received rave reviews. The fireplace definitely adds to the atmosphere. Be sure to call ahead and make reservations. Another favorite is Potomac's **Old Angler's Inn** (10801 MacArthur Blvd.; 301/365-2425). This country inn, within walking distance of the C&O towpath, features regional cuisine with a French accent. In the winter, try to snag a spot next to the fireplace. In the summer and spring, take advantage of the outside terrace. Atmosphere here comes at a steep price; dinner for two can easily cost $100.

The Iron Gate (1734 N St., N.W.; 202/737-1370), a Middle-eastern restaurant in an old carriage house just off Dupont Circle, is another place to woo your sweetheart. In the summer, take advantage of its wonderful courtyard. Meals are just as romantic in the winter when you can sit indoors in a cozy, dark room with a fireplace.

To cap off an evening out with a drink and a bit of jazz, stop by **Cafe Lautrec** (2432 18th St., N.W.; 202/265-6436). You cannot miss

My Favorite Restaurants
by Secretary of Commerce Ronald H. Brown

Tony Cheng's Mongolian Barbecue
I go there so often they want to bronze my gold card. Select your own meal from dozens of ingredients and spices, watch the Mongolian Chef stirfry it for you on a wok the size of center court.

Mr. K's
Mr. K's for "the usual." Four, five or six courses, chef's choice, but always including Peking Duck. You will not be hungry again in an hour.

Enzo's
Fantastic kitchen, especially [when it comes to] veal and seafood. Forget the menu, just ask the waiter "what's good?"

Cafe Atlantico
Caribbean food, trendy decor, modest tabs. See, be seen, eat seafood.

Crisfields (The original location)
No atmosphere at all—just the best seafood in America.

The Palm
(Not just because they have my picture on the wall.) Cholesterol city. Steak, potatoes, and a crowd right out of Who's Who.

---

this building—a mural of Lautrec is painted on the front. This cafe has nightly live entertainment and on the weekends, tap dancing on the bar.

If you are in the mood for something a little quieter to finish off the evening why not consider a coffee bar. You will have to look closely to spot **Dolce Finale**—it is tucked underneath Petitto's in Woodley Park (2653 Connecticut Ave., N.W. 202/667-5350). This tiny basement cafe, with seating for just over a dozen people, has excellent desserts and is open until 1:30 a.m. on weekends.

All-Night Diners
Unfortunately, if you are likely to get the midnight munchies, your choices are pretty limited. Georgetown's French cafe, **Au Pied de**

Cochon (1335 Wisconsin Ave., N.W.; 202/333-5440) is open round the clock. **Bob & Edith's Diner** in Arlington (2310 Columbia Pike; 703/920-6103) offers night owls the regular diner fare: eggs, coffee, waffles, pies and interesting patrons. You will find a fairly large menu and wonderful desserts at **The Amphora** (377 Maple Ave., Vienna; 703/938-7877). Each booth comes with an individual juke box. The old suburban stand-by, **Tastee Diner,** is also open 24 hours a day, seven days a week, with locations in Fairfax (10536 Lee Highway; 703/591-6720), Silver Spring (8516 Georgia Ave.; 301/589-8171), Laurel (118 Washington Blvd.; 301/953-7567) and Bethesda (7731 Woodmont Ave.; 301/652-3970).

The Afterwords Cafe (1517 Connecticut Ave., N.W.; 202/387-3825) in Dupont Circle can be a perfect place to go for dessert and coffee any night. On weekends, the cafe, which is attached to Kramerbooks, stays open all night. Besides the excellent desserts, the Afterwords Cafe offers a selection of vegetarian and southwestern dishes. **The American City Diner** (5532 Connecticut Ave., N.W.; 202/244-1949) is also open around the clock on Fridays and Saturdays.

☐ **BARS**

The Traditional Bar Scene

When Washingtonians want to engage in a friendly game of bar golf or go on a more casual pub crawl, they head for the busy streets of Georgetown. You will find almost every kind of bar here—from prep to crunch muffin. Prices reflect the neighborhood's trendy status. Old Town's King St. draws much the same crowd. In Dupont Circle, the bars around 19th and M Sts. are the place to go. Below is a list of some of Washington's notable bars.

The Brickskeller Inn (1523 22nd St., N.W.; 202/293-1885) boasts over 500 different types of beer from all over the world. The Brickskeller is a better place to go to catch up with a long-lost pal than to pick up a new friend. Unlike most bars, no one mills about or dances; instead the host will ask you to choose a table. The Brickskeller also serves food, but stick with the beer.

The Bottom Line (1716 Eye St., N.W.; 202/298-8488) features free munchies (tacos, buffalo wings and egg rolls) on weekdays, making this a popular watering hole for nearby workers. On the weekends, college students pack this bar to drink and dance. **Quigley's** (1825 Eye St., N.W.; 202/331-0150) attracts much of the same crowd, with dancing on Tuesday, Friday and Saturday nights and live entertainment on Thursday nights. American University students hang out at its second location near Tenleytown at 3201 New Mexico Ave., N.W. (202/966-0500). I once mistook the **Third Edition** (1218 Wisconsin Ave., N.W.; 202/333-3700) in Georgetown for a bookstore. Instead, it is a hot-spot for the college crowd, especially on the weekends. Expect to pay a $5 cover on the weekends.

Several bars around 19th and M Sts. make up one of the better-known pick-up spots, inspiring the area's unpleasant nickname "Herpes Triangle." Washingtonians and suburbanites flock to **Madhatter** (1831 M St., N.W.; 202/833-1495), **Sign of the Whale** (1825 M St., N.W.; 202/785-1110) and particularly **Rumors** (1900 M St., N.W.; 202/466-7378). Another popular pick-up joint is **Mr. Days** (1111 19th St., N.W.; 202/296-7625), just off 19th St. in the back alley. **DeJaVu** (2119 M St. N.W.; 202/452-1966) attracts a slightly older and more international crowd. Just a few blocks away is **The Front Page** (1333 New Hampshire Ave., N.W.; 202/296-6500). It lacks the reputation of the M St. bars, yet draws large crowds of yuppies and post-yuppies to its happy hours.

Happy hours at **Jaimalito's Cantina** (3000 K St., N.W.; 202/944-4400) and **Ha' Penny Lion** (1101 17th St., N.W.; 202/296-8075) promise a stunning quotient of the well-dressed per square foot. Jaimalito's seems to attract an extremely good-looking, affluent crowd, while Ha' Penny Lion caters to a slightly younger group.

A lot has been brewing at the corner of 11th and H Sts., N.W. A lot of beer, that is, since the **Capital City Brewing Company** (202/628-2222) opened. This restaurant and bar serves all kinds of beer, most of which are brewed on the premises. A rotating production schedule ensures that there are lots of new ales, pilsners and porters to try on a regular basis. The menu ranges from steaks, sausages and burgers to salmon, shrimp and other seafood. The brewery has a mostly young, professional crowd and a popular happy hour.

If you are looking for a bar with live music, venture over to **Grog & Tankard** (2408 Wisconsin Ave., N.W.; 202/333-3114). A wide variety of local talent can be seen here. Different nights of the week feature different types of music: Mondays are Grateful Dead nights, Tuesdays are blues and Wednesdays feature progressive music. Showtime is around 9:30 p.m. Cover charges vary between $2 and $5 depending on the night.

Bethesda residents hang out at **Malarkey's** (7201 Wisconsin Ave.; 301/951-9000) and **Nantucket Landing** (4723 Elm St.; 301/654-7979) and shoot pool at **Shootz** (4915 St. Elmo Ave.; 301/654-8288), a pricy billiard hall. Afterwards, they trek out to the **Silver Diner** (11806 Rockville Pike; 301/770-2828) in Rockville for late-night snacking.

In Adams Morgan, the best places to go for a beer without giving up your entire wallet are **Stetson's** (1610 U St., N.W.; 202/667-6295) and **Millie & Al's** (2440 18th St., N.W.; 202/387-8131). Stetson's serves Tex-Mex fare and is a popular hangout among young Democrats. At Millie & Al's, you can relive college days in a smoky barroom cluttered with cheap pitchers of beer.

Several bars line Pennsylvania Ave. between 2nd and 7th Streets on Capitol Hill. Among them you will find the **Tune Inn** (202/543-2725) and **Hawk 'n Dove** (202/543-3300). Both cater to the budgets of congressional staff and interns, who make up the majority of the crowd. Several congressmen are occasionally known to join their staffers at these spots, especially the Tune Inn. Other staffers trek over to **My Brother's Place** (237 2nd St., N.W.; 202/347-1350) near the Labor Department. At nearby Union Station, **Fat Tuesday's** (Lower level; 202/289-6618) serves daiquiris and is a good place to hang out before going to the movies. **Tiber Creek Pub** (15 E St., N.W.; 202/638-0900) sells beer by the half-yard or yard, which translates into 24 or 48 ounces. People go there for the quantity more than anything else.

Whitey's (2761 North Washington Blvd.; 703/525-9825) is the place to go in Arlington. A young crowd comes to enjoy beer, live music and a large back room with a pool table, pinball machines, dart boards and fooz ball tables, turning this neighborhood bar into a neighborhood traffic jam on the weekends. Whitey's is easy to spot, just look for its neon "EAT" sign out front.

> **A Few Miscellaneous Suggestions...**
>
> To keep tabs on what is going on in Washington's world of food, fun and frolic, you can read "On the Town" in the Weekend section (Friday edition) of *The Washington Post*. For specific information about restaurants, nothing can beat Phyllis Richman's weekly restaurant review in *The Washington Post's* Sunday magazine. *Washingtonian Magazine* also reviews restaurants and frequently publishes lists of the top restaurants.

Bardo Rodeo (2000 Wilson Blvd.; 703/527-9399) is Arlington's new kid in town. Located in the old Olmstead Oldsmobile building, Bardo never got around to removing the Olmstead sign or the car/jukebox that pokes through the front window. Simply put, this place is huge, occupying the old showroom and the garage, with tons of outdoor seating to boot. Topping it off is Bardo's on-tap selection of 35 beers, as well as root beer, hard cider and 40 kinds of bottled beer.

A short distance from Bardo Rodeo, two new bars serve a similarly broad selection of beer in much smaller environs. **Strangeways** (2830 Wilson Boulevard; 703/243-5272), adorned with pictures of balding men and imitations of Picasso paintings, is a cozy, funky place to hang out. Check out their dozens of beers on a Sunday night, when the crowd is not so big and there is a better chance of finding the pool table free. You can also visit the **Galaxy Hut** (2711 Wilson Boulevard; 703/525-8646) as an alternative to gigantic Bardo. This bar is similar to Strangeways—a smaller, strangely-decorated place with a wide selection of beers on tap. Bring some quarters for the lava-lamp jukebox.

Irish Pubs

Washington has several excellent Irish pubs. The biggest and most popular is **Ireland's Four Provinces,** commonly referred to as the Four P's (3412 Connecticut Ave., N.W.; 202/244-0860), in Cleveland Park. In addition to good folk singers and good food, the Four P's offers Guinness on draft. On the Hill, staffers and Georgetown law students hang out at **The Dubliner** (4 F St., N.W.; 202/737-3773) and **Kelly's Irish Times** (14 F St., N.W.; 202/543-5433). Other favorites include **Murphy's of D.C.** (2609 24th St., N.W.; 202/462-7171); **Murphy's Grand Irish Pub** (713 King St., Alexandria; 703/548-1717); **Ireland's Own** (132 N. Royal St., Alexandria; 703/549-4535) and **Flanagan's Irish Pub** (7637 Old Georgetown Road, Bethesda; 301/986-1007).

Gay Bars and Restaurants

The Dupont Circle area is very much the center of Washington's gay community. Along with several bookstores and the Whitman Walker Clinic, Dupont Circle is home to several of the city's gay restaurants and bars. On 17th St., **JR's Bar & Grill** (1519 17th St., N.W.; 202/328-0090) attracts the young, preppie crowd. Its popular happy hours draw a regular following. Along this strip on 17th St. you will find several gay-oriented restaurants: **Annie's Paramount Steak House** (1609 17th St., N.W.; 202/232-0395), **Trio's** (1537 17th St., N.W.; 202/232-6305), **Boss Shepherd's** (1527 17th St., N.W.; 202/328-8193) and around the corner, **Cafe Luna** (1633 P St., N.W.; 202/387-4005). Capitol Hill also has a few restaurants that cater to the "festive" crowd. **Two Quail** (320 Massachusetts Ave., N.E.; 202/543-8030) is an excellent restaurant for dates and **Mr. Henry's** (601 Pennsylvania Ave., S.E.; 202/546-8412) serves burgers and beer in a relaxed atmosphere. Of all these, Annie's is the place to see and be seen.

JR's patrons cross Dupont Circle to go dancing at **Badlands** (1415 22nd St., N.W.; 202/296-0505). A much larger dance floor awaits at **Tracks** (1111 1st St., S.E.; 202/488-3320), but you will have to travel to get there. Be careful when you go, Tracks is located in a rough neighborhood.

The Levi/Leather crowd hangs out at **D.C. Eagle** (639 New York Ave., N.W.; 202/347-6025). The newly renovated **Fireplace** (2161 P St., N.W.; 202/293-1293) is currently in vogue, attracting mostly the Levi/Leather crowd. Those looking for country and western bars will have to make a trip up to the Hill. **Remington's,** at 639 Pennsylvania Ave., S.E., (202/543-3113), is one of the friendliest bars in the city. Nearby **Wild Oats** (539 8th St., S.E.; 202/547-9453) brings in much of the same crowd. As is true in a number of big cities, gay bashing is no stranger to Washington, so be careful and pay attention to where you walk.

The French Quarter Cafe (808 King St.; 703/683-2803) in Alexandria—commonly referred to just by its address—caters to gay suburbanites. No similar bar has yet opened in Maryland's suburbs. One historical note: 808 King St. was the first bar in Virginia to successfully challenge Virginia's law forbidding liquor to be served to gays. Believe it or not, this happened all the way back in October 1991. No misprint.

Coffee Bars

Espresso machines all over town are now busier than ever churning out espresso, latte and cappuccino. Now, San Franciscans who complain that they miss Peet's can get a real cup of coffee at Quartermaine Coffee Roasters. And Seattlites, who used to have to drive to Nordstrom to get their fix, can go to the oh-so familiar Starbucks. For the rest of us, the coffee invasion has been an educating experience.

The most obvious proof of the speed with which the coffee industry has struck in the Washington, D.C. area is the invasion of the Seattle-based **Starbucks.** In less than a year, Starbucks has opened a multitude of shops: 3430 Wisconsin Ave., N.W., 202/537-6879; 1501 Connecticut Ave., N.W., 202/588-1280; 532 King St., Old Town Alexandria, 703/836-2236; 5438 Westbard Ave., Bethesda, 301/718-6339; 10100 River Road, Potomac, 301/299-9226; 5748 Union Mill Road, Clifton, 703/802-0494.

Quartermaine Coffee Roasters (3323 Connecticut Ave., N.W.; 202/244-2676) plans similar growth. Unlike Starbucks, which ships its roasted beans from Seattle, Quartermaine's roasts its coffee at their plant in Rockville. Its Bethesda store is located at 4817 Bethesda Ave. (301/718-2853). If you are interested in taking a tour of the roasting plant, just call 301/230-4600.

A relative old timer, **Racheli's** original location (1350 19th St., N.W., 202/659-8069) was aimed primarily at the morning commuter; no seating, just coffee and pastries to go. With more space and an expanded menu, Racheli's second location (1020 19th St. N.W.; 202/466-7860) is great if you would like to relax and sit down while enjoying your latte.

Dupont Circle also hosts **Kramerbooks & Afterwords Cafe** (1517 Connecticut Ave., N.W.; 202/387-3825), which aims to please the hungry bookworm. Kramer's is two places in one: a bookstore and a cafe. Aside from cakes and pastries, Kramer's offers an eclectic, somewhat pricy dinner menu and is most known as a late night hangout after everything else closes: the cafe and bookstore are open all night Fridays and Saturdays. A second location (4201 Wilson Blvd.; 703/524-7227) recently opened in Arlington within sight of the Ballston Metro. It features an indoor and outdoor cafe and stays open until just 3:00 a.m. on the weekends.

Across the street, **Ferrara** (1528 Connecticut Ave., N.W.: 202/232-1107) serves up some of the best cappuccino in D.C. Ferrara is small inside, but has tables outside for drinking espresso and watching everyone else rush in and out of the Metro.

The owner of the **Java House** (1645 Q St., N.W.; 202/387-6622) says his emphasis is on coffee and he stocks over 70 kinds of beans to prove it. This place has been selling flavored and gourmet coffee from all over the world for three years. The beans are roasted and flavored on the premises. Indoor and outdoor seating is available for those who want to take advantage of the light menu.

Just around the corner is a great place to enjoy your favorite coffee drink on a cool evening: the storefront at **Cafe Blanca** (1523 17th St., N.W.; 202/986-3476) opens up, blending the interior with the sidewalk. The decor is inspired by the movie "Casablanca," complete with spinning ceiling fans and Humphrey Bogart murals.

On the same block, the **Pop Stop** (1513 17th St., N.W.; 202/328-0880) offers a more off-beat atmosphere. The walls and floors of this two-story coffee bar are painted with brightly-colored scenes and psychedelic patterns to offset the mixed bag of old upholstery, chairs and mismatched end-tables. There is plenty of seating inside, but if the decorations are too much for your eyes, you can join the crowd that is always seated at the tables in front. In the summer, the iced-coffee drinks are a great change.

Zig Zag Cafe (1524 U St., N.W.; 202/986-5949) is perhaps the most hip coffee bar in town. Located in the up-and-coming U St. corridor, this cafe hosts a young artistic crowd. Zig Zag is below street level and crowded with old tables, chairs and benches. On Fridays and Saturdays, Zig Zag is open until 4:00 a.m.

☐ THE CLUB SCENE

Tracks is an institution (1111 1st St., S.E.; 202/488-3320). Three dance areas (two inside and one outside) fill over 20,000 square feet. The outdoor dance area plays a mix of music and indoors, one dance floor gyrates to techno music while the other plays mostly alternative. Dress down: jeans in the winter and shorts in the summer. Cover charges on Friday and Saturday nights are $5. Tracks is not in the best of neighborhoods; if you drive, it is worth it to pay $3 or so for parking in one of the makeshift parking lots.

The Fifteenth Street corridor, just above the White House, has become a popular ground for new clubs. Within a few blocks, you will find **The Spy Club** (805 15th St., N.W.; 202/289-1779), **15 Minutes** (1030 15th St., N.W.; 202/408-1855) and **Zei** (1415 Zei Alley, N.W.; 202/842-2445). The Spy Club's entrance is in an alley off 15th St. The club recently had a facelift and is trying to change its image—away from Ralph Lauren to industrial. By day, 15 Minutes is Rothchild's Cafeteria and at night, this low-key club offers a mix of live and recorded music in its various rooms. The music ranges from progressive to rock to blues to jazz. Cover charges on Friday and Saturday nights ($6) include a free buffet. When you walk into Zei, you are greeted with a jumble of images—a tower of TVs, girls dancing on pedestals and lots of attitude. (A $750 memberhsip allows you to skip the line out front and relax in their private club, two floors above the dance floor.) This explains the name, Zei which is Greek for "he lives." This club plays mostly dance and disco.

The Fifth Column (915 F St., N.W.; 202/393-3632), **The Vault** (911 F St., N.W.; 202/347-8079) and **The Ritz** (919 E St., N.W.; 202/638-2582) are not far away. Despite their geographic proximity, they offer different types of music and attract different crowds. The Fifth Column is probably the closest thing Washington has to a New York club. A younger, more mixed group frequents its next-door neighbor, The Vault. At the Ritz, a fashionably-dressed crowd dances on five dance floors to jazz, top 40, reggae, hip hop and Motown.

Adams Morgan, too, has its share of nightclubs. A mon-eyed Euro-crowd frequents **IKON** (2424 18th St., N.W., 202/328-7194) upstairs from the restaurant, Cities. **Heaven and Hell** (2327 18th St., N.W.; 202/667-4355) are close by. Not surprisingly, Hell is downstairs and Heaven is upstairs. In Heaven, a young crowd dances to progressive music; the faintly-lit Hell fosters drinking and talking.

One of Adams Morgan's best-known clubs is **Kilimanjaro** (1724 California St., N.W.; 202/328-3838). Despite its African name, Kilimanjaro plays a mix of music but concentrates mostly on Caribbean themes. On weekdays before 8:00 p.m., Kilimanjaro offers a happy hour (complete with food). Kilimanjaro carefully controls its two dance floors; the second one opens only when the first is completely packed. This guarantees that you will always experience that club crush, bringing you all too much in touch with your neighbors. Cover charges for live acts start at $15.

Do you want to go out or would you rather eat bugs? Well, **The Insect Club** (625 E St., N.W.; 202/347-8884) happily caters to both tastes by offering drinks, dancing and edible insects. In addition, the

---

For the budget-minded as well as the adventurous, the **Entertainment Guide** is a wonderful resource. These coupon books (one for Virginia/D.C. and another for Maryland/D.C.) offer discounts at hundreds of restaurants, as well as many area theaters and concert halls. The Entertainment Guide costs about $40, but practically pays for itself with just three restaurant visits. Entertainment Guides can be purchased directly from the publisher by credit card (703/207-0770). If you prefer to see the Entertainment Guide before you purchase it, you can peruse it at People's Drugs, Waldenbooks, Brentanos and Drug Emporium stores.

dim lighting and small rooms and hallways give this place the feel of some kind of hive or nest when its crowded.

There is always a line at **Chief Ike's Mambo Room** (1725 Columbia Rd., N.W.; 202/332-2211) in Adams Morgan on weekends, so consider getting there early if you want to get in at all. Ike's is very casual, very crowded and very dark. The DJ "Stella Neptune" is a big attraction for two reasons: she only plays disco music from the '70s and she is the hottest DJ in town.

For an evening a little outside the mainstream, try the newly-opened **Black Cat Club** (1831 14th St., N.W.; 202/667-7960). The Black Cat is owned and operated by musicians and leans toward underground and alternative music, although it also has jazz and blues on certain weeknights.

Chapter 6
Beyond the Job

Even though a city dominated by workaholics, Washington has a surprisingly large number of social, cultural, educational, recreational and entertainment resources. You can join any of a multitude of organizations—everything from biking and hiking clubs to volunteer organizations to affiliations with the Smithsonian and Kennedy Center. Organizations provide a great way to meet new friends while taking part in your favorite activities.

Organizations to Join

Washington's cultural and recreational organizations are always looking for new members. Below is a list of some of the organizations unique to Washington.

■ 1869 Society
Corcoran Gallery of Art
17th & New York Ave., N.W.
202/638-3211
Metro: Farragut North (Red) or Farragut West (Orange & Blue)
Membership Fee: $65

The Corcoran, one of Washington's great private museums and renowned for its collection of American art, sponsors monthly events for the public. The 1869 Society, named after the year the museum was founded, hosts events that mix art and socializing. Events usually cost $15. You do not have to be a member to attend, but members are entitled to discounted rates, usually $5 off.

■ American Film Institute (AFI)
Kennedy Center
New Hampshire Ave. at Rock Creek Parkway, N.W.
202/785-4600 (recorded schedule of upcoming events)
202/828-4000 (membership information)
Metro: Foggy Bottom (Orange & Blue)
Membership Fee: $15

Great for cocktail conversation! Washingtonians love to boast about the American classics or foreign or avant garde films they have just seen in AFI's 220-seat theater. Members receive advance information about screenings through *Preview,* a monthly magazine and a one-dollar discount on all movies. Usually two different films are shown each night ($5 each for members; $6 for the general public). AFI also sponsors advance screenings of upcoming movies.

■ BRAVO!
Kennedy Center
New Hampshire Ave. at Rock Creek Parkway, N.W.
202/416-7838
Metro: Foggy Bottom (Orange & Blue)
Membership Fee: $25

BRAVO! helps raise money for the Washington Opera. Through lectures, trips and special events, members can socialize and learn more about the opera. BRAVO! also sponsors an annual black-tie "Valentines Ball" at one of the embassies in town. This fund-raiser generally draws a crowd topping 750.

■ Capitol Hill Restoration Society
1002 Pennsylvania Ave., S.E.
202/543-0425
Metro: Eastern Market or Potomac Ave. (Orange & Blue)
Membership Fee: $20 (individual) or $25 (family)

The CHRS is dedicated to the preservation and historical restoration of the Capitol Hill neighborhood. One of the more activist-oriented groups in the city, it meets the first Wednesday of each month for lectures and discussion regarding various architecture or restoration topics.

■ FANS (Friends Assisting the National Symphony)
Kennedy Center
New Hampshire Ave. at Rock Creek Parkway, N.W.
202/416-8100
Metro: Foggy Bottom (Orange & Blue)
Membership Fee: $50 (Sustainer level)

Symphony enthusiasts may want to join FANS, which hosts several social events throughout the season to promote the National Symphony. "In Celebration," a black-tie fund-raiser kicking off the opening week of the National Symphony subscription season, is their biggest event of the year. For $125, members dine with a celebrity at a Washington-area home, attend the concert and cap off the evening at a dessert reception with members of the orchestra.

■ Phillips Contemporaries
Phillips Collection
1600 21st St., N.W.
202/387-2151
Metro: Dupont Circle (Red)
Membership Fee: $75

Phillips Contemporaries promotes activities related to contemporary art and to the collection itself. Membership allows you and a friend to attend any of the museum's regular public programs (approximately four per month) and the Contemporaries' Evenings (generally one a month) at the Phillips, as well as gallery walks throughout the Dupont Circle area and visits to artists' studios and private collections. At the end of the season, the Contemporaries hosts a painting-inspired fund-raiser.

■ Smithsonian Institution Resident Associate Program (RAP)
Smithsonian Institution
202/357-3030
Metro: Smithsonian (Orange & Blue)
Membership Fee: $40 (individual); $50 (double); $55 (family)

The Resident Associate Program links the Smithsonian Institution with the Washington community and has the largest variety of social and cultural events of any group in town. In addition to classes offered through its Campus on the Mall program, RAP sponsors special evening lectures, concerts, tours of Washington and environs, films and theatrical performances. *The Smithsonian Associate* magazine will keep you informed of the latest programs and events. In addition to advance notice of events (which often do sell out), you also get substantial discounts and a 10% discount in the Smithsonian's many souvenir shops.

■ Ski Club of Washington, D.C. (SCWDC)
5309 Lee Highway
Arlington
703/532-7776
Membership Fee: $35 (individual); $55 (double)

Most people do not associate Washington with skiing (lack of snow during the winter provides one good reason, lack of a suitable nearby mountain another); however, SCWDC members do not let that slow them down. Over 6,000 members make the Ski Club of Washington the largest year-round ski club on the Eastern Seaboard. The Ski Club offers a host of social and recreational activities, including wine and cheese tastings, swing/ballroom dance lessons, hikes, tennis parties, biking trips and, yes, skiing (lessons and excursions). Call 703/532-7776 and leave your name and address to receive a membership application and a SKI-O-GRAM (you will have to call to find out what this is).

■ State Societies

Lonely for home or people who pronounce the letter "r" just like you do? Then join your home state society. Nominal membership fees (around $15 a year) will guarantee you an invitation to every one of their social events. For more information on your state society, you can call the National Conference of State Societies at 301/249-6666.

■ Women's Information Network (WIN)

202/347-2827
Membership Fee: $20

WIN is a Democratic, pro-choice women's response to the old boy network. Formed in the summer of 1989, WIN currently has over 2,000 members who participate in its lectures, events and committee meetings. Most events are free. WIN members have access to a job bank and they receive *The Winning Slate,* a monthly newsletter filled with legislative news, upcoming WIN events, committee reports and announcements of members' latest professional accomplishments. WIN's two big fund-raisers, each drawing over a thousand people, are the Winter Gala and "Women Opening Doors for Women," a cocktail and dinner party that helps young professionals network.

■ World Affairs Council of Washington, D.C.

1726 M St., N.W.
202/293-1051
Metro: Dupont Circle or Farragut North (Red)
Membership Fee: $40

The World Affairs Council sponsors lectures and programs about international policy issues. In addition to monthly lectures from luminaries such as former President Ronald Reagan, former CIA Director William Webster, former Secretary of State George Shultz,

Queen Noor of Jordan, Prime Minister Mahathir of Malaysia and former British Defense Secretary George Younger, the Council offers a monthly series of programs for young professionals. These lectures, held at various Downtown hotels and embassies, cover a wide variety of topics and feature academic and business leaders, journalists and members of the diplomatic corps.

Volunteer Activities

Two groups, **D.C. Cares** (202/663-9207) and **Doing-Something** (202/393-5051), bring volunteering right to your doorstep (well, actually your mailbox). Catering to the lifestyles of busy Washingtonians, these organizations send members long lists of volunteer projects each month. Members then sign up for the projects that interest them by contacting the specific project's volunteer coordinator. Volunteer coordinators fill you in on the details: how to get there and what to wear and bring. Most projects are performed before or after weekday work hours, or on weekends, at locations throughout the District. Projects include working with children, the elderly, the homeless, the disabled and AIDS sufferers, as well as caring for the environment. Although volunteers are given total flexibility, they are encouraged to make volunteering a regular commitment. Both groups will also help you to coordinate your own volunteer project with friends or co-workers.

Before any new D.C. Cares' volunteers begin working on projects, they must complete a one-hour orientation that describes D.C. Cares and its different projects. Projects fall into three categories: regular monthly projects involving the ongoing monthly commitment of volunteers; special one-day projects designed to meet a particular short-term community need; and individual projects requiring a larger commitment (such as tutoring a homeless child). In addition, volunteers receive training, education and follow-up support designed to enhance their experience. Orientations are at 6:15 p.m. on Tuesday nights and 7:00 p.m. on Wednesday nights at the D.C. Cares offices at 2300 N St., N.W.

> **Political Organizations**
>
> If you are interested in getting involved with either the Democratic or Republican parties, call the **Democratic National Committee** (202/863-8000) or the **Republican National Committee** (202/863-8500). These organizations will also be able to put you in touch with other political groups from their side of the aisle.

DoingSomething takes a more casual approach to volunteering and does not require volunteers to attend an orientation. After volunteers have finished their projects, they often get together to discuss their experiences over pizza and beer. DoingSomething is still completely volunteer-run, so you should expect to talk to an answering machine when you call to get on their mailing list.

For a more hands-on approach, contact the volunteer clearinghouse in your community (phone numbers and addresses below). Clearinghouses serve as information banks for prospective volunteers, providing details on hundreds of community service opportunities. Counselors who interview you will inform you of the available projects in your community and give you the names and phone numbers of contacts at organizations. Most clearinghouses recommend that you come in to browse through their files.

Alexandria Volunteer Bureau
801 North Pitt St., Suite 102
703/836-2176
Metro: Braddock Road (Yellow & Blue)

Arlington County Volunteer Office
2100 Clarendon Blvd., Suite 314
703/358-3222
Metro: Court House (Orange)

D.C. Volunteer Clearinghouse
1313 New York Ave., N.W., Room 303
202/638-2664
Metro: Metro Center (Red, Orange & Blue)

Volunteer Center of Fairfax County
10530 Page Ave.
Fairfax, VA
703/246-3460
Metro: Vienna (Orange)

Montgomery County Volunteer and Community Service Center
401 Fleet St., Room 106
Rockville, MD
301/217-4949
Metro: Rockville (Red)

Prince George's County Voluntary Action Center
6309 Baltimore Ave., Room 305
Riverdale, MD
301/779-9444
Metro: Prince George's Plaza (Green)

Non-Degree Classes

Take advantage of having the **Smithsonian Institution** in your backyard. Their **Campus on the Mall** (202/357-3030) program offers courses in the arts, humanities, the sciences and studio arts, together with a vast offering of lecture series. Some of the classes offered in recent semesters include: The Magic of Shakespeare, the Architecture of Turkey, Educational Reform, Interior Design and the Literature of English Landscape. Many courses include guided tours of local museums and art galleries. Some courses even conclude with receptions at appropriate embassies. Classes usually meet at one of the Smithsonian museums on the Mall once a week (on weeknights) for six to eight weeks. Virtually all locations are easily accessible by Metro. Resident Associate Program members pay approximately $60 to $150 per course.

Georgetown University (202/687-5942) offers some of the best non-credit classes for adults, from Women in Western Political Thought to Screen Writing for Film and T.V. Movies to Chinese. There are courses in art history, studio arts, theater, music, literature, writing, communication, classics, religion, psychology, philosophy, history, international affairs, languages, economics, personal finance, science, computers and professional development. (Whew!) The prices will not shock you, either. They range from $65 to $200 per course. Classes are held nights and weekends. On-campus parking is available at a discounted rate with a valid non-degree student ID.

Another great bargain is the **U.S. Department of Agriculture** (202/720-5885). The USDA offers over a thousand courses per year in fifty subject areas intended to assist government and other organizations increase their efficiency and effectiveness. Anyone can enroll in any of these classes, though, for an average of $200 per class. Most classes are held weeknights at various federal office buildings Downtown. All locations are accessible by Metro.

Through its **Center for Career Education and Workshops** (CCEW), **George Washington University** (202/994-5299) also offers non-credit professional training courses. In addition to courses in fields such as desktop publishing and financial planning, CCEW sponsors FSE, GRE, GMAT and LSAT test-prep courses that are much cheaper than Stanley Kaplan or the Princeton Review. Most CCEW courses cost between $300 and $350. Courses usually last eight weeks and convene in the basement of a Downtown office building at 2020 K St., N.W. Enrollment in regular undergraduate and graduate courses at GWU as a non-matriculating student costs $490 per credit hour. If the price does not scare you away, stop by the information desk in the lobby of Rice Hall at 2121 Eye St., N.W., to pick up a course catalog and schedule.

Also on the expensive side, **American University** (202/885-2500) offers all of its regular undergraduate and graduate courses to qualified non-degree students at the hefty price of $506 per credit hour. All classes are given at the main campus at 4400 Massachusetts Ave., N.W. Non-degree students have access to the AU libraries and to the shuttle bus from the Tenleytown Metro (Red line). For an additional $25 fee, you can also purchase a pass to use the sports center (swimming pool, racquetball courts and weight room).

The District's only public university, **University of the District of Columbia** (UDC; 202/274-5000) offers both academic and non-academic classes at its main campus at 4200 Connecticut Ave., N.W. District residents have a substantial advantage: $153 per course versus $487 for non-residents. For professional development and leisure courses, call (202/274-5179).

Suburbanites get the same advantages at their community colleges. **Northern Virginia Community College** (Alexandria Campus 703/845-6200; Annandale Campus 703/323-3000; Woodbridge Campus 703/878-5700) and **Montgomery College** (Rockville 301/279-5000; Takoma Park 301/650-1300; Germantown 301/353-7700) offer a wide variety of credit and non-credit courses and seminars. Virginia residents can expect to find course catalogs stuffed in their mailboxes regularly. Budgetary pressures have forced Montgomery County to cut back on their extensive mailing activities, so you will have to pick up catalogs and applications at any of MC's campuses. Course prices are $44 per credit hour for Virginians and $57 for Montgomery County residents.

First Class (202/797-5102) offers numerous, inexpensive off-beat classes which convene anywhere from one to four times. First Class courses cost $20 to $30 and most meet at their Dupont Circle office, 1522 Connecticut Ave., N.W. Recent classes have included Mastering the Art of Spelling, Bob Levey's Inside Look at Washington and Guerrilla Dating Tactics. First Class distributes its brochures in drop boxes at Metro stations, stores and restaurants around town.

International Washington

On a tight budget but still interested in seeing the world? Visit some of Washington's many foreign embassies, many of which are located along Massachusetts Ave. Since many embassies are too small to host public events, they often join forces with institutions such as the International Monetary Fund Visitor's Center and the World Bank to sponsor activities.

Below is a sample of some of the embassies or cultural centers which sponsor events. You can call any embassy's public information officer or cultural department to get on its mailing list.

Australian Embassy	202/797-3000
1601 Massachusetts Ave., N.W.	
Austrian Embassy	202/895-6700
3524 International Court, N.W.	
British Embassy	202/462-1340
3100 Massachusetts Ave., N.W.	
Canadian Embassy	202/682-1740
501 Pennsylvania Ave., N.W.	
Colombian Consulate	202/387-8338
2118 Leroy Place, N.W.	
Danish Embassy	202/234-4300
3200 Whitehaven St., N.W.	
French Embassy	202/944-6000
4101 Reservoir Rd., N.W.	
Greek Embassy	202/332-2727
2211 Massachusetts Ave., N.W.	
Indonesian Embassy	202/775-5200
2020 Massachusetts Ave., N.W.	
Irish Embassy	202/462-3939
2234 Massachusetts Ave., N.W.	
Israeli Embassy	202/364-5500
3514 International Dr., N.W.	
Italian Embassy	202/328-5500
1601 Fuller St., N.W.	
Japan Information & Culture Center	202/939-6900
1155 21st St., N.W.	

Mexican Cultural Institute   202/728-1628
2829 16th St., N.W.
Portuguese Embassy   202/328-8610
2125 Kalorama Rd., N.W.
Royal Netherlands Embassy   202/244-5300
4200 Linnean Ave., N.W.
Swiss Embassy   202/745-7928
2900 Cathedral Ave., N.W.
Turkish Embassy   202/659-8200
1714 Massachusetts Ave., N.W.

Sports & Recreation
■ Bicycling

Bicyclists should have no problem pursuing their avocation. Hundreds of miles of bike trails criss-cross the metropolitan area. Michael Leccesse has written an excellent guide for recreational and serious cyclists alike, entitled *Short Bike Rides In and Around Washington, D.C.* It details bike rides of various length and difficulties with maps, pictures and thumbnail descriptions of each. (Globe Pequot Press; $9.95).

    Many cyclists favor a picturesque fifteen-mile stretch between Georgetown and Great Falls on the C&O Towpath. On the other side of the Potomac, the paved Mount Vernon Bike Trail rambles eighteen miles from Roosevelt Island to George Washington's plantation. The Washington & Old Dominion (W&OD) trail extends from Alexandria to Leesburg. Rock Creek Park provides another prime location, especially on weekends when cyclists can cruise car-free sections of Beach Drive.

    One of the largest recreation areas in Maryland is the Beltsville Agricultural Park, just north of Greenbelt. This is a huge tract of government land, criss-crossed by miles of two-lane country roads. It is perfect for bicycling and on weekends you will usually see more bicycle traffic than automobiles. To get there, take the Kenilworth Ave. exit on the Beltway.

    Mountain bikers may not be satisfied with riverside or park routes. Instead, they can tackle the unrestricted system of challenging trails around Sugarloaf Mountain just outside the northwest corner of Montgomery County. To get to Sugarloaf, take I-270 north to Route 109. Follow Route 109 three miles to Comus Rd., make a right and drive another three miles.

Chapter Six | Beyond the Job

Rentals If you do not have your own bicycle, you can rent one at **Fletcher's Boathouse** (4940 Canal Rd. N.W.; 202/244-0461), **Thompson Boat Center** (2900 Virginia Ave., N.W.; 202/333-4861) or **Swain's Lock** (301/299-9006).

Maps The District's Department of Documents (Suite 520, 441 4th St., N.W.; 202/727-5090) publishes bike trail maps. They cost $3. You can pick them up or order them by mail.

Clubs Potomac Pedalers Touring Club (202/363-8687)
National Capital Velo Club (301/588-2087)

■ Running

Thousands of Washingtonians squeeze a run into their lunch hour along The Mall, East Potomac Park, the Mount Vernon Trail or Rock Creek Park. A few runners even opt for a diabolical sprint up the imposing flight of stone steps featured in "The Exorcist" on M St. in Georgetown.

Triathlons take place in Reston, Virginia and Columbia, Maryland. The **Tri-Maryland Triathlon Club** (410/882-6103) plans the running/biking and swimming/running "No Frills" Biathlon Series at sites throughout Maryland.

Clubs D.C. Road Runners (703/241-0395)
Montgomery Country Road Runners Club (301/353-0200)
National Capital Track Club (301/948-6905)
Northern Virginia Running Club (703/644-5364)

■ Tennis

Tennis buffs can play on the same courts that have hosted McEnroe tantrums and Navratilova slams at the **Washington Tennis Center,** at the corner of 16th & Kennedy Streets, N.W. (202/722-5949). A large plastic bubble permits winter play on five of the hard courts. Fees for outdoor courts range from $3.25 to $8 an hour. Indoor court fees climb sharply to $15 to $24 per hour. You should definitely plan ahead, since courts are available to the public on a first-come, first-served basis and must be reserved one week in advance.

Public tennis courts are widely available, both in the District and beyond. **Hains Point's East Potomac Tennis Center** (202/554-5962) has nineteen outdoor and five indoor courts. You can also play at the outdoor courts at Pierce Mill in Rock Creek Park (202/426-6908). Several Georgetown tennis courts, on R St. between 30th and 31st, are open on a first-come, first-served basis. Members of Congress and their staff head to the Hill's Garfield Park, 3rd and I Streets, S.E., to play a few sets. Federal Reserve Board Chairman Alan Greenspan plays his game at one of the least well-known public courts in town: the outdoor tennis court on D St., N.W. right across from the State Department. Time slots are distributed to employees and the public through a lottery system. You can sign up in person at the Federal Reserve Bank (Constitution & 20th, N.W.; 202/452-3357). For a list of all of the public tennis courts in your area, you can call your city's or county's recreation department.

Clubs   Mid-Atlantic Tennis Association (703/560-9480)

■ Golf

Golfers can tee off at **East Potomac Park Golf Course** (202/863-9007). This Hains Point facility has two nine-hole courses and one eighteen-hole course. Green fees are very reasonable: $13 for eighteen-holes on the weekend. Rolling hills and tree-lined fairways characterize the eighteen-hole golf course in **Rock Creek Park** (202/882-7332), located at Rittenhouse and 16th Streets, N.W. Suburbanites can stroll the links closer to home at public courses in Alexandria (6700 Telegraph Rd.; 703/971-6170), Reston (11875 Sunrise Valley Dr.; 703/620-9333), Silver Spring (9701 Sligo Creek Parkway; 301/585-6006)and Potomac (Falls Rd.; 301/299-5156). If you can afford the fees, Washington's country clubs have some superb golf courses.

Resources   D.C. has its own bimonthly golf magazine, *Metro Golf* (202/663-9015). Besides the usual tips and golf book reviews, *Metro Golf* posts an extensive listing of local tournaments (both open and members only) so that you can hone your game in competition.

Clubs   Rock Creek Golf Club (202/882-7332)

■ Miniature Golf

For those who consider the best kind of golf the type where you have to putt up a hill, past the windmill and through Snoopy's dog house, **Hains Point** is the District's only outdoor miniature golf course. At the Post Office Pavilion you can putt through replicas of Washington-area monuments at **City Golf** (East Atrium, Bottom Floor, 1100 Pennsylvania Ave., N.W.; 202/898-7888). In the suburbs, miniature golf courses are more profuse. Some of the best include: **Upton Hill Regional Park** (6060 Wilson Blvd., Arlington; 703/237-4953), **Cameron Run Regional Park** (4001 Eisenhower Ave., Alexandria;

703/960-0767) and **Putt Putt Rockville** (130 Rollins Ave., Rockville; 301/881-1663).

■ Horseback Riding

City slickers can enjoy seventeen miles of bridle paths in **Rock Creek Park,** winding through some of Washington's best scenery (202/362-0118). The escorted trail rides are $17. Rock Creek also offers lessons at all levels. **Wheaton Regional Park** (301/622-3311) also offers horseback riding ($15 per person). Guided hour-long trail rides are given three times every Sunday afternoon. Make sure to wear long pants and call ahead for reservations.

Equestrian Enterprises (Great Falls, Virginia; 703/759-2474) offers guided trail rides for adults through Great Falls Park and riding lessons for beginners and those with experience. You have to call ahead to book one of the two-hour trail rides ($38 per person).

Clubs   Capitol Hill Equestrian Society (202/828-3035)

■ Hiking

Trails paralleling the Potomac River in Great Falls Park provide great terrain and striking vistas for some of the area's best hiking. Those looking for something closer in should head to the C&O Canal in Georgetown. Trails also meander through Roosevelt Island, the wildlife sanctuary just across the Potomac from the Lincoln Memorial.

Clubs   Sierra Club (202/547-2326)
Potomac Appalachian Trail Club (703/242-0965)
Potomac Backpackers Association (703/524-1185)

■ Swimming

If you do not have access to a pool, relief from Washington's hot, muggy summers can be found in any one of the area's public swimming pools. One of the city's finest, the **Georgetown pool** (202/282-2366) is just off Wisconsin at 34th St. and Volta Place, N.W. It is open during the summer from Tuesday to Friday (1:00 to 8:00 p.m.) and on the weekends from noon to 7:00 p.m. Other public pools are the indoor **Marie H. Reed Learning Center** pool at 2200 Champlain St., N.W. (202/673-7771) or the indoor **Capitol East Natatorium** at 635 North Carolina Ave., S.E. (202/724-4495).

Arlington's high schools all have indoor pools open to the public for lap swimming on a pay-as-you-swim basis. You can try **Washington-Lee** (1300 North Quincy St.; 703/358-6262), **Wakefield** (4901 South Chesterfield Rd.; 703/578-3063) or **Yorktown** (5201 North

28th St.; 703/536-9739). One swim costs $3 (for county residents) and a book of twenty swims can be purchased for $45. Non-residents are welcome but must pay a slightly higher fee.

The **Montgomery Aquatic Center** (5900 Executive Blvd.; 301/468-4211) has a 200-foot long waterslide. Water lovers can also enjoy swimming in the Center's 50-meter pool and relaxing in either of its two hot tubs. For county residents, admission is just $4 for adults and $3.25 for children. If you do not live in Montgomery County, fees will be $6 for adults and $5 for children.

In Silver Spring, the **Martin Luther King Swim Center** (1201 Jackson Rd.; 301/989-1206) has a 42-yard pool, eight 25-yard lanes and a teaching pool. After your swim, you can relax in their hot tub. For residents, swims are $3.25 for adults and $2.75 for children. Nearby the **Fairland Aquatic Center** (13820 Old Gunpowder Rd.; 301/206-2359) boasts a 50-meter Olympic size pool and a 20-person jacuzzi. Swims here are also reasonably priced: $2.50 for adults and $1.50 for children.

Clubs   Nearly every public pool has a Masters Swimming group for adults. You can receive coaching, a private swimming lesson several times a week and periodically the chance to compete.

■ Boating and Sailing

The waters of the C&O Canal and the Potomac River (downstream from the Chain Bridge) cater to the romantic soul with canoeing and boating from May to October. You can rent both canoes and rowboats for $8 per hour at **Fletcher's Boathouse** (202/244-0461). A bit further downstream near Washington Harbour, **Thompson Boat Center** (2900 Virginia Ave., N.W; 202/333-4861) rents canoes ($6/hour), sculls ($13/hour), kayaks ($7/hour) and two-person Sunfish($12/hour). Thompson's proximity to the Georgetown waterfront and the Mall makes it the best starting point for watercraft tours of the city. If you would like to paddle around the Tidal Basin, you can rent a two-person paddle-boat at the **Tidal Basin Boathouse** (1501 Maine Ave., S.W.; 202/484-0206) for $7 an hour. **The Washington Sailing Marina** (703/548-9027), a mile south of National Airport, gives lessons and rents windsurfers and sailboats. Further down the George Washington Parkway, the **Mariner Sailing School** at the Belle Haven Marina (703/768-0018) offers sailing lessons and rents canoes, kayaks, windsurfers and sailboats.

Clubs   Washington Canoe Club (202/333-9749)

Canoe Cruisers Association of Greater Washington (301/656-2586)

Resources Flooding or severe weather can curtail these water activities. Before you venture out, you may want to call 703/260-0505 for the marine forecast.

■ Ice Skating

With the elegant Willard Hotel as a backdrop, ice skaters glide across the ice at the outdoor **Pershing Park Ice Rink** (202/737-6938). This outdoor rink at Pennsylvania Ave. and 14th St., N.W., is just a short stroll from the White House. A few blocks away, winter enthusiasts can enjoy skating at the **National Sculpture Garden Ice Rink** (Constitution & 9th St., N.W.; 202/371-5340) or at the **Reflecting Pool** in front of the Lincoln Memorial. Fees for skating at Pershing Park and the National Sculpture Garden are around $4; skating on the Reflecting Pool is free. Montgomery County has several outdoor rinks: **Wheaton Regional Park Ice Rink** (301/649-2703), the **Bethesda Metro Ice Center** (301/656-0588) or **Rockville's Cabin John Ice Rink** (301/365-2246). Cabin John is open year-round. Virginians can skate year round at the **Fairfax Ice Arena** (703/323-1131).

Clubs Hockey players should get in touch with Washington's only hockey league, **Hockey North America** (703/471-0400), to find out about joining a team.

■ Skiing

During the winter, cross-country skiers pick up where walkers and joggers left off on the C&O Canal Towpath, in Rock Creek Park or on the Mall. Of course, snow in D.C. is relatively rare. So, if you enjoy skiing, pack up the car and head out of town. Downhill skiing requires some serious driving to reach the slopes. While Virginia and Maryland have their own slopes, Eastern Pennsylvania, about 200 miles away, is one of your best bets.

Pennsylvania
Blue Knob, Claysburg	814/239-5111
Doe Mountain, Macungie	215/682-7108
Hidden Valley, Somerset	800/458-0175
Seven Springs, Champion	800/452-2223
Ski Liberty, Fairfield	717/642-8282
Whitetail, Mercersburg	717/328-9400

Virginia
Bryce Mountain, Basye	703/856-2121
Massanutten, Harrisonburg	703/289-9441

Wintergreen, Wintergreen   800/325-2200
Maryland
Wisp, Deep Creek Lake   301/387-4911

Clubs Ski Club of Washington, D.C. (703/532-7776–office; 703/536-TAPE–weekly recording of events)

Resources You can call the Post-Haste Hotline at 202/334-9000 (extension 4300) to hear the latest ski conditions.

■ Sporting on the Mall

The vast expanse of the Mall, especially around the Washington Monument, is the staging ground for many sports activities. Recreational team sports, particularly softball, have become as vital to politicking and deal-making as the K St. power lunches. Interns, legislative aides, partners and associates can be seen battling it out on the Mall grounds, both in and out of uniform. Most teams are co-ed and low-key. You should ask around your office to see about joining a team.

Resources Congressional Softball League (202/544-3333)

■ Health Clubs

Most of the national health club chains have opened pools and exercise rooms here. Some area entrepreneurs have started their own health clubs. You do not have to go far to see **Sport & Health** centers, for example. Sport & Health facilities vary in their features, but all offer exercise rooms and aerobics classes. When you are given the sales pitch, ask about the discount available to members of George Washington University's HMO or Group Health Association. In addition, with more HMO's encouraging regular exercise, check if your health insurance plan offers a discount at any health club or rebates on premiums for health club membership.

Hotels, too, have gotten into the act. Most of the larger hotels offer exercise rooms and pools to both their guests and to local residents. Of these, the **Four Seasons' Fitness** Club (202/944-2022) has one of the poshest set-ups. Full memberships ($3000 initiation fee and $180/month) are sold out; only associate memberships allowing daytime use of the club are currently available ($1750 initiation fee and $180/month).

Several health clubs offer special attractions which make them particularly popular among Washingtonians. **The National Capital YMCA** (202/862-9622) is one of the fanciest YMCA's you will ever work out in, with prices to match ($200 initiation fee and $60/month).

In this modern, seven-story building at the corner of 17th & Rhode Island Ave., N.W., you can swim in a 25-meter lap pool, jog around the indoor track or play basketball, racquetball or squash. In addition, the Y has a large workout room with free weights (including Keiser weights) and Nautilus machines.

If you were a Congressperson and tired of all the scampering and scurrying around on the House floor, where would you go to sweat? Hill staffers scrounge to pay the initiation fee ($299) and monthly dues ($69) just to work out with congressional heavyweights and Supreme Court justices at the **Washington Sports Club** (214 D St., S.E.; 202/547-2255), just a few blocks from the House office buildings.

If you want to exercise at the largest facility in the area, check out the **Worldgate Athletic Club** (13037 Worldgate Dr.; 703/709-9100) in Herndon, Virginia, near Dulles Airport. It has a 25-yard lap pool, an indoor driving range and putting green, basketball, squash, racquetball and tennis courts, weights, Cybex and exercise machines—not to mention a sauna, steam room and whirlpool.

Many flock to **Olympus Fitness Center** (in the back parking lot of Seven Corners Shopping Center, Falls Church; 703/241-2255) because of the club's hours: it is open daily from 5:00 a.m. to midnight. While there is no pool or racquetball court, the gym has every imaginable exercise machine and piece of weight-lifting equipment.

Fit Physique offers a wide variety of aerobic exercise classes including Aerobic Funk, Body Contouring and Fit 'n' Firm (all at 1500 Massachusetts Ave., N.W., First Floor; 202/659-5959). Fit Physique offers two payment options: by the class ($11 per class) or in a block (for example, 36 classes for $234).

Skiers should investigate **Aspen Hill Club** (14501 Homecrest Rd., Silver Spring; 301/598-5200). Their ski training center, complete with an indoor ski simulator, will help keep you in shape for the slopes. The club's basketball, racquetball and tennis courts, as well as its indoor lap pool, track, free weights, Nautilus, hot tub and sauna will not hurt your skiing either.

Professional Sports

Liberal or conservative, Democrat or Republican, the nation's capital has one unifying force—the National Football League's **Washington Redskins**. Few teams' followers are as devoted as Redskin fans. When they play Dallas, you will hear of little else all week. Unless you go as a guest or pay scalpers' exorbitant prices, though, chances of seeing a Redskins game at RFK (Robert F. Kennedy Memorial Stadium) are slim at best. Tickets are so hot that people fight over them in divorce settlements and pass them along in wills. You may want to get on the waiting list for season tickets. At least your children will see the games. (Really — right now it does take about a generation to get off the waiting list.) But get on the list anyway, when the new Stadium is built that should move about 20,000 names off the list. The perennial sell-outs guarantee that all games will be televised. But if you still want to be there, tickets can be found. The classified section of the *Post* and the *Times* regularly list single game and season ticket packages. If you do plan to see a game, Metro is the best and cheapest way to get to RFK (Orange/Blue: Stadium/Armory).

One side benefit to Washington's Redskin-mania is that the stores are pretty quiet during games. For non-football fans, Sunday afternoons can be an excellent time to shop, check out the latest show at the National Gallery of Art, go to the movies or do just about anything unimpeded by the usual crowds.

Washington also hosts professional basketball and hockey teams. The **Bullets** (basketball) and **Capitals** (hockey) play at the USAir Arena (301/350-3400) in Landover, Maryland. Seats are easy to come by, except for play-off games (though the Bullets making the playoffs in recent years has been more of a problem than getting seats). The Caps have played pretty well of late. To get there, take the Beltway (I-95) to exits 15 or 17 and follow the signs to the arena. Unfortunately, there is no mass transit to the game.

Since the Senators left in 1971, Washingtonians have longed for a baseball team they could call their own. They lost their most recent quest to Miami and Denver, so unless the San Diego Padres sell or the National League expands again, it is still Baltimore or bust for local major league baseball. The American League **Baltimore Orioles** (410/685-9800) play in the wonderful new downtown ballpark, Oriole Park at Camden Yards (or simply Camden Yards). Already Camden Yards is a model for the next generation of stadiums. Even if you are not an Orioles fan, you cannot help but have a great time at this ballpark.

Camden Yards is also far more convenient to D.C. than Memorial Stadium was. To get to Camden Yards by car, take I-95 North to Baltimore. From I-95 take the I-395 exit and follow the signs; the new stadium is just off the highway. Officials recommend, though, that you take public transportation if you can. MARC runs special trains between the new stadium and Union Station. Since the Stadium is only a short stroll away from Inner Harbor, it is fun to make a day of it. Parking is cheap and you can hang out in Inner Harbor or nearby Little Italy before heading over to the game.

The Orioles regularly sell out, therefore you should plan ahead. Washingtonians (who provide the O's with nearly a third of their attendees) can go to the convenient **Orioles Baseball Store** (914 17th St., N.W.; 202/296-2473) for tickets and memorabilia. Players make personal appearances at the store so call and check out when you can do a little bird-watching. You can also purchase tickets over the phone through TicketMaster (202/432-SEAT).

For National League games, you will have to do some traveling. Philadelphia hosts the closest team, the **Philadelphia Phillies** (215/463-1000). Travel north on I-95 and follow the signs to downtown Philly. Veteran Stadium (the "Vet") is located on the southside just off the interstate and you can make the trip in a manageable two hours.

The more adventurous may want to try the four to five hours to see the **New York Mets** at Shea Stadium (718/507-8499), the **New York Yankees** in the Bronx (718/293-6000) or the **Pittsburgh Pirates** in Three Rivers Stadium (800/ BUY-BUCS).

Those who prefer the small-town charm of the minor leagues have plenty of options near D.C. The **Prince William Cannons** (a Yankees farm club; 703/590-2311) and the **Frederick Keys** (an Oriole farm club; 301/662-0013) play in the Class A Carolina league, they both compete against the now famous Durham Bulls. Tickets are cheap, parking plentiful and it is a good place to take children.

In 1994, Bowie will host the **Bowie Baysox** (301/805-6000), an Oriole farm team, playing in the AA Eastern league. Last year, the Baysox played at Memorial Stadium and the year before that in Hagerstown, Maryland, as the Suns.

Directions to the Cannons Take I-95 South to exit 160 (Lake Ridge/ Occoquan). Turn left on Davis Ford Rd. and go approximately six miles to Prince William County Stadium in Woodbridge.

Directions to the Keys Take I-270 North to exit 31A (Frederick's Market St.). The ballpark, The Harry Grove Stadium, is on the left, just next to the highway exit.

Directions to the Baysox Take Route 50 East to 197 East. The Stadium is just off 197 at the junction of Route 50 and Route 301.

The **Professional Golfer's Association** (PGA) tour swings into Washington for the **Kemper Open,** traditionally held in late May. The Tournament Player's Club at Avenel in Potomac, Maryland (301/469-3737) hosts the event, which has attracted Greg Norman, Tom Kite, Hale Irwin and many other top pros.

Many of the world's top male tennis players travel to the Capital in July for the **Newsweek Classic** (it comes sufficiently after Wimbledon so that usually a few top players arrive). The top women players show up in September for the **Champions' Challenge.** Both events are held at the Washington Tennis Center at the corner of 16th & Kennedy Streets, N.W. Tickets can be purchased through Pro Serv (703/276-3030).

Cycling fans will not want to miss the **Tour DuPont** races in mid-May. World famous cyclists like Greg LeMond, Alexi Grewal and Davis Phinney participate. The Washington course has yet to be finalized, but it will undoubtedly be a multi-lap race, which means lots of action—several times over—for spectators.

Each February, past and future Olympic medalists assemble at George Mason University for the **Mobil 1 Invitational Track and Field Meet.** It is one of the major events of the indoor track and field circuit. Seating is limited and tickets go quickly. For ticket information, call 703/993-3270.

Serious runners may want to begin training for Washington's biggest marathon. In late October, the **Marine Corps Marathon** tests the mettle of more than a few good men and women. The race begins at the Iwo Jima Memorial in Rosslyn and finishes 26 miles later at the same spot. Thousands participate each year. The entrance fee is $25. For more information, you should call 703/690-3431.

College Athletics

There are many schools in and around Washington with excellent, nationally-competitive athletic programs. The **University of Maryland's** basketball teams play their home games at Cole Field House on the Maryland campus. The **Terrapins** compete in the Atlantic Coast Conference against schools like Duke, North Carolina and Virginia. Maryland's football team has perennially been competitive but has fallen on tough times the past few years and has been trying to rebuild. Tickets for either sport can be ordered in advance by phone (301/314-7070) or mail (P.O. Box 295, College Park, Maryland 20741).

The USAir Arena in Landover hosts the **Georgetown Hoyas** men's basketball team (202/687-4692). Contests against Big East Conference rivals sell out quickly. Tickets can be purchased at Georgetown or through TicketMaster (202/432-SEAT).

George Washington University's Colonials (men's basketball team; 202/994-DUNK) had a stellar year in 1993, advancing to the NCAA Sweet Sixteen. Watch out for seven-foot-one star player Yinka Dare! The Colonials play at the Smith Center (600 22nd St., N.W.) Tickets are available from TicketMaster (202/432-SEAT).

Area Departments of Recreation

Alexandria	703/838-4343
Arlington County	703/358-3322
District	202/673-7660
Fairfax County	703/324-4386
Montgomery County	301/217-6800
Prince George's County	301/699-2400

Theater

Washington once had the reputation of being a weak theater town, but that has changed over the past decade. This is now a prime pre-Broadway tryout spot and a regional theater scene for which no apologies are necessary. Stars such as Thomas Hulce, Stacy Keach and Kelly McGillis make regular appearances at the Shakespeare Theatre at the Lansburgh and the Helen Hayes Awards have become an institution honoring local theater.

The Kennedy Center (202/467-4600), perched along the banks of the Potomac not too far from the Lincoln Memorial, houses many cultural events and programs in its six-theater complex. Plays and comedies are usually performed in the **Eisenhower Theater.** The **National Symphony** performs in **Concert Hall,** the Washington Opera in the **Opera House. The Terrace Theater** is reserved for concerts and plays. Theater groups and dance troupes perform experimental works in the **Theater Lab.** All kinds of movies, from advanced screenings to retrospectives, can be seen at the **American Film Institute Theater** (202/828-4000). Since 1987, the Kennedy Center's **Cabaret Theater** has performed a comedy whodunit called "Shear Madness." This interactive play, set in D.C., lets the audience play armchair detective. The humor is based on local events and people.

The National Theatre (1321 Pennsylvania Ave., N.W.; 202/628-6161), a few blocks from the White House, attracts Broadway previews and touring Broadway hits. The newly-renovated **Warner Theatre** (13th and E Sts., N.W.; 202/783-4000) hosts many musicals and concerts.

Although shows at the National Theatre and Kennedy Center may command the headlines, the irreplaceable theater gems for Washington theatergoers are the Arena and Shakespeare Theaters. Theater in the round is the best-known facet of **The Arena Stage** (6th and Maine, S.W.; 202/488-3300). The Arena has been providing some of the most consistently terrific playgoing in the Capital. Arena's own acting company produces a variety of plays, including classics, modern plays and the occasional musical. The Arena complex has a standard stage, the Kreeger Theatre, and a performance space, the Old Vat Room.

Shakespeare's D.C. home is the **Shakespeare Theatre at the Lansburgh** (450 7th St., N.W.; 202/393-2700). Popularity forced this first-rate theater company to move from its original stage at the Folger Library to its new, larger accommodations two years ago and it has been onward and upward ever since. The new theater holds twice as many people. Each season, the company produces three Shakespearian plays and one penned by someone other than the Bard. If you were to pick only one theater to subscribe to, the Shakespeare is an excellent choice. The quality is superb and the price not astronomical. If the performance is sold out, standing room only tickets are usually available for $10. These tickets go on sale one hour before the performance.

Each year, the **Ford's Theatre** (202/638-2941), best known as the site of President Lincoln's assassination, performs big-name, family-oriented shows and musicals. Ford's Theatre is a national monument and the small Lincoln museum in the basement is worth a trip to Ford's. The historical merit of visiting Ford's Theatre often outweighs the theatrical merit.

Studio Theatre (1333 P St., N.W.; 202/332-3300) offers off-beat comedy and drama on its two small stages. Studio is one of several small theaters in the 14th St. Theater District. This unofficial district is famous for its daring and experimental theater companies. Neighbors of the Studio Theatre, the **Woolly Mammoth** (1401 Church St., N.W.; 202/393-3939) and **The Source Theatre** (1835 14th St., N.W.; 202/462-1073) attract local thespian groups and occasionally produce the works of local playwrights. In Northern Virginia, the **Signature Theatre** (3806 South Four Mile Run Dr.; 703/820-9771) has acquired a terrific reputation for its productions, especially of Stephen Sondheim musicals (this comparatively small company produced the first local staging of Sondheim's offbeat "Assassins.") Ticket prices at all of these theaters are generally pretty low.

The award-winning Grupo de Actores Latino Americanos performs at the **GALA Hispanic Theatre** (1625 Park Rd., N.W.; 202/234-7174). They present three plays a season by Latin American or Spanish authors. One of these productions is performed in both Spanish and English and the others are done in Spanish with simultaneous English translation.

Each summer, Rock Creek Park and the Shakespeare Theatre sponsor a free play at the **Carter-Barron Amphitheater** (16th St. and Colorado Ave., N.W.; 202/426-6837). The production is usually a restaging of one of the Shakespeare Theatre's recently-produced works. During the rest of the summer, the Carter-Barron is home to a series of free concerts and musical recitals from classical to jazz to pop.

If you are looking for discount theater tickets, half-price tickets can be purchased (cash only) the day of the show at **Ticketplace** (12th and F Sts., N.W.; 202/842-5387). To get to Ticketplace, take the Red, Orange or Blue line to Metro Center. Given the high demand, Ticketplace can afford to have limited hours; it is only open Tuesday through Friday from noon to 4:00 p.m. and on Saturdays from 11:00 a.m. to 5:00 p.m. You can also look into standing room tickets or being an usher by checking with the box offices of the individual theaters.

Regular-price tickets can be purchased either at the theater box offices or over the phone through **TicketMaster** (202/432-7328) or **Telecharge** (800/233-3123).

Concerts

To find out about upcoming concerts, listen to your favorite radio station or check the newspapers, especially the *City Paper*. Popular performers, particularly rock groups, play at **RFK Stadium** (202/547-9077), **USAir Arena** (301/350-3400), **George Mason's Patriot Center** (703/993-3033), **Warner Theatre** (202/783-4000) and **Constitution Hall** (202/638-2661).

Smaller concerts play **Lisner Auditorium** at George Washington University (202/994-1500) and the **Bayou** (3135 K St., N.W.; 202/333-2897). The reputation of Alexandria's **Birchmere** (3901 Mount Vernon Ave., Alexandria; 703/549-5919) has been growing even though the space remains small. If you can get in, though, you will enjoy the live music, ranging from folk to country to blues. Calling ahead could get you tickets to see bands play now that will be nationally known later. Tickets range from $6 to $35 and you can call TicketMaster (202/432-SEAT) to order yours. The **Merriweather Post Pavilion** (301/982-1800) in Columbia, Maryland, is similar to Wolf Trap, but is a little wilder because it does not have to get the Park Service's approval for shows.

During the summer, outdoor concerts are held at Wolf Trap's Filene Center, universally known just as **Wolf Trap** (703/255-1860). Wolf Trap generally books classical, folk and country performers, as well as storytellers and comedians. If the weather is good and you are not particular about seating arrangements, buy lawn tickets. You can bring a blanket, some food and wine and have a picnic while you listen to the music. **The Barns of Wolf Trap** (703/938-2404), which sponsors indoor concerts and shows, is their winter solution. The **Carter-Barron Amphitheater** (202/426-6837) also holds outdoor concerts.

During the summer, area monuments, various art galleries and churches host free concerts. The **Smithsonian** (202/357-2700) frequently sponsors classical concerts. Big band aficionados attend performances on the grounds of the Washington Monument. If you have time during the day, the **Corcoran Gallery of Art** (202/638-3211) sponsors free summertime jazz. The **Washington National Cathedral** (202/537-6200) hosts free choral and chamber music concerts. From time to time, they also offer lunchtime concerts.

Jazz

Unfortunately, Washington's jazz scene is not what it was back in the days of Duke Ellington. Today, the jazz scene is off the beaten path, but still alive. One of the most popular clubs attracting top musicians is **Blues Alley** (1073 Wisconsin Ave., N.W.; 202/337-4141). An evening at Blues Alley can be quite expensive; covers range from $13 to $31.50, depending on the show and there is a $7 food and beverage minimum per person. Nearby, **One Step Down** (2517 Pennsylvania Ave., N.W.; 202/331-8863) is slightly less expensive, with a $5 to $12.50 cover and a two-drink minimum. **Takoma Station Tavern** (6914 4th St., N.W.; 202/829-1999) features live jazz nightly and charges no cover, just a two-drink minimum. **The Saloon** in Georgetown (3239 M St., N.W.; 202/338-4900) features local jazz bands seven nights a week. This is probably the most economical choice, since cover charges are only $2 to $3 and food and drink prices are reasonable.

The Best Places to go for Free Movies
BY BILL HENRY

The best is the National Gallery of Art in the new(er) East Wing Building Theater. Aesthetically pleasing and blessed with a large screen and good sound system, the NGA shows art documentaries during the week and feature films on weekends (usually 2:00 p.m. on Saturdays and 6:00 p.m. on Sundays). Some of the recent programs have included a Sergei Eisenstein retrospective, the films of Andrezej Wajda, pre-New Wave French films and a silent series with live orchestra.

The Hirshhorn Museum's auditorium on Thursday and Friday evenings mixes up a great blend of the offbeat, avant-garde and the unnerving by showing a program of movies that few commercial theaters could risk. No matter which week you go, whether it be a feature or documentary, it will always be a challenging piece of work brought to you by someone who genuinely cares about the cinema.

Just across the street at the National Air and Space Museum, you can see science fiction and aviation features projected onto the monster IMAX screen of NASM's Langley Theatre. They have a movie almost every Friday (except during the summer) and you might be able to catch anything from one of the **Star Trek** features to **Twelve O'Clock High**. And you could not ask for a bigger screen or better projection.

What it lacks in size it makes up for in impact and popularity at the appropriately-named Mary Pickford Theater in the Library of Congress' Madison Building. A tiny auditorium with less than 70 seats, the Pickford makes up for its shortcomings with the continent's largest film selection—every film ever submitted to the Library of Congress for registration. They show movies several weeknights and have had some terrific series in recent years including one dedicated to small town America and another looking at the cinema images of Native Americans. You need to make reservations early (202/707-5677), but even if you are shut out, go and wait—there are almost always no-shows.

Bill Henry is the film reviewer for **The Hill Rag** on Capitol Hill. The hardest working movie critic in town, he regularly sees 500 movies each year. He says that video is bad and the best movie he has even seen is Woody Allen's "Crimes and Misdemeanors" with "Citizen Kane" a close second.

Comedy

People are always poking fun at Washington. Who can blame them? Many of the things that go on here are pretty outrageous. A few local comedy clubs and comedy troupes should keep you in good spirits. The newest comedy stop is the local version of the nationally-known **Improv** (1140 Connecticut Ave., N.W.; 202/296-7008). The Improv will get everyone short of a Jerry Seinfeld or a Dennis Miller (who will opt for the Lisner Auditorium or Constitution Hall). But beware, after paying the $10 admission charge, you will be invited to overpay for food and beverages.

The Comedy Cafe (1520 K St., N.W.; 202/638-JOKE) books a mix of national and local talent. Wednesday and Thursday nights are open-mike nights. Watch out! In addition to comedy, there is a strip joint in the basement of this three-story townhouse.

Drawing from local talent, both **Gross National Product** (301/587-4291)and the **Capitol Steps** satirize Washington's politics. Gross National Product performs improv at the **Bayou** (3135 K St., N.W.; 202/333-2897). Tickets are $15 per person. The Capitol Steps, a nationally-known musical parody group made up of current and former Congressional staffers, can be seen at **Chelsea's** (1055 Thomas Jefferson St., N.W.; 202/298-8222) most weekends. Tickets for the show and dinner cost $45 per person. If you opt to eat dinner elsewhere, the show will still cost $30 per person. Although an evening with the Steps is a bit pricy, they are just terrific. For a less expensive dose of the Capitol Steps, watch for one of their frequent specials on PBS, wait for one of their shows on NPR or buy one of their compact discs.

Movies

Washington is a terrific movie town. It is one of the few places where movie theaters survived the video revolution (although in a greatly diminished state). There are a goodly number of first-run houses, a sizable collection of theaters specializing in art house and off-beat product, and an annual local film festival (Filmfest D.C.).

The prize of Washington movie-going is the **American Film Institute Theater** in the Kennedy Center (202/785-4601). Hundreds of movies, new and old, from Hollywood or elsewhere play the AFI annually. The only problem is that you will not have enough time for all the movies you want to see there.

Whenever Washingtonians are polled, the **Uptown Theatre** (3426 Connecticut Ave., N.W.; 202/966-5400) generally gets the most votes as Washington's best movie theater. A remnant of the art deco period, the Uptown has not split its huge screen into three or four TV screens. The theater shows both first-run movies and, occasionally, classics like "Lawrence of Arabia" and "2001: A Space Odyssey."

But the **Avalon** just up the street (5612 Connecticut Ave., N.W.; 202/966-2600) may be even better. Renovated in the mid-'80s with a brand new sound system, the Avalon has a better screen than the Uptown. The Uptown was built for an old curved Cinemascope screen and since curved screens are no longer made, The Uptown has had to replace the original with a series of one-inch strips running floor to ceiling. This can be distracting if you sit in the first few rows. The Avalon shows first-run movies.

The **Cineplex Odeon 4000 Wisconsin Ave. Cinemas** (4000 Wisconsin Ave., N.W.; 202/244-0880) serves as a terrific example of how you can build a modern multiplex with a little pizzazz. They have six screens and show mostly first run commercial movies. Occasionally, a little art house fare sneaks in. The seats are super-comfy and the presentation quality markedly superior.

The **AMC Union Station** (50 Massachusetts Ave., N.E.; 703/998-4AMC) is the only movie house in the northeast quadrant of the city. When the idea was first floated to have a movie theater in the basement of the renovated train station, it was met with some skepticism. Time has proven the naysayers wrong. Nine spacious and popular theaters now cater to an under-served part of the city. Each theater is named (rather than numbered) after a famous movie house from Washington cinema history.

Both the **Arlington Cinema 'n Drafthouse** (2903 Columbia Pike; 703/486-2345) and the **Bethesda Theatre Cafe** (7719 Wisconsin Ave.; 301/656-3337) serve beer, wine and munchies during shows. Both show second-run movies and admission costs around $4 on the weekends and $3 during the week. Radio station DC 101 sponsors dollar nights on Monday at each. On Sundays during the fall, Redskins games take over the screen and admission is free. Bring an ID; they card.

The Key (1222 Wisconsin Ave., N.W.; 202/333-5100) and **The Biograph** (2819 M St., N.W.; 202/333-2696) in Georgetown show independent and foreign films. Both are ideal places to brush up on your French, Spanish or German. The Biograph plays more offbeat stuff (and thanks to a new lease should continue playing into the next century), while the Key plays more mainstream art house fare. Those who really love their serious cinema should look into the Key's Sunday Cinema Club. Members see new, unreleased (mostly foreign) movies on Sunday mornings with free coffee during the showing and a discussion session following.

The **Cineplex Odeon Jenifer** (5252 Wisconsin Ave., N.W.; 202/244-5703) still shows movies for just $1.25. The Jenifer is a great place to catch a movie that you may have missed when it first came out. You can take the Red line to Friendship Heights; the theater is steps from the Jenifer Street exit. Other than the Jenifer, the other second-run houses are in the suburbs.

Special Events and Festivals

■ Martin Luther King Jr.'s Birthday
The National Park Service sponsors an annual ceremony in honor of Dr. Martin Luther King at the Lincoln Memorial, the site of his 1963 "I Have A Dream" speech.

■ Chinese New Year Parade
Celebrate the Chinese New Year in Chinatown by watching the fireworks and the elaborately-costumed parade participants.

■ Smithsonian Kite Festival
Bring your kite to the west side of the Washington Monument and fly it with hundreds of others.

■ Cherry Blossom Festival
A week-long event to celebrate this rite of spring in Washington. Many of the events are geared towards tourists, and you might not want to fight the crowds to see them, but try to take a walk around the Tidal Basin to see the cherry trees in bloom. The cherry blossoms rarely coincide with the festival itself. Depending on the weather, the blossoms peak between mid-March and mid-April.

■ Duke Ellington Birthday Celebration
Celebrate the music of this D.C.-born jazz star with a concert at Freedom Plaza (13th St. and Pennsylvania Ave., N.W.).

■ Filmfest DC
It is the District's version of Cannes. Over fifty-five international and American independent films are shown in movie theaters all over town. Watch *The Washington Post* or the *City Paper* for information.

■ Malcolm X Day
A day to honor Malcolm X in Anacostia Park, along the Anacostia River in Southeast. Food, speakers, music and exhibits.

■ Gay Pride Day
A march through Downtown to promote gay rights and awareness. The march begins at 16th and W Sts., N.W., and ends at N and 24th Sts., N.W.

■ Festival of American Folklife
At this annual festival, the Smithsonian presents a slice of American folklife. The festival usually lasts two weeks (last week in June through the first week in July) and is held on the Mall in front of the Museums of Natural History and American History.

■ Fourth of July
A day full of Washington's best freebies. During the day, listen to a dramatic reading of the Declaration of Independence and watch the Fourth of July parade down Constitution Ave. The National Symphony Orchestra performs on the West Lawn of the Capitol Building at around 8:00 p.m. The main event occurs afterwards—a tremendous fireworks display on the Mall. If you intend to watch the fireworks from the Mall itself, plan on going early in the day to stake out a spot. Virginians congregate at the Iwo Jima Memorial for a superb view of the fireworks across the river. Many prefer to avoid the crowds and watch from the roofs of their apartment or office buildings.

■ Adams Morgan Day
A street festival along 18th St., N.W., (above Florida Ave.) on the second Sunday in September that celebrates the multi-ethnic flavor of this neighborhood.

■ Halloween
Georgetown is the place to be for Halloween if you like to mingle in a huge, drunken mob. Watch this gentrified neighborhood go crazy. Wisconsin Ave. and M St. are closed off to vehicular traffic as thousands of costumed pedestrians descend upon an eight-block area. This event is not for the faint of heart, but can be lots of fun.

■ National Christmas Tree Lighting
Join the President and a few thousand tourists for this annual ritual on the Ellipse, south of the White House.

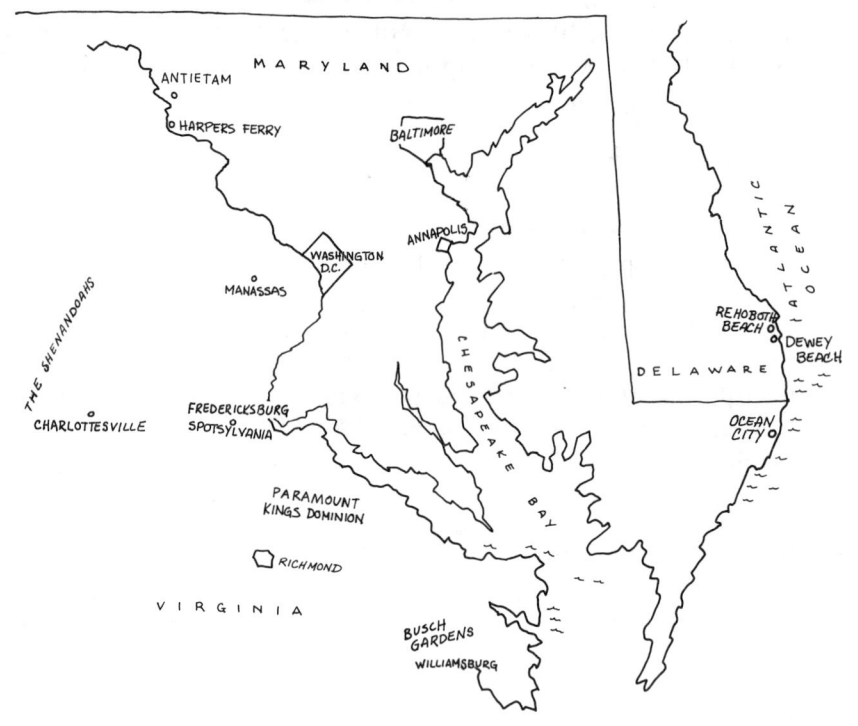

Chapter 7

Washington Weekends

Washington is a great place, with a tremendous amount going on both within the Beltway and closeby, but it takes an affirmative effort to take advantage of it.

Besides word of mouth, one of the best ways to learn about weekend goings-on is to check the Weekend section of *The Washington Post* (Friday edition). The Weekend section details special events, local exhibits, movie and theater listings and sports events. Washington's *City Paper* is also an excellent resource. In addition to its regular column, "City Lights," which highlights the week's best events, the *City Paper* contains numerous advertisements to help you find some of the area's best nightlife.

☐ Entertaining Visitors

You would be surprised to find out how many Washingtonians have never been to the top of the Washington Monument or taken a cruise on the Potomac. "It is just for tourists!" claims one Hill staffer, expressing a wide-felt local attitude. Just for tourists, you say? You would be surprised at what you are missing. If you need an excuse, wait for guests or family to arrive for a visit, but you can also take a break from your routine anytime to see some of the tourist sights. You will get a whole new perspective on the city.

The Weekend Tourist

For a quick overview of Washington, start at the Mall. This sweeping avenue of gardens, museums and revered monuments extends from the **Lincoln Memorial** to the **U.S. Capitol.** Some of the Smithsonian's best museums sit here, as well as the beautiful Botanic Gardens. The new **Holocaust Memorial Museum** is not far away on 14th St., S.W., near the river.

The Lincoln Memorial, Washington Monument and the Capitol are all open on the weekends. If you visit the **Washington Monument,** it is well worth it to wait in line and take the elevator to the top for a panoramic view of the city. Favorite museums at the **Smithsonian** include the **Air and Space Museum,** the **Museum of Natural His-**

tory and the **American History Museum.** Air and Space highlights include shows at the Planetarium and the IMAX theater. A word of warning, a good lunch can be hard to find in the Smithsonian cafeterias. The museum is free, so it is easy to leave at lunch time and head for more interesting fare on the Hill past the Capitol Building.

The **East and West Buildings of the National Gallery of Art** face each other at the corner of Constitution Ave. and 4th St., N.W. The West Building houses works from the thirteenth to the early twentieth century, including paintings by Raphael, Rembrandt and Monet. Across the street, I.M. Pei's East Building displays modern art and the museum's special exhibits. An underground tunnel allows you to move easily between the East and West Buildings. From the National Gallery you can walk across the Mall to the exotic atrium at the **Botanic Gardens.**

The **National Archives** is further down Constitution Ave. at 8th St., N.W. There you can see the original Declaration of Independence, the U.S. Constitution and the Bill of Rights. The **National Museum of American Art** and **National Portrait Gallery** are also close by on 8th St. between G and F.

During the spring and summer months, you will share the Mall with thousands of visitors. To avoid the crowds, you may want to follow a less-traveled path. You can walk up to the **Capitol Hill** area and tour the **Library of Congress,** the **Folger Shakespeare Library** and the **Supreme Court** (only open on weekdays). Round out the day with a trip to **Eastern Market,** Washington's oldest market, at the corner of 7th and C Streets, S.E. Eastern Market is particularly fun on weekends, with local artists plying their wares alongside the meat, cheese, fruit and vegetable vendors. Many people on the Hill stroll around Eastern Market on the weekends to pick up food or to have a meal at the Market Lunch. On your way there, you may want to stop at any hotel and pick up *Shaw's Guide to Capitol Hill.* This free pocket guide has an excellent map of the neighborhood.

Further off the tourist track, **Dupont Circle** houses dozens of small art galleries and interesting museums. The Dupont Circle-Kalorama Museum walk, an informal self-guided tour around the area stops at the **Phillips Collection,** the **Textile Museum,** the **Woodrow Wilson House,** the **Historical Society of Washington, D.C.,** the **Anderson House** and the **Fondo del Sol Visual Arts Center.** A brochure mapping out this tour can be obtained at any of these museums. Several of the museums rely on private donations and ask for contributions at the door.

Georgetown's **Dumbarton Oaks,** at 32nd and R Sts., N.W., maintains spectacular public gardens. Adjacent to the gardens, the Dumbarton Oaks Museum houses somewhat incongruously one of the country's best pre-Columbian and Byzantine collections. If your guest is someone special, you might want to stroll down nearby **Lover's Lane** (daylight hours only).

The **National Cathedral** awaits if you continue up Wisconsin Ave. about a mile from Georgetown. The Cathedral dominates the skyline and was finally completed in 1990 after almost eighty years construction. If you go, take time to wander through the gardens behind the Cathedral and maybe over to St. Albans School next door, where Vice President Gore received his high school education.

Another major facet of Washington's tourist attraction is its African-American heritage. **The Frederick Douglass National Historic Site** (1411 W St., S.E.) on Cedar Hill was the last residence of the black statesman and abolitionist. The **Anacostia Museum** (1901 Fort Place, S.E.) focuses on African-American art, culture and history.

Once you venture outside the District, more sites await nearby. **Arlington National Cemetery** rests silently across the Potomac from the Lincoln Memorial. Originally Robert E. Lee's home, it was turned into a cemetery for fallen Union soldiers and now is the last resting place for casualties of war, veterans and their spouses. You can wander the grounds and watch the changing of the guard as they keep vigil over the Tomb of the Unknowns. The eternal flame burns in remembrance of President Kennedy who is buried there. His brother Robert rests nearby beneath a simple white cross against a gentle-sloping, grass-covered hill.

Some visitors prefer a quick motorized preview on a red, white and blue **Tourmobile** (202/554-7950). The Tourmobile cruises through Washington and stops at its most popular sights: the White House, the Capitol, the Smithsonian, the Bureau of Engraving and Printing, Jefferson Memorial, Lincoln Memorial, Arlington Cemetery and the Kennedy Center. Tours of Washington and Arlington Cemetery are $8.50 per person.

And finally, if you are looking to take a cruise on the Potomac, there are several companies in the area that will transport you past the monuments and other shoreline attractions in addition to providing dinner and dancing.

The Dandy (703/683-6090 information, 703/683-8076 reservations) sails from Prince St. in Old Town Alexandria for a three-hour dinner cruise past the monuments, the Kennedy Center and Georgetown. Prices range from $47 to $55 and the boat departs at 7:00 p.m. You can float away on a luncheon cruise as well, costing around $30 and departing between 11:30 a.m. and 12:30 p.m.

For a trip with an historical twist, take the **Spirit of Mount Vernon** to George Washington's Mt. Vernon estate. The captain will point out landmarks along the way and you will have two hours to explore the mansion and its gardens before returning to Washington. The sister ship **Spirit of Washington** sails down the Potomac to Alexandria past the monuments and Old Town while live bands play music from the Forties to the Nineties or the staff performs in a Caberet-style show. Both ships are part of the Potomac Spirit fleet (202/554-1542 recorded information; 202/554-8000 reservations) and depart from Pier 4 at 6th and Water Sts., S.W. Cruises aboard the Spirit of Mt. Vernon cost $20 and run daily at 9:00 a.m. and 2:00 p.m. The Spirit of Washington is more expensive, ranging from $25 for a luncheon cruise to $45 dollars for an evening sail. It departs daily at 11:30 a.m. and 6:30 p.m.

The **Admiral Tilp** takes you on a narrated sight-seeing cruise along Old Town's Waterfront. The Admiral Tilp has several cruises that sail from behind the Torpedo Factory Arts Center, usually departing every hour on the hour. Reservations are recommended for the short trips, which cost $6 for adults. Call the recording at 703/548-9000 for more information.

Cruise times for all of these ships vary depending upon the time of year and the day of the week. You should probably call ahead to check specific departures for the cruise you want to take.

Exploring Beyond the Beltway

Below, you will find some basic information about day and weekend trips in the Mid-Atlantic area. For more detailed information, you may want to purchase a guidebook for a particular area or get in touch with local chambers of commerce or visitors' centers.

The Beach

The Maryland and Virginia beaches are only several hours from the city and are a haven for heat-weary D.C. residents every summer.

Renting beach houses along the coast is a popular summer tradition in Washington. Often couples or groups of friends will rent a house for the summer. Call the local chambers of commerce or visitors'

Chapter Seven | Washington Weekends

A Native's Favorite Tourist Attractions
BY DEREK MCGINTY, HOST/EXECUTIVE PRODUCER THE DEREK MCGINTY SHOW ON WAMU 88.5 FM

The Washington Monument
I grew up here, but I never get tired of the view from what is by law the tallest structure in town. For the more adventurous (and well-conditioned), I believe they will still let you walk down the stairs. Summer nights are the best.

The Vietnam Veterans Memorial (a.k.a. The Wall)
This list of all of the American soldiers killed in the Vietnam War remains the most moving of the local monuments. Especially since family members and friends still leave mementos such as cans of beer, flags and flowers. In memory of... it becomes positively eerie if visited at night.

The Smithsonian Air and Space Museum
Not only is the history of space exploration featured in this magnificent modern building, but there is a specially designed movie theater showing incredible flicks such as the now famous "To Fly." Don't even think about going on weekends, though, it's too crowded.

The New Warner Theatre
An expensive facelift has made this grand old lady the best place in town to hear a musical performance. It only holds two to three thousand people... and as far as I can see, there is not a bad seat in the house and the acoustics are phenomenal. Pray that your favorite group is booked there and not at the cavernous Constitution Hall.

Tysons Corner Mall II: The Galleria
Yeah, I know its just a shopping mall, but its the best upscale mall in the area, featuring Saks Fifth Avenue and Macy's, not to mention a huge number of small specialty shops and restaurants. Fun even to visit if you can't afford to buy much. A close second is the Pentagon City Mall. Great stores and its right on the Metro at the stop of the same name.

The National Zoo
This one is for the kids. A lot of walking, some pretty good animals and although it does not measure up to its bigger counterparts in cities like San Diego, it also lacks the admission fee charged by those fancier animal housing establishments.

centers and ask for information on rentals. You can also check the classified section of *The Washington Post* for leads on seasonal rentals.

If you want to rent a group beach house and find yourself without interested friends, then Beach Night at Rumors will be a good place to start. Each spring, the restaurant Rumors and a publication called *The Beach House Directory* sponsor a beach night once a week to bring prospective renters and rentees together. People who want to rent a beach house or who are looking for people to share a place get one color name tag. People with places to rent wear a different color. Both groups mingle, drink and strike deals. As the manager put it, Beach Night is "an excuse to meet a lot of people, get a little buzzed and perhaps get a beach house for the summer." If you rent a beach house, you will be listed in *The Beach House Directory* (a who's who of the Dewey, Rehobeth, Bethany and Lewes Beaches). To find out more about the directory and to check the time and location of Beach Night, you should call 202/362-8227.

■ Ocean City, Maryland

Distance 153 miles

Visitors' Center 800/62-OCEAN

Directions Take Route 50 East all the way into Ocean City.

Ocean City's summer weekend population can swell to as much as 200,000 as Washingtonians seek relief from the humidity. Like most beach resorts, Ocean City offers plenty of recreational choices: amusement parks, fishing, sailing, miniature golf and a few movie theaters.

The Coastal Highway (Route 1), Ocean City's main thoroughfare, houses a multitude of hotel rooms and condo units. The strip does not lack restaurants either; you can choose from over 160 of them. If you plan to visit during the summer months (May to mid-September), your best bet is to make your reservations early and stay for the entire weekend. Many hotels require a minimum stay of two to three nights during the peak season.

Ocean City ends its summer with SunFest, an annual bash held the third weekend after Labor Day. The city sets up four large circus tents filled with food vendors, bands, entertainers and arts and crafts booths.

Many area high school students participate in "Beach Week" at Ocean City after graduation. Unless you are up to dealing with thousands of newly-graduated high school seniors, it is best to avoid Ocean City during the first two weeks of June.

■ Rehoboth Beach/Dewey Beach, Delaware
Distance   125 miles
Chamber of Commerce   800/441-1329
Directions   Take Route 50 East to Route 404 through Delaware to Route 1.

Rehoboth is not nearly the size of Ocean City, but it offers many of the same activities on a smaller scale. This beach resort attracts mostly families and couples. Like Ocean City, the restaurants along Rehoboth's boardwalk keep most beach-goers happy, both in terms of price and variety.

Since Rehoboth is only about a two-and-a-half-hour drive from the District, adventurous Washingtonians sometimes pack a round trip into a one-day excursion. If you opt to do this, you should leave early (preferably before dawn) to avoid the summer-long traffic jam at the Bay Bridge. If you do plan to stay for just the afternoon, you should bring plenty of quarters. Costly parking meters must be fed every two hours.

Just south of Rehoboth is the even smaller community of Dewey Beach. Dewey Beach is about a ten-minute drive from downtown Rehoboth and is only two blocks wide. Many visitors choose to rent a cottage in Dewey (since it tends to be much quieter than Rehoboth) and migrate to the Rehoboth boardwalk and beach during the day.

> **Bed & Breakfasts**
>
> Bed & Breakfasts (B&Bs) offer weekend escapes from $60 to $150 (or more) per night in the myriad small towns and villages within a few hours from the District. To locate potential B&Bs, you may want to consult a guidebook. *America's Wonderful Little Hotels and Inns* (St. Martin's Press) is one of the best I have seen. This guide reports guests' impressions of local B&Bs, as well as prices, phone numbers and directions. *The Washington Post* runs several pages of B&B advertisements in the back of its Sunday Magazine. The Virginia Office of Tourism (202/659-5523) can provide information on B&Bs in Virginia and even book your rooms. If you are planning a trip in the fall when the foliage is changing, during apple picking season or over a holiday weekend, you should make your reservations a few weeks in advance.

Annapolis

Distance   30 miles

Annapolis & Anne Arundel County Visitors' Bureau
410/280-0445

Directions from D.C.   Follow U.S. 50 East to Route 70 (Rowe Blvd.) and follow signs to Annapolis.

Even though Annapolis is the capital of Maryland, it remains a quaint, touristy town. Maryland's capitol building, the circular, red-brick **State House** (410/974-3400) gives free tours at designated times. This is a good place to start if you are interested in learning about the city's past. It is the oldest state house in continuous legislative use in the country. Students of history will be amazed and appalled by the prominent statue of Chief Justice Roger Taney on the State House grounds.

The **U.S. Naval Academy** (410/263-6933) is also in Annapolis. The Naval Academy Guide Service (410/267-3363) offers walking tours of the Academy. Visit the Academy Visitors' Center at Ricketts Hall, Gate 1, for tour information. Otherwise, just wander past the buildings and along the waterfront on your own.

Students at **St. John's College** (410/263-2371) study the "Great Books" of Aristotle, Euclid and Thucydides. In front of McDowell Hall stands The Liberty Tree, a four-hundred-year-old tulip tree. The Sons of Liberty met beneath its branches in the days leading up to the Revolutionary War.

If you saw the television mini-series or read the book *Roots*, then you should try to visit the Kunta Kinte Plaque. The plaque is located at the head of the city dock and commemorates the 1767 arrival of Alex Haley's famous ancestor.

If shopping is your passion, you can walk along the streets and browse in some of Annapolis' upscale stores. Clothes stores compete with antique shops for your business, with several kitschy tourist shops thrown in. There are few more relaxing pastimes than spending a lazy spring or summer afternoon feasting on crab cakes and beer in one of the restaurants around the main square. To pursue this pleasure, you can stop by the **Old Towne Restaurant** (105 Main St.; 410/268-8703) or **Buddy's Crabs & Ribs** (100 Main St.; 410/626-1100). For a big date or some other special occasion, cap off your visit with dinner at the **Treaty of Paris** (16 Church Circle; 410/263-2641), one of Annapolis' finest restaurants. Dinner for two can easily cost around $80.

Baltimore

Distance 45 miles

Visitors' Center 410/837-4636 or 800/282-6632

Directions from D.C. Take the Beltway to I-95 North; to get to the Inner Harbor, just follow the signs. On weekdays, you can take the MARC commuter train from Union Station to either Camden or Pennsylvania Station in Baltimore. For more information, call 800/325-RAIL. Amtrak (800/USA-RAIL) will also take you from Union Station to Baltimore's Pennsylvania Station.

Baltimore is probably best known to District residents as the home of Washington's adopted baseball team, the Orioles, and the setting of Barry Levinson's film, "Diner". Located only 45 miles north of the District, Baltimore offers many surprises to the visitor, combining its heritage as a seaport with the bustle of a city revitalized in the 1980's.

The **Inner Harbor** is the city's visitor mecca. A brick walkway six blocks long winds along the waterfront past many of Baltimore's tourist attractions, including **Harborplace,** the **National Aquarium,** the frigate *Constellation,* the **Maryland Science Center** and the **Maritime Museum.**

Most of the food and shopping at the Inner Harbor can be found at **Harborplace** (Pratt and Light Sts.; 410/332-4191) and **The Gallery** (200 East Pratt St.). If you have been to Quincy Market in Boston, South St. Seaport in New York City or Pier 39 in San Francisco, the set-up will probably look familiar. All three Inner Harbor buildings are packed with food kiosks, cafes and touristy specialty stores. In the summer, musicians, jugglers and magicians often stroll around the harbor's promenade to entertain visitors.

The **Maryland Science Center** (601 Light St.; 410/685-5225) is an exciting museum if you enjoy hands-on or participatory exhibits. The Science Center also boasts a planetarium and five-story IMAX theater. Adult admission is $8.50 and child admission is $6.50.

The modernist, triangular-shaped **National Aquarium** (Pier 3/Pratt St.; 410/576-3800) houses over 5,000 aquatic animals and a tropical rain forest exhibit. The National Aquarium is one of Baltimore's main tourist attractions. On weekends, the ticket line can take over an hour, so unless you plan to get there early, you may want to consider ordering tickets in advance. Either way, be prepared for sticker shock. The Aquarium is extremely expensive: $11.50 for adults and $7.50 for children.

Next to the Aquarium, the **Baltimore Maritime Museum** (410/396-3854), offers a self-guided tour of the *U.S.S. Torsk* submarine, noted for sinking the last warship in World War II, and the lightship *Chesapeake*, which once served as a floating lighthouse. Another nautical attraction is the frigate *Constellation*. Launched from Baltimore Harbor in 1797, the *Constellation* was the U.S. Navy's first commissioned ship.

If you are even remotely a baseball fan, you will by now be familiar with one of the game's gems, **Oriole Park at Camden Yards** (410/685-9800). A short stroll from the Inner Harbor and just off I-95 coming up from Washington, this park's convenience is only surpassed by its marvelous ambiance. You do not need to be a fan of the Orioles, or even of baseball, to have a great time there. If you have the patience to wait in the long lines you can get some of Boog Powell's barbecue in the walkway beyond right field.

Sports fans can take advantage of the sports bar, **Balls** (200 West Pratt St.; 410/659-5844) right across the street from Camden Yards. Baseball fans might be interested in stopping by the **Babe Ruth Birthplace and Baltimore Orioles Museum** (410/727-1539) at 216 Emory St. on the way to the ballgame.

If you are looking for restaurants with a little more atmosphere and authenticity than the national chains in Inner Harbor, venture into nearby **Little Italy.** Located five blocks from the Inner Harbor, this neighborhood has over a dozen restaurants, ranging from inexpensive pizza parlors to elegant, somewhat pricy Italian restaurants. President Carter's favorite was **Chiapparelli's** (237 South High St.; 410/837-0309). Another highly recommended restaurant, though it does not boast the presidential seal of approval, is **Sabatino's** (901 Fawn St.; 410/727-9414).

The World Trade Center (401 East Pratt St.; 410/837-4515) offers a terrific view of the harbor and most of Baltimore from its 27th floor (dubbed "The Top of the World"). For a different view of the harbor, *The City Clipper,* a replica of an 1854 topsail schooner, offers early evening and midnight cruises.

Washingtonians who have been to Baltimore often tend to skip the touristy atmosphere of the Inner Harbor and head straight for one of Baltimore's historic districts. **Fells Point's** 200 years of maritime history is visible in every tavern, antique store, restaurant and home. The city has been renovating the area, so some stores and restaurants have yet to reopen. The best taverns and restaurants are often the hardest to find. You will have to look hard for **The John**

Steven at 1800 Thames St. (410/327-5561). This pub offers little to look at on the outside, but serves some of Baltimore's best seafood inside. **Bertha's** (410/327-5795), at 734 South Broadway, is a favorite yuppie watering hole where area residents gather to eat mussels and take in some jazz.

While sailors and shipbuilders roamed Fells Point in the nineteenth century, merchants and shoemakers occupied **Federal Hill**. This historic neighborhood is only a five-minute walk south down Light St. from the Inner Harbor. Cannons were placed on top of Federal Hill during the Civil War to protect the harbor and an observation tower was built to herald arriving ships. Today, the park offers a good view of the harbor and a quiet place to picnic. Dozens of family-owned stalls, some handed down for generations, ply their trade at Federal Hill's Cross St. Market. Each stall features something different: seafood, cheese, bread, barbecue, cookies and pastries.

Baltimore is also home to the first architectural monument honoring George Washington. This 178-foot obelisk stands on the 700 block of North Charles St. at Mount Vernon Place. Its architect, Robert Mills, later designed the more famous Washington Monument.

Another notable Baltimore sight is **Fort McHenry** (East Fort Ave.; 410/962-4299), where America's successful defense against the British in 1814 inspired Francis Scott Key to write "The Star Spangled Banner." You can stroll around the grounds for free but must pay $2 for adult admission to the Fort.

Once you have seen the Smithsonian, it is hard to compare other art galleries and museums. Still, **Baltimore's Art District** offers visitors plenty to see plus an added attraction: no crowds. The Art District is located on Charles St., about three-quarters of a mile from the harbor. Among more than a dozen museums and galleries you will find Baltimore's gem, the **Walters Art Gallery** (600 North Charles St.; 410/547-9000). This museum houses one of the largest private collections in the world spanning 5,000 years of artistic endeavor. The museum is open from 11:00 a.m. to 5:00 p.m. on Tuesdays through Sundays and adult admission is $4. Art aficionados will also not want to miss the **Baltimore Museum of Art** (410/396-7101), which features a collection of French Impressionist paintings and a sculpture garden. The museum is located just off North Charles St. on Art Museum Drive. Most of these museums and galleries are free to the public. A few do charge nominal admittance fees.

Charlottesville

Distance 110 miles
Chamber of Commerce 804/295-3141
Directions I-66 West to Route 29 South all the way to Charlottesville.

This is Thomas Jefferson's city. Jefferson's home, **Monticello,** (804/295-8181) reflects his many interests and hobbies. You will quickly learn of Jefferson's wide-ranging interests, horticultural pursuits and quirks as you wander through his house and gardens. The estate sits on a mountain top overlooking the city. Admission to Monticello is $8 and includes a guided tour. From Monticello, you can see parts of "Mr. Jefferson's University," otherwise known as **The University of Virginia** (804/924-7969) or UVA. Jefferson founded the university, which was chartered in 1819. The grounds of the campus consist mostly of neo-classical buildings, white porticos and carefully manicured grounds. The Lawn, the focal point of the University, is listed (at least by UVA grads) among the greatest architectural sites in the world. The school boasts a strong scholastic reputation as well as fine athletic teams, particularly in women's basketball, men's soccer and football.

Charlottesville was also home to James Monroe. Monroe's estate, **Ash Lawn** (804/293-9539), famous for its boxwood gardens and strolling peacocks, has the atmosphere of an early nineteenth-century working plantation. Jefferson personally selected the site for Monroe's house and, on a clear day, you can see Monticello from the front porch of Ash Lawn. Admission for adults is $6.

If you decide to visit either Ash Lawn or Monticello, you will probably pass by **The Historic Michie Tavern** (804/977-1234). It is on Route 53 about half a mile from Monticello. The tavern opened in 1784 and still offers native Virginia wine and fine southern cooking.

Charlottesville's Historic District is a favorite of students and tourists. By no means expansive, the downtown mall makes for a nice late afternoon stroll. You probably will not want to spend more than a couple of hours here. Still, the mall is the highlight of the Historic District and is home to antique stores, small shops, art galleries and a few good restaurants. The **Old Historic Hardware Store** (804/977-1518) is an interesting place to dine. If you go there, be sure to try the challenge of drinking one of their meter beers. **The Court Square Tavern** (804/296-6111) offers more than 100 imported beers and a decent Shepherd's Pie.

Central Virginia hosts dozens of festivals and annual celebrations, but the **Foxfield Steeplechase** is Charlottesville's pride and joy. Virginians come from all over each spring and fall.

The Shenandoahs

    Distance   75 miles
    Shenandoah National Park   703/999-2229
    Directions   Take Route 66 West to U.S. 340. Follow signs to the park.

I-66 heads straight west through Virginia's countryside to the Blue Ridge Mountains. In the fall, people love to drive along Skyline Drive in Shenandoah National Park. Skyline Drive offers breathtaking, panoramic views of the Piedmont and Shenandoah Valleys and the mountains beyond. Recreational activities at Shenandoah National Park include camping, hiking and fishing. *The Guide to Skyline Drive* ($4.50) contains information about park accommodations and activities. If you stop in Front Royal, you can replenish yourself with a great meal at **Dean's Steakhouse** (708 South Royal Ave.; 703/635-1780). Dean's serves steak they way it should be served: lots of it with little fuss and a big baked potato. The warm pecan pie makes for an excellent dessert.

    In the fall as the leaves are changing, you can also take part in Virginia's apple-picking season. You can either pick your own at various orchards or stop by one of the numerous roadside stands.

Williamsburg

    Distance   150 miles
    Visitors' Center   800/HIS-TORY
    Directions   Take I-95 South to I-64 East.

Williamsburg, originally the capital of Virginia, was a training ground for the men who led America to independence. In this small city, George Washington, Thomas Jefferson, Patrick Henry and George Mason helped frame the structure of America's government. Here, the House of Burgesses adopted Virginia's Resolution for Independence in May 1776, which led to the adoption of the Declaration of Independence the following July in Philadelphia.

    It is easy to picture these events in **Colonial Williamsburg;** life goes on much as it would have nearly 200 years ago. Thanks to generous donations from the late John Rockefeller, Jr., most of the original town was completely restored in the late 1920's and early 1930's.

Along its streets you will find all of the makings of a colonial town: houses, shops, taverns, gardens and even a church. Costumed actors give the town its human dimension as they recreate details of daily eighteenth-century life. In the historic district, **King's Arms** comes highly recommended for either lunch or dinner. And for fun, eighteenth-century style, stop by **Chowning's Tavern** (804/229-2141) where you can drink ale, eat peanuts and play games from the era including, the Most Wonderful Game of Goose and the Game of Life.

To get the most out of this excursion, you should plan on staying two or three days. A Patriot Pass ($29; $17.50 for children) allows access to Williamsburg for up to a year. During the summer and the Christmas season you should call ahead for reservations.

The **College of William and Mary,** the second-oldest college in the United States, has been an integral part of Williamsburg since 1693. The Sir Christopher Wren Building houses the oldest classrooms in the country.

Civil War History

Many famous Civil War battle sites, such as **Antietam, Manassas** (Bull Run to Northerners), **Fredericksburg** and **Spotsylvania,** are within an hour's drive or so of the District. The National Park Service provides excellent guided tours of each site as well as detailed maps for walking tours on your own. These battlefields make for great day trips, especially since most of them are surrounded now by quaint towns, many with antique shops cheaper than anything you could find inside the Beltway. Manassas is an exception, since the area around it has succumbed to fast food restaurants and auto dealers.

In West Virginia, just a little over an hour from here, you can visit **Harpers Ferry** (304/535-6298), the site of John Brown's famous raid. Harpers Ferry perches above the confluence of the Potomac and Shenandoah Rivers where three states meet—Maryland, Virginia and West Virginia. The town remained a strategic location throughout most of the Civil War. Today, Harpers Ferry has been converted into a museum town where you can stroll from building to building. Many are just as they would have appeared in 1859. There are few better experiences than walking along the Shenandoah River nearby. To get to Harpers Ferry, take I-270 North to Route 340 West.

Gettysburg (717/334-6274) is approximately 78 miles north of the District; take 270 North to 15 North. Visitors can trace the three-day battle with an organized tour group or through a number of walking tours. While you are there, be sure to see the Cyclorama exhibit. This ten-minute film shown inside a circular auditorium depicts Pickett's charge with a sound and light program.

If you are up to reliving history, a number of local groups regularly recreate Civil War battles, usually on battle anniversary dates. Re-enactments are taken seriously in these parts, so if you are interested, be prepared to commit many weekends and a fair amount of money to experience the elements and the food as did the soldiers of the day. For information about re-enactments, you can consult *The Washington Post* Weekend Section or write to Civil War News, P.O. Box C, Arlington, MA 02174. Civil War News publishes a monthly newsletter that features schedules of re-enactments.

Amusement Parks

Three large amusement parks entice thrill-seeking Washingtonians. **Paramount Kings Dominion** (804/876-5000), just 75 miles south of D.C., offers the shortest trip. Kings Dominion boasts five theme areas (similar to the Disney parks) and the infamous Anaconda roller-coaster, which curves snakelike through six loops and an underwater tunnel. Admission is $26.95 for adults and $18.95 for children aged three to six. Take I-95 South to Doswell, Exit 98.

Chocoholics will feel like they have reached heaven visiting **Hershey Park** (800/HER-SHEY) in Hershey, Pennsylvania. Besides its 50 rides, Hershey Park also offers a narrated tour through the chocolate-making process. This was somewhat disappointing, since you get nowhere near the chocolate factory to see the real thing. There is, however, a gift shop the size of a warehouse devoted entirely to chocolate at the end of the tour. Admission to the tour is free. Adult admission to Hershey Park costs $23.95. Admission is $14.95 for children three to eight years old. Hershey Park is about 150 miles north of the District. Take I-95 North to 695 (the Baltimore Beltway). Follow 695 West to 83 North. Take 83 to 322 (Harrisburg) and follow this until you see the exit for Hershey Park Drive.

Finally, you can take a step back in European history at **Busch Gardens, The Old Country** (800/772-8886), about 165 miles south of the District in Williamsburg, Virginia. In addition to nine re-created hamlets that portray life in Old World Europe, the park offers many other attractions, including several roller coasters, such as The Loch Ness Monster and Big Bad Wolf. Adult admission costs $27.95 and children aged three through six pay $21.50. Take I-95 South to I-64 all the way to Williamsburg. Follow signs to Busch Gardens, The Old Country.

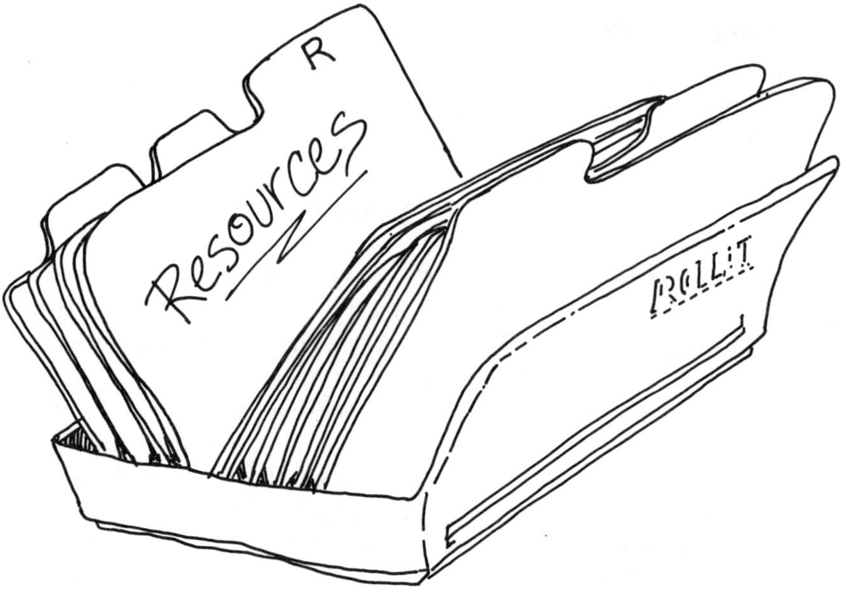
R
Resources
ROLLIT

Chapter 8

Resources

This chapter provides a quick reference for useful phone numbers and important practical information.

■ AAA Potomac   703/222-6000

AAA Potomac comes in handy not only when your car breaks down, but also when you need maps or triptiks.

■ AIDS Hotline   202/332-AIDS
    HIV Testing   202/332-3926

Provides information about confidential HIV testing locations throughout the metropolitan area.

■ Alexandria - City Government   703/838-4000

■ American Association of   202/434-2277
    Retired Persons (AARP)

Provides helpful public information on insurance, consumer fraud and travel.

■ Area Codes

Although Washington (202), Northern Virginia (703) and neighboring parts of Maryland (301) have different area codes, all calls within a thirty-mile radius of the Washington Monument are local. You do not have to dial "1" but you have to use the area code. Calls to Baltimore (410) and Richmond (804) will be billed as long-distance calls.

■ Arlington County - Government   703/358-3000

■ Art Galleries

    Ansel Adams Collection   202/833-2300
    Arthur Sackler Gallery   202/357-4880
    Corcoran Gallery of Art   202/638-3211
    Freer Gallery   202/357-1300

Holography Collection	202/667-6322
National Gallery of Art	202/737-4215
National Museum of African Art	202/357-4600
Renwick Gallery	202/357-2700
Torpedo Factory Art Center	703/838-4565

■ Auto Registration

For $40 the **United States Vehicle Registration Service** (202/342-2558) will obtain a title, registration and parking permit for your car in the District, Maryland or Virginia. Double the amount and you can get your car inspected too.

■ Auto Repair

Washington

Distad's Amoco 823 Pennsylvania Ave., S.E.	202/543-0200
Spring Valley Exxon 4866 Massachusetts Ave., N.W.	202/364-6370

Maryland

Auto Centro Foreign Car Repair 7406 Westmore Rd., Rockville	301/340-2444
Brittain's Auto 14630 Southlawn Lane, Rockville	301/340-0116
Burnt Mills Exxon 10711 Columbia Pike, Silver Spring	301-593-1036
Central Brake-Alignment 924 Wayne Ave., Silver Spring	301/587-8881
Cloverly Shell Auto Care 15541 New Hampshire Ave., Silver Spring	301/384-4140
Glenmont Exxon 12321 Georgia Ave., Silver Spring	301/949-1494
Marv & Mike's Transmission 11508 Schuylkill Rd., Rockville	301/770-7051
Murray's Auto Clinic 939 Gist Ave., Silver Spring	301/585-7557
Satellite Motor 8109 Mayor Lane, Silver Spring	301/585-7876
Snider and Company 1303 Grude Dr., Rockville	301/340-3038

Wrenchmasters Auto Center   301/424-7574
1081 Taft St., Rockville

Virginia
Action Automotive   703/780-3388
8150 Richmond Highway, Alexandria
Autotech   703/442-0166
1524-G Springhill Rd., McLean
Cherrydale Motors   703/527-5511
3412 Lee Highway, Arlington
Foreign Auto Services   703/591-5225
3180 Draper Dr., Fairfax
Herb's Auto Repair   703/532-3455
802 South Washington St., Falls Church
Lee-Lex Service Center   703/534-5797
5747 Lee Highway, Arlington
Mack's VW Repair   703/528-3010
3912 North 5th Rd., Arlington
Mount Vernon Auto   703/780-3446
8853 Richmond Highway, Alexandria

An invaluable guide to good local auto repair shops is put out by *Washington Consumer Checkbook* magazine. This survey covers hundreds of area auto repair shops and lists types of cars serviced, range of services, hourly labor charges and recommendations as to best values with regard to price and quality of service. You can call WCC (733 15th St., N.W.; 202/347-7283) to order a copy ($6.95).

■ Auto Train   800/872-7245

Amtrak runs a daily auto train that will transport you and your car non-stop from Virginia to Florida. You must accompany your car on this journey. One-way coach fare is $125 per person and $175 per car.

■ Babysitting

Many local colleges will allow you to list your babysitting jobs at their career centers or student employment offices. Hourly rates average between $5 and $7.

Georgetown University   202/687-4187
Howard University   202/806-6100
University of Maryland   301/314-8324

American University (202/885-1800) provides a list of students available for babysitting. The list costs $1.

■ **Bethesda-Chevy Chase Government Center**   301/986-4325

■ **Booted Vehicle (D.C.)**   202/727-5000

■ **Car and Truck Rental**

Most national car rental companies have offices in the metropolitan area. Rentals out of Arlington promise the lowest rates.

Alamo	800/327-9633
Avis	800/331-1212
Budget	800/527-0700
Hertz	800/654-3131
National	800/227-7368

■ **Car Wash**

Car washes in the District are hard to come by. My favorite, **Flagship Car Wash** at 4432 Connecticut Ave., N.W., in Van Ness, (202/363-4960) does an excellent job. Car washes include a free vacuuming.

■ **Consumer Information**

Talking yellow pages (703/ADS-1001) can be used to find out more information about businesses in the area. Operators tell you the phone number, address and any special news (sales or promotions) related to the business you inquired about.

Better Business Bureau   202/393-8000

The BBB will send you a free report on any business you are concerned about. You can call them day or night, but be sure to have the main phone number of the company in question in order to file for a report.

Washington Consumers' Checkbook   202/347-9612

A consumer's guide for Washingtonians. This nonprofit organization analyzes how local gas stations, dry cleaners, dentists, doctors and restaurants measure up. Their findings are published in their magazine, *Washington Consumers' Checkbook*. This is a great source for locating a reputable plumber, car mechanic, bank or dentist. Call to subscribe or order back issues.

■ **D.C. Government**   202/727-1000

■ **Dentists' Referrals**

District	202/547-7615
Montgomery County	301/460-0500

    Prince George's County 301/731-7333
    Northern Virginia 703/642-5297

■ **Dial-a-hike** 202/547-2326

■ **Dial-a-museum** 202/357-2020

■ **Dial-a-park** 202/619-PARK

■ **Dogs and cats**
The Dog Owner's Guide to Washington (Edington-Rand Press; $14.95) is an excellent resource for dog and cat owners.

■ **Errands**
If you do not have enough time to do all your errands, you may want to call **The Errand Specialist** (703/448-9748). Dot Woodbury has been running errands for over a decade. The charge is $18 per hour plus 26¢ per mile.

■ **Fairfax County** 703/246-2000

■ **Falls Church City Government** (City Manager) 703/241-5001

■ **Food Delivery**
Another innovation in the food industry, delivery services will bring meals from your favorite restaurants to your front door.

Takeout Taxi promises to deliver dinners from any of 150 restaurants to your door in less than an hour.

    Herndon, Reston, Sterling 703/435-3663
    Alexandria 703/719-9409
    Arlington 703/908-0700
    Fairfax 703/204-0002
    Mannassas 703/369-1000
    District 202/986-0111
    Bethesda-Rockville 301/571-0111

If you live in Dupont Circle or on the Hill, **A La Carte Express** (202/546-8646) will deliver to you from over a dozen District establishments, including Duke Ziebert's.

■ **Foreign Currency**
Foreign currency can be purchased at several Downtown banks, including **Thomas Cook Currency Services** (1800 K St., N.W.;

202/872-1427), **Riggs National Bank** (17th and H Sts., N.W.; 202/835-6000), or **Ruesch International** (825 14th St., N.W.; 202/408-1200).

The American Express Travel Service sells foreign currency as well as its trademark travelers' checks. You will find its offices at 1150 Connecticut Ave., N.W. (202/457-1300), 1776 Pennsylvania Ave., N.W. (202/289-8800), 1001 G St., N.W. (202/393-0095) and Mazza Gallarie (5300 Wisconsin Ave., N.W.; 202/364-4000).

■ Gay and Lesbian Resources

The Washington Blade (202/797-7000) has an extensive listing of weekly and monthly events. Copies are free and can be picked up around town, especially in Dupont Circle. Annual subscriptions ($25) guarantee that you will not miss an issue.

The Whitman-Walker Clinic (202/797-3500) offers a wide range of health-related services, including anonymous HIV testing and counseling, dental care, pharmacy, massage therapy and a gay men's venereal disease clinic.

Gay and Lesbian Hotline	202/833-3234
Gay and Lesbian Switchboard	202/628-4667
Gay and Lesbian Switchboard (TDD)	202/628-4669
Gay Religious/Spiritual Organizations	
Affirmation (Methodist)	202/462-4897
Bet Mishpachah (Jewish)	202/833-1638
Church of the Disciples (MCC)	202/387-5230
Dignity (Catholics)	202/332-2424
Integrity (Episcopalians)	301/953-9421
Lutherans Concerned	703/971-4342
Presbyterian	301/345-0324
Quakers	202/483-3310
Unitarians for Lesbian/Gay Concerns	301/776-6891

■ Hospitals

District

D.C. General Hospital   202/675-5000
Massachusetts Ave. & 19th St., S.E.
Capitol Hill   202/675-0500
700 Constitution Ave., N.E.
Columbia Hospital for Women   202/293-6500
2425 L St., N.W.
George Washington Medical Center   202/994-1000
901 23rd St., N.W.

Georgetown University Hospital 202/342-2400
3800 Reservoir Rd., N.W.
Howard University Hospital 202/865-6100
2041 Georgia Ave., N.W.
Psychiatric Institute 202/965-8550
4228 Wisconsin Ave., N.W.
Sibley Memorial Hospital 202/537-4000
5255 Loughboro Rd., N.W.

Maryland
Doctor's Hospital of PG County 301/552-8118
8118 Good Luck Rd., Lanham
Holy Cross Hospital 301/905-0100
1500 Forest Glen Rd., Silver Spring
NIH - Clinical Center 301/496-2563
9000 Rockville Pike, Bethesda
PG Hospital Center 301/618-2000
3001 Hospital Dr., Cheverly
Suburban Hospital 301/530-3100
8600 Old Georgetown Rd., Bethesda
Washington Adventist Hospital 301/891-7600
7600 Carroll Ave., Takoma Park

Virginia
Alexandria Hospital 703/379-3000
4320 Seminary Rd., Alexandria
Arlington Hospital 703/558-5000
1701 N. George Mason Dr., Arlington
Dominion Hospital 703/536-2000
2960 Sleepy Hollow Rd., Falls Church
Fairfax Hospital 703/698-1110
3300 Gallows Rd., Falls Church

■ **Insurance Helpline** 800/942-4242
Call if you have any questions or complaints.

■ **International Newspapers & Magazines** 202/332-1489
The Newsroom at 1753 Connecticut Ave., N.W., in Dupont Circle has the best selection of foreign and national newspapers.

■ Lawyers Referral Service

State bar associations will help you find a lawyer if you need one. In the District, call 202/626-3499; Northern Virginia, 800/552-7977; Montgomery County, 301/279-9100; Prince George's County, 301/952-1440.

■ Libraries/Research Facilities

American University/Bender Library	202/885-3200
Catholic University/Mullen Memorial Library	202/319-5077
George Washington University/Gelman Library	202/994-6558
Georgetown University/Lauinger Library	202/687-7452
Historical Society of Washington	202/785-2068
Library of Congress	202/707-5000
Martin Luther King Memorial Library	202/727-1111
National Archives	202/501-5402
National Geographic Society Library	202/857-7783
University of the District of Columbia	202/282-3091

■ Locksmith

Maryland Lockmasters (301/423-1880) is available 24 hours a day to unlock or repair locks in Washington and parts of Maryland. Stranded Northern Virginians can call **Baldino's Lock & Key Service** at 703/550-0770.

■ Mail   City Post Office: 202/682-9595

If you need your letter to get there just a little bit faster, you can get an edge on the mail service and bring it to the **Sectional Center** at 8409 Lee Highway in Merrifield, Virginia (703/698-6300), the place where all the mail is sorted before it goes to your regional post office.

■ Maps and Guides

For a free map of the District, you can call the **Committee to Promote Washington** (202/724-4091) or the **D.C. Department of Tourism** (202/727-4511).

■ Medical Services

Doctors' Referral (Metro area)	202/362-8677
Planned Parenthood Clinic (District)	202/483-3999
Northern Virginia	703/820-3335
Silver Spring	301/588-7933
Rape Crisis Hotline (District)	202/333-7273
Northern Virginia	703/527-4077

Montgomery County	301/738-2255
Suicide Hotline (District)	202/223-2255
Northern County	703/525-4077
Montgomery County	301/738-2255

■ Montgomery County - Government   301/217-6500

■ Music Reviews   202/334-9000 (extension changes daily)
Listen to excerpts of albums reviewed by *The Washington Post*. Check the Style section of the *Post* on Sunday and Wednesday and the Weekend section on Friday for the latest extension.

■ News   202/334-9000
Free telephone information services courtesy of *The Washington Post*. For hourly AP News, enter 5000. For an abridged version of the news, dial extension 5100. AP Financial news (ext. 3002), Stock Quotations (ext. 2000) and Sports Scores (ext. 4100) are also available.

■ Package Delivery
PackageMan (703/276-7400) delivers packages locally. Their five-dollar, five-hour, five-pound package delivery (within the metropolitan area) is a quick and cheap way to get things around town.

If you need to send your package beyond the Washington area, packages can be mailed from **UPS** (301/595-9090), **Federal Express** (301/953-3333) or **DHL Worldwide Express** (202/296-6950). Each has offices throughout the region.

■ Parking Tickets
Dorsey & Associates, Inc. (202/842-2881) helps individuals and businesses handle parking tickets and moving violations in the District. Their fee is $20 per ticket ($50 per moving violation and $75 if an accident is involved). Your savings usually exceed this fee.

■ Parks
Fort Washington Park	301/763-4600
Great Falls Park (Maryland)	301/299-2026
Great Falls Park (Virginia)	703/285-2964
Glen Echo Park	301/492-6282
Pohick Bay Regional Park	703/339-6100
Rock Creek Park	202/426-6829
Wheaton Regional Park	301/946-7033

■ Party Supplies

Virginia owns and operates all liquor stores in the state. You can purchase beer and wine in the grocery store but all other alcohol in Virginia must be purchased at the ABC liquor stores.

The best place to go to buy either quantity or quality is **Rodman's Drugs** (202/363-3466) at 5100 Wisconsin Ave., N.W.

■ Passports   202/647-0518

Passport applications or renewals can be filed at 1425 K St., N.W., weekdays from 9:00 a.m. to 4:00 p.m.

■ All-Night Pharmacies

Several **People's Drug** stores are open 24 hours a day:

District
Dupont Circle, 7 Dupont Circle, N.W.	202/785-1466
14th St. Area, 1121 Vermont Ave., N.W.	202/628-0720

Virginia
Arlington, 3133 Lee Highway	703/528-3617
Falls Church, 8124 Arlington Blvd.	703/560-0719

Maryland
Bethesda/Chevy Chase, 6917 Arlington Rd.	301/656-2522

■ Photographs of Washington   202/707-5640

And almost anything else. The Library of Congress lets you make prints from their photography collection (the largest in the world). Go to the Prints and Photographs Reading Room in the Madison Building to see the archives. Bring your order to the Photo Duplication Office in the Adams Building. Reprints are only $12 for an eight-by-ten picture. Allow four to six weeks for prints to be ready.

■ Police (Non-Emergency Calls)

Alexandria	703/838-4444
Arlington	703/558-2222
Bethesda/Chevy Chase	301/652-9200
District	202/727-4326
Falls Church	703/241-5054
Prince George's County	301/336-8800
Silver Spring	301/565-7744

■ Prank Phone Calls   202/508-7556
Call the Annoying Calls Bureau to report annoying or prank phone calls and phone harassment.

■ Prince George's County - Government   301/350-9700

■ Recycling Hotlines
District	202/727-5856
Montgomery County	301/590-0046
Northern Virginia	703/358-6570
Prince George's County	301/925-5963

■ Radio Stations
WTEM (Sports)	570 AM	301/770-5700
WMAL (News/Talk)	630 AM	202/686-3100
WTOP (News)	1500 AM	202/895-5000
WAMU (National Public Radio)	88.5 FM	202/885-1030
WDCU (Jazz)	90.1 FM	202/282-7588
WETA (Classical, National Public Radio, American Public Radio)	90.9 FM	703/998-2790
WARW (Rock 'n Roll Oldies)	94.7 FM	703/866-4636
WASH (Adult Contemporary)	97.1 FM	202/432-0097
WHFS (Progressive)	99.1 FM	301/731-0991
WWDC (Rock)	101.1 FM	202/432-1101
WCXR (Classic Rock)	105.9 FM	202/432-1059
WJFK (Talk/Rock)	106.7 FM	202/432-1067
WRQX (Adult Contemporary)	107.3 FM	202/432-1073

■ Religious Organizations
Buddhist	202/829-2423
Catholic Information Center	202/783-2062
Episcopal Diocese of Washington	202/537-6555
Friends Meeting of Washington	202/483-3310
Islamic Center	202/332-8343
Jewish Information & Referral Service	301/770-4848
Lutheran - Washington, D.C. Synod	202/543-8610
Presbyterian (National Capitol)	202/244-4760
Unitarian Church of Arlington	703/892-2565
United Methodist - District Superintendant	301/589-8772

Catholic Young Adults Club (703/841-2759) sponsors sports activities, trips, dances, etc. They also offer a complimentary newsletter.

Jewish Information & Referral Service offers a welcome package. You can call 301/770-4848 to receive yours.

■ Roses   202/842-1000
RosExpress will deliver roses (red, white, yellow, pink and peach) anywhere in the metro area. Same-day delivery if order is placed before noon.

■ Ski Conditions   202/334-9000 (ext. 4300)
Find out ski conditions in the metropolitan region and around the country for free.

■ Sporting Events - Professional
USAir Arena (Bullets, Capitals)	301/350-3400
RFK Stadium (Redskins)/D.C. Armory	202/547-9077
Oriole Park at Camden Yards (Orioles)	410/685-9800
TicketMaster	202/432-7328

■ Taxis
District
Capitol Cab	202/546-2400
Diamond Cab	202/387-6200
Yellow Cab	202/544-1212

Virginia
Arlington Yellow Cab	703/522-2222
Alexandria Yellow Cab	703/549-2500
Fairfax Yellow Cab	703/941-4000
Red Top Cab	703/522-3333

Maryland
Tri-County Cab	301/248-2073

Maryland - Prince George's County
Checker Cab	301/270-6000
Yellow Cab	301/864-7700

Maryland - Montgomery County
Checker Cab	301/816-0066
Yellow Cab	301/984-1900

■ Theater & Arts
Arena Stage	202/488-3300
Shakespeare Theatre at the Lansburgh	202/393-2700

Ford's Theatre	202/638-2941
Kennedy Center	202/416-8000
American Film Institute	202/828-4000
National Symphony	202/416-8100
Washington Opera	202/416-7800
National Theatre	202/628-6161
Smithsonian	202/357-2700
Studio Theatre	202/332-3300
Warner Theatre	202/783-4000
Washington Ballet Company	202/362-3606
Wolf Trap	703/255-1900

■ TicketMaster 202/432-SEAT (7328)

The easiest way to order tickets for the theater, sporting events and concerts. Be prepared to pay a $3 to $4 surcharge per ticket.

■ Time

Accurate to the second, call 844-1212.

■ Tourist Sights

Capitol	202/224-3121
Library of Congress	202/707-8000
National Zoo	202/673-4800
Smithsonian	202/357-2700
Supreme Court	202/479-3000
White House	202/456-2200

■ Transportation

Airports

BWI	301/261-1000
Dulles	703/661-2700
National	703/685-8000

The **Washington Flyer Express** shuttles passengers to and from Dulles and National airports as well as other Downtown locations and Metro stops. Call 703/685-1400 for more information.

Buses

DASH (Alexandria)	703/370-3274
Fairfax Connector (Fairfax County)	703/339-7200
Greyhound/Trailways	202/289-5191
Metrobus	202/637-7000
Ride-On (Montgomery County)	301/217-7433

Metro	202/637-7000
Trains	
Amtrak	800/872-7245
MARC Commuter Rail (MD)	800/325-7245
Metroliner	800/523-8720
Virginia Railway Express	703/497-7777

■ TV Stations

WRC	Channel 4	NBC
WTTG	Channel 5	FOX
WJLA	Channel 7	ABC
WUSA	Channel 9	CBS
WDCA	Channel 20	IND
WETA	Channel 26	PBS
WHMM	Channel 32	PBS
WFTY	Channel 50	IND

■ Vistors' Centers

Maryland   You can get tourist information about Maryland (410/333-6611), including material about the Eastern Shore and Maryland beaches. Be sure to order the Maryland Free Travel Kit. It includes a calendar of events, a map of the state, coupons and a travel and outdoor guide.

Virginia   The Virginia Division of Tourism (202/659-5523) operates an office at 1629 K St., N.W. This branch is open on weekdays from 8:30 a.m. to 5:00 p.m.

Washington   1455 Pennsylvania Ave., N.W. in the Willard Collection Shopping Complex (202/789-7038). Open Monday through Saturday from 9:00 a.m. to 5:00 p.m. Stop by to pick up free maps and brochures about D.C. To hear a recorded message listing daily events, call 202/737-8866.

■ Weather   936-1212

Washington weather can change fast. After a few months here, you will know why Washingtonians have this number memorized.

■ Zip Codes   202/682-9595

Local and national information.

Index

A.V. Ristorante 123
AAA Potomac 112
Adams Morgan 13
Adams Morgan Spaghetti Garden 124
Aditi 123
Afterwords Cafe, The 139, 144
Air and Space Museum 179
Airports 73
Alexandria 37
AMC Union Station 175
American Cafe 116
American City Diner 139
American Film Institute 149, 174
American food 115
American History Museum 180
American International Newsstand 88
American pub food 117
American University 5, 27, 156
American University Park 27
Amphora, The 139
Amusement parks 193
Anacostia Museum 181
Andalusian Dog 135
Annapolis 186
Annie Sez 99
Annie's Paramount Steak House 143
Antietam 192
Antiques 79
Appliances 84
Arena Stage 11, 170
Arlington 30
Arlington Blvd. 64
Arlington National Cemetery 181

Arlington Cinema 'n Drafthouse 175
Arlington Co-op 96
Armand's 128
Atlantic Futon 83
Au Pied du Cochon 121, 138
Austin Grill 128
Auto insurance 110
Aux Fruits de Mer 121
Avalon, The 175

Bacchus 126
Badlands 143
Bakeries 94
Baltimore Washington Parkway 66
Ballston 34
Ballston Common 34, 97
Baltimore 166, 187
Baltimore Orioles 166, 187
Bangkok Garden 132
Bangkok Orchid 132
Bardo Rodeo 142
Barns of Wolf Trap, The 172
Bars 139
Baseball 166
Basketball 166
Bay Bridge Market Place 98
Bayou, The 171, 174
Beach Drive 75
Bed Store, The 83
Bed, Bath & Beyond 84
Beds 82
Beltway, The 63
Best 84
Bethesda 47
Bethesda Co-op 95
Bethesda Crab House 131
Bethesda Theatre Cafe 175
Bicycling 75, 158

Bike-on-Rail 75
Biograph, The 175
Birchmere 171
Black Cat Club 147
Bloomingdale's 79, 96, 97
Blue Point Grill 132
Blue Ridge Outlet Center 98
Blues Alley 172
Boating 162
Bob & Edith's Diner 139
Bombay Delight 123
Bombay Palace 123
Bonifant Books 90
Borders Books 89
Boss Shepherd's 143
Botanic Gardens 180
Bottom Line, The 139
Brass Beds & Bedding 83
BRAVO! 150
Breads Unlimited 94
Brickskeller Inn, The 139
Brooks Brothers 98
Bullfeathers 118
Bureau of Motor Vehicles (BMV) 101
BWI Airport 74

Cable TV 86
Cactus Cantina 127
Cafe Blanca 144
Cafe La Ruche 121
Cafe Lautrec 137
Cafe Luna 143
Cafe Pettito's 124
Cafe Saigon 134
California Pizza Kitchen 130
Calvert Cafe 126
Campus on the Mall 151, 155
Candey Hardware 85

Capital City Brewing Company   140
Capitol Hill   8, 180
Capitol Hill Books   90
Capitol Hill Restoration Society   150
Capitol Steps   174
Carter-Barron Amphitheater   171, 172
Casey's Bar and Grill   117
Cathedral   26
Center for Career Education and Workshops (CCEW)   155
Chapters Literary Bookstore   89
Charlie Chiang's   120
Charlottesville   190
Cheesecake Factory   115
Chelsea's   174
Chesapeake Seafood Crab House and An-Loc Landing Vietnamese Restaurant and Pho   131
Chesapeake Village   98
Chevy Chase Pavilion   96
Chief Ike's Mambo Room   147
China Cafe   120
China Inn   120
Cities   135, 146
City Lights of China   120
City Paper   3, 87, 179
City Place   50, 97
Civil War   192
Clarendon   33
Clearance centers   81
Cleveland Park   19
Cleveland Park 20008   87
Clyde's   117
Colesville Road (Route 29)   66
Columbia Pike   65
Comedy Cafe   174
Connecticut Ave.   17, 61
Conran's Habitat   78
Constitution Hall   171
Corcoran Gallery   149, 172
CORT   81, 82
Court House   33
Crisfield's   131

Crown Books   88
Crystal City   36

D.C. Cares   153
D.C. Eagle   143
Da Domenico Ristorante   124
Dancing Crab, The   131
Dandy, The   181
DASH   37, 72
Dean & DeLuca   24, 91
DeJaVu   140
Democratic National Committee   153
Dezzenio Futon   83
DoingSomething   153
Dolce Finale   138
Dominique's   122
Door Store   78
Driver's license   101
Duangrat's   132
Dubliner, The   142
Duke St.   65
Duke Ziebert's   136
Dulles International Airport   73
Dumbarton Oaks   181
Dupont Circle   15, 139, 180

East-West Highway (Route 410)   66
Eastern Market   10, 180
El Prognero   87
El Tamarindo   127
Electricity   86
Embassies   157
Enriqueta's   128
Ethnic markets   93
Evans   84

Faccia Luna   129
Fairfax City   41
Fairfax Connector   40, 72
Fairfax County   39
Falls Church   40
FANS   150
Farecards   68
Fashion Centre at Pentagon City   35, 97

Fat Tuesday's   141
Ferrara   144
Fettosh   126
Fifth Column   146
Filene's Basement   96, 98
Firehook Bakery and Coffee House   95
Fireplace   143
First Class   156
Fish, Wings & Tings   124
Fish Market   132
Fitz & Floyd Factory Outlet   84
Five Guys   119
Foggy Bottom   21
Folger Shakespeare Library   9, 180
Fondo del Sol Visual Arts Center   180
Food Co-ops   95
Food for Thought   4, 132
Football   165
Ford's Theatre   170
Fortune Chinese Seafood Restaurant   121
Four P's   142
Frager's Hardware   85
Frederick Douglas National Historic Site   181
French Quarter Cafe, The   143
Fresh Fields   41, 49, 92
Friendship Heights   29
Front Page, The   140
Futons   82
Futons by Shonin   83

GALA Hispanic Theatre   171
Galaxy Hut   142
Galileo   137
Galleria at Tysons II   40, 97
Gangplank, The   131
Garrett's   117
GEICO   110
Generous George's Positive Pizza Place   130
George Mason University   41, 171
George Washington Parkway   65

210

Index

George Washington Univ. 6, 7, 21, 155, 169
George's 126
Georgetown 23
Georgetown University 6, 7, 155, 169
Georgetowner, The 87
Georgia Ave. 61, 66
Geppetto's 129
Germaine's 135
Gettysburg 192
Giant Supermarkets 91
Ginza 83
Glover Park 25
Glut Food Co-op 55, 96
Golf 160
Good Fortune 120
Gourmet Vietnam 134
Greenbelt 55
Grog & Tankard 140
Gross National Product 174
Guards, The 117

H Street Hideaway 125
Ha' Penny Lion 140
Hamburger Hamlet 119
Handicapped parking permit 104
Hard Times Cafe 116
Hardware stores 85
Harpers Ferry 192
Hawk 'n Dove 118, 141
Health clubs 164
Health's A Poppin 134
Heaven and Hell 146
Hechinger's 85
Hecht's 79, 81, 97
Hecht's Clearance Center 81
Henry St. 65
Herndon 44
Hershey Park 193
Hibiscus Cafe 125
Hiking 161
Hill Rag 4, 87
Hillary's 117
Historical Society of Washington, D.C. 180
Hockey 163, 166
Hogate's 131
Hogs on the Hill 119

Horseback Riding 161
Houston's 117
HOV 63, 65
Hub, The 79
Hunan Gourmet 126
Hunan Number One 121

I Matti 123
i Ricchi 123
Ice skating 163
Ikea 77
IKON 146
Il Forno Pizzeria 129
Il Pesce 131
Il Radicchio 123
Improv 174
Income taxes 111
Insect Club 146
Interstate 66 (I-66) 64
InTowner, The 4, 87
Ireland's Own 142
Iron Gate, The 137
Italian Kitchen, The 124

J. Paul's 117
Jaimalito's Cantina 140
Jaleo 135
Java House 144
Jean-Louis at the Watergate 136
Joe Theismann's 118
Jos. A. Bank Clothiers 98
JR's Bar & Grill 142
Julio's 130

Kabul Caravan 126
Kabul West 126
Kelly's Irish Times 142
Kennedy Center 169
Kent Narrows Factory Stores 98
Key, The 175
Kilimanjaro 146
King St. 65
Kiss & Ride 71
Kitchen Bazaar 84
Korean Times 87
Kosher restaurants 125
Kramerbooks 89

Li'l Pub 119
La Brasserie 137
La Colline 137
La Lomita 128
La Lomita Dos 128
Lebanese Taverna 126
Lambda Rising 90
Landmark Center 97
Lantern Bryn Mawr Bookshop 90
Lauriol Plaza 127
Lavandou Cuisine Provencal 122
Laws Antique World 80
Le Bistro Francais 122
Le Gaulois Cafe Restaurant 137
Le Lion d'Or 136
Le Mistral 121
Library of Congress 9, 173, 180
Linsey's Bon Apetit 119
Lisner Auditorium 171
Loehmann's 99
Lord & Taylor 96, 97, 98
Lover's Lane 181
Luigi's 130
Lulu's 116

Macy's 79, 97
Madhatter 117, 140
Madurai 123
Maggie's New York Style Pizzeria 129
Maison Blanche 122
Malarkey's 141
Map Store, The 59, 90
Market, The 83
Marlo Furniture 79
Marvelous Market 21, 92
Mattress Discounters 82
Mazza Gallerie 96
McLean Gardens 26
McLean Providence Journal 87
Membership clubs 94
Merriweather Post Pavilion 172
Meskerem 121
Metrobus 71

211

Metrorail 66
Millie & Al's 141
Miniature golf 160
Montego Bay 124
Montgomery College 156
Montgomery County 46
Montgomery Mall 97
Montgomery Ward 83
Morrison Clark Inn 137
Morton's of Chicago 136
Movies 173, 174
Mr. Days 140
Mr. Henry's 143
Mr. K's 136
Mr. Smith's 117
Mr. Yung's 120
Mount Rainer 54
Murphy's Grand Irish Pub 142
Murphy's of D.C. 142
Museum of Natural History 179
My Brother's Place 141
Mystery Books 90
Mystery Bookshop 90

Nam-Viet 134
Nantucket Landing 141
National Airport 73
National Archives 180
National Cathedral 26, 180
National Museum of American Art 180
National Portrait Gallery 180
National Theatre 169
Natural Gas 86
Neiman Marcus 79, 97
Newspapers 86
Newsroom, The 88
Nora's 134
Nordstrom 79, 97
Northern Virginia Community College 156
Nuthouse 126

Ocean City 184
Odeon Cafe 124
Old Ebbitt Grill 118
Old Glory 119
Olsson's Books and Records 89
One Step Down 172
One Stop News 88
Old Angler's Inn 137

Palm, The 136
Pan Asian Noodles 125
Paolo's 124
Paramount Kings Dominion 193
Park & Ride 71
Parking 62
Parking Tickets 62
Paru's Indian Vegetarian Restaurant 134
Patrick St. 65
Peking Gourmet 119
Pentagon City 35, 97
Perry's 125
Phillip's Flagship 131
Phillips Collection 151, 180
Phillips Contemporaries 151
Phone service 85
Pik-a-Pita 127
Pines restaurants 124
Pizzeria Paradiso 129
Planet Fred 118
Planet Hollywood 118
Pleasant Peasant 116
Ploy 132
Politics and Prose 89
Polly's Cafe 117
Pop Stop 145
Potomac Mills 77
Price Club 94
Prime Rib, The 136

Quartermaine Coffee Roasters 19, 144
Queen Bee 135
Quigley's 139

Racheli's 144
Radio Free Italy 130
Rajaji 123
Recreation News 88
Red Sage, The 137
Red Sea 121
Red, Hot & Blue 118
Reeves Bakery 95
Registering to Vote 112
Registering your Car 102
Rehoboth Beach 185
Remington's 143
Renters' Insurance 111
Renting furniture 82
Republican National Committee 153
Residential Parking Permit 103
Reston 43
RFK Stadium 10, 166, 171
Ride-On 72
Rio Grande Cafe 128
Ristorante Piccolo's 137
Ritz, The 146
Rock Creek Parkway 61, 63
Roll Call 4, 87
Rosslyn 31
Route 270 64
Royal Dragon, The 126
Rumors 140, 184
Running 159
Rush hour traffic 63

Safeway 91
Saks Fifth Avenue 79, 96, 97
Saloon, The 172
Sam's Club 94
Sassafras 99
Scan International 78
Shakespeare Theatre at the Lansburgh 170
Shenandoahs 191
Shirley Highway (I-395) 64
Sholl's Colonial Cafeteria 136
Shootz 141
Shopping malls 96
Sidney Kramer Books 89
Sign of the Whale 140
Signature Theatre 170
Silver Diner 141
Silver Spring 49

Ski Club of Washington, D.C. 151, 164
Skiing 163
Slick Willy's 118
Smithsonian Institution 151, 172, 179
Smithsonian Resident Associate Program (RAP) 151
Smitty's Servistar 85
Softball 164
Source Theatre 170
South Austin Grill 128
Spirit of Mount Vernon 182
Spirit of Washington 182
Sports Focus 87
Spring Valley 27
Spy Club, The 145
Starbucks 27, 144
State of the Union 135
Stetson's 141
Steve Windsor 98
Strangeways 142
Strosnider's Hardware 85
Strosnider's Kemp Mill Paint and Hardware 85
Studio Theatre 170
Supreme Court 8, 180
Sutton Place Gourmet 92
Swimming 161
Syms 99

Tako Grill 125, 134
Takoma Park 52
Takoma Park Silver Spring Co-op 95
Takoma Station Tavern 172
Tastee Diner 139
Taxicabs 61
Tennis 159
Textile Museum 180
Third Edition 140
Three Pigs Barbeque 119
Thrift Shops 80
Tiber Creek Pub 141
Tiberio 136
TicketMaster 167, 169, 171
Ticketplace 171
Tiempo Latino 87
Timberlake's 117

Today's Man 98
Tombs, The 117
Tony and Joe's Seafood Place 131
Tony Cheng's Mongolian Restaurant 120
Tony Cheng's Seafood Restaurant 120
Topkapi Restaurant 127
Tourmobile 181
Tracks 143, 145
Traffic circles 62
Travel Books and Language Center 90
Trio's 143
Trover Books 88, 89
Tune Inn 141
Two Quail 143
Tysons Corner 40, 97

U.S. Department of Agriculture (USDA) 155
University of District of Columbia (UDC) 20, 156
Unkai 125
Uptown Bakers 19, 95
USAir Arena 166, 171
Utopia 135

Van Ness 20
Vault, The 146
Viet Huong 135
Vietnam Georgetown Restaurant 135
Virginia Hardware 85
Virginia Railway Express 72

Waccamaw Pottery 84
Wal-Mart 84
Warehouse Bar & Grill, The 132
Warner Theatre 170
Washington Afro-American 87
Washington Antiquarian Booksellers Assoc. 90
Washington Blade, The 4, 87
Washington Citizen 3, 87
Washington Informer 87
Washington Jewish Week 87

Washington Monument 179
Washington Post, The 3, 4, 86, 141, 179
Washington St. 65
Washington Times, The 3, 4, 87
Washingtonian Magazine 88, 141
Well-Dressed Burrito 136
White Flint Mall 96
Whitey's 141
Wild Oats 143
Wilson Blvd. 64
Williamsburg 191
Wisconsin Ave. 23, 24, 48, 61
Wolf Trap 172
Women's Community Bakery 96
Women's Information Network (WIN) 152
Woodley Park 17
Woodrow Wilson Bridge 64
Woodrow Wilson House 180
Woodward & Lothrop (Woodie's) 79, 81, 96, 97
Woolly Mammoth 170
World Affairs Council 152

Yesterday's Books 90
Yosaku 125

Zebra Room 129
Zed's 121
Zei 145
Zig Zag Cafe 145
Zimmerman and Sons Hardware 85
Zorba's Cafe 126